Also by Sherman Alexie

Novels

The Absolutely True Diary of a Part-Time Indian
Flight
Reservation Blues
Indian Killer

Stories

Blasphemy
War Dances
Ten Little Indians
The Toughest Indian in the World
Indian Killer
The Lone Ranger and Tonto Fistfight in Heaven

Poetry

What I've Stolen, What I've Earned
Face
Dangerous Astronomy
Il powwow della fine del mondo
One Stick Song
The Man Who Loves Salmon
The Summer of Black Widows
Water Flowing Home
Seven Mourning Songs for the Cedar Flute I Have Yet to Learn to Play
First Indian on the Moon
Old Shirts & New Skins
I Would Steal Horses
The Business of Fancydancing

Picture Books

Thunder Boy Jr.

You Don't Have to Say You Love Me

A Memoir

SHERMAN ALEXIE

LITTLE, BROWN AND COMPANY

LARGE PRINT EDITION

Little, Brown and Company
Hachette Book Group
1290 Avenue of the Americas, New York, NY 10104
littlebrown.com

First Edition: June 2017

Little, Brown and Company is a division of Hachette Book Group, Inc. The Little, Brown name and logo are trademarks of Hachette Book Group, Inc.

The publisher is not responsible for websites (or their content) that are not owned by the publisher.

The Hachette Speakers Bureau provides a wide range of authors for speaking events. To find out more, go to hachettespeakersbureau.com or call (866) 376-6591.

Endpaper photograph of Lillian Alexie's quilt (1994) by Emily Rieman

ISBN 978-0-316-27075-5 (hc) / 978-0-316-39677-6 (large print) / 978-0-316-55664-4 (signed ed.)
LCCN 2016958327

10 9 8 7 6 5 4 3 2 1

LSC-C

Printed in the United States of America

For Arnold, Kim, Arlene, and James

You Don't Have to Say You Love Me

1.

Forty Knives

IN 1972 OR 1973, or maybe in 1974, my mother and father hosted a dangerous New Year's Eve party at our home in Wellpinit, Washington, on the Spokane Indian Reservation.

We lived in a two-story house—the first floor was a doorless daylight basement while the elevated second floor had front and back doors accessible by fourteen-step staircases. The house was constructed by our tribe using grant money from the U.S. Department of Housing and Urban Development, more tersely known as HUD. Our family HUD house was new but only half finished when we moved in and remains unfinished, and illogically designed, over forty years later. It was worth $25,000 when it was built, and I think it's probably worth about the same now. I don't speak my tribal language, but I'm positive there are no Spokane Indian words for *real estate appreciation.*

The top floor of our HUD house contains a tiny bathroom with an unusually narrow door and a small windowless kitchen, both included as afterthoughts in deadline sketches hurriedly drawn by a tribal secretary who had no architectural education.

I didn't grow up in a dream house. I lived in a wooden improvisation.

On the top floor with the kitchen and bathroom, there is also a minuscule bedroom that was shared by my little sisters, identical twins, during childhood. My sisters, Kim and Arlene, never married and nearly fifty years old now, have never lived more than one mile apart, so perhaps they cannot escape their twinly proximity.

Also on the top floor of our HUD house is the master bedroom, where my late father slept alone, and a disproportionately large living room, where my late mother slept on a couch.

My late father, Sherman Alexie, Sr., was a Coeur d'Alene Indian. He was physically graceful and strong, adept at ballroom waltzes, powwow dancing, and basketball. And always smelled of the smoke of one good cigar intermingled with dozens of cheap stogies. As a teenager, he began to resemble the actor Charles Bronson, and that resemblance only increased with age. Introverted, depressed, he spent most of his time solving crossword puzzles while watching TV.

My late mother, Lillian Alexie, crafted legendary quilts and was one of the last fluent speakers of our tribal language. She was small, just under five feet tall when she died. And she was so beautiful and verbose and brilliant she could have played a fictional version of herself in a screwball Hollywood comedy if Hollywood had ever bothered to cast real Indians as fictional Indians.

I don't know if my parents romantically loved each other. I am positive they platonically loved each other very much.

My mother and father slept separately from the time we moved into that HUD house in the early 1970s until his death from alcoholic kidney failure, in 2003. And then my mother continued to sleep alone on a living room couch—on a series of living room couches—until her death, in 2015. My parents were not a physically affectionate couple. I never saw, heard, or sensed any evidence—other than the existence of us children—that my mother and father had sex at any point during their marriage. If forced to guess at the number of times my parents had been naked and damp together, I would probably say, "Well, they conceived four children together, so let's say they had sex three times for keeps—the twins only count for one—and four times for kicks."

My big brother, Arnold, and I each had our own mostly finished basement bedrooms. But he spent much of his time living and traveling with a family of cousins like they were surrogates for his parents and siblings. I love my brother, but he sometimes felt like a stranger in those early years, and I imagine he might say the same about me in our later years. Never married, but in a decade-long relationship with a white woman, he is loud and hilarious and universally beloved in our tribe.

The furnace and laundry rooms, also in the basement, are cement-floored with bare wood stud walls. Dug five feet into the ground, our basement flooded with every serious rainstorm and has smelled of mold, and subsequent disinfectant fluids, from the beginning of time.

My little brother, James, who is also our second cousin, was adopted by my parents when he was a toddler. Fifteen years younger than me, he would eventually take over my bedroom after I went away to college. He was so starved when we got him that he would devour any food or drink in his vicinity, including other people's meals. While we were distracted, he once drank my father's sixty-four-ounce Big Gulp of Diet Pepsi in one long pull. He was only three years old. We thought it was funny. We didn't ponder why a kid would come to us so very thirsty.

James was only five years old when I moved away from the reservation. So I think I have been more like his absent uncle than his big brother.

Smart and handsome and thin and also married to a white woman, James has a master's degree in business.

Ah, my little brother is my favorite capitalist.

But that inexpertly constructed HUD house was still a spectacular and vital mansion compared to the nineteenth-century one-bedroom house where I spent most of the first seven years of my life. That ancient reservation house didn't have indoor plumbing or electricity when my parents, siblings, and I first moved in, along with an ever-changing group of friends, cousins, grandparents, aunts, and uncles.

I most vividly remember my half sister, Mary. She was thirteen years older than me and seemed more like a maternal figure than a sibling. Even more beautiful than our gorgeous mother, Mary was a charming and random presence in my life. She was profane and silly and dressed like a hippie white girl mimicking a radical Indian. In later years, I would learn that Mary's randomness and charm—and her eventual death in a house fire—were fueled by her drug and alcohol addictions. I didn't yet know that romantic heroes—famous and not—are usually aimless nomads in disguise. Mary's father lived in Montana, on the Flathead Indian Reservation, so she sometimes lived with him and sometimes lived with us and sometimes shacked up with Indian men who reeked of marijuana and beer or with white men who looked like roadies for Led Zeppelin. A mother at fifteen, Mary gave her baby, my niece, to our aunt Inez to raise. My niece is only a few years younger than me, and I still don't understand why my mother didn't take her into our home. My parents raised one of our cousins as a son, and my sisters would eventually raise another cousin as a daughter. So why didn't our niece become our sister? I never asked my parents those questions. But, in writing the first draft of this very paragraph, I realized for the first time that my father, so passive in nearly all ways, might have said no to raising a granddaughter who was not his biological relative. I feel terrible for considering this possibility. Could my father have done such a thing? Could he have been such an alpha lion? I don't know. I don't think so. I hope not. So why didn't my mother raise her granddaughter? I doubt that I'll ever be able to answer that question. There are family mysteries I cannot solve. There are family mysteries I am unwilling to solve.

Before her death, my mother told me that she liked to sleep alone on a couch in her later years because she'd only slept in crowded beds and bedrooms for most of her younger life. I never would have thought of a lumpy couch as a luxury, but my mother certainly did. Sometimes, when I was little and afraid and screaming from yet another nightmare, I would fitfully sleep on a smaller couch in the HUD house living room near my mother's larger couch.

Born hydrocephalic, with abnormal amounts of cerebral spinal fluid crushing my brain, I had surgery at five months to insert a shunt and then had it removed when I was two. I suffered seizures until I was seven years old, so I was a kindergartner on phenobarbital. I have alternated between insomnia and hypersomnia my whole life. I begin dreaming immediately upon falling asleep, a condition called shortened REM latency that can be a precursor, indicator, cause, and result of depression. I have always been haunted by nightmares. By ghosts, real or imagined. I have always heard voices, familiar and strange. I was officially diagnosed as bipolar in 2010, but I think my first symptoms appeared when I was a child.

For Christmas in 1976, when I was ten, I received a plastic Guns of Navarone battle play set with Allied and Nazi soldiers, cannon, tanks, and planes. I added my own Indian and U.S. Cavalry toy soldiers and manically played war for twenty-two hours straight. My parents didn't stop me. They didn't tell me to go to bed. My mania was accepted. In the context of my family, I wasn't being odd. Rather, I was behaving like my mother, who would often work on her quilts for even longer sleepless stretches.

I often stayed awake all night reading books and writing stories and playing the board games I invented. If I was especially agitated and lucky, I would have a new graph-paper notebook and I would carefully color in thousands of squares, one by one, until I was calm enough to sleep.

I think I inherited my bipolar disorder from my mother. I believe she was haunted by ghosts, too. I also believe she has become a ghost, either as a supernatural being or as a hallucination caused by my various mental illnesses and medications or as the most current and vivid product of my imagination.

Thing is, I don't believe in ghosts. But I see them all the time.

"You slept on that living room couch for years," my mother's ghost said to me while I was writing this memoir. "You never used your basement bedroom until you were eleven or twelve. I had you sleep close to me because you had those seizures. And I had to keep you safe. And I had to give you medicine in the middle of the night. And because you were always scared."

"That's not how I remember sleeping," I said. "I remember moving into the basement bedroom on my first night."

"You used to wet your bed," my mother's ghost said. "You wet the couch until you were thirteen, I think."

"I stopped wetting the bed long before that," I said.

"Do you remember that I would lay down a shower curtain on the couch and then lay down your sheets and blanket?" my mother's ghost asked.

"That was only in the old house," I said. "Never in the HUD house."

"It was in both places," she said. "You had bladder issues even when you were awake. Do you remember when you drove to Spokane with your cousins for a birthday party? But you were too nervous to go into a house filled with city Indians you didn't know? So you stayed outside in the car and peed your pants because you were too scared to go to the bathroom in a stranger's house?"

I lied and said, "I don't remember that happening."

"I think you forget things on purpose," my mother's ghost said.

I do remember when the white men in gray overalls installed the first indoor toilet in our ancient nineteenth-century house, but I can't recall when the place was wired for electricity and the first light-bulb was switched on.

When performing for crowds, I like to say, "When I was a kid, I shared an outhouse with sixteen Indians. But I only remember fourteen of them."

That primitive house was infinitely better than the series of filthy highway motels and filthier down-town hotels in and around Spokane where we'd sometimes stay for days or weeks whenever my parents had extra money, or a temporary job, or needed a sad-ass sabbatical from reservation life.

My parents sold blood for money to buy food.

Poverty was our spirit animal.

Once, when he was only five or six, my big brother told my aunt that he was going to hock all of our fur-niture to the pawnshop, just like "Mom and Dad al-ways do," so he could buy Kentucky Fried Chicken.

My aunt, the white one, told me that story. My big brother doesn't remember it.

He said, "That chicken thing sounds more like something you'd write in a book than something I would say for real."

I vividly remember moving from that old house into our HUD house only fifty yards away. The front and back stairs were not yet built, so we had to climb a ladder to get into the place. Ludicrous, I know, but it felt magical. I remember a photograph of us four children posing on the ladder. We looked more like mesa-dwelling Hopi Indians than salmon-fishing Spokane Indians.

My little sister doesn't remember that photograph. She doubts it exists.

"You're always making up stuff from the past," she said. "And the stuff you imagine is always better than the stuff that actually happened."

"That's just a fancy way of calling me a liar," I said.

"If the moccasin fits, then wear it," she said.

I don't recall the moment when I officially became a storyteller—a talented liar—but here I must quote Simon Ortiz, the Acoma Pueblo writer, who said, "Listen. If it's fiction, then it better be true."

Simon, a beautiful storyteller, doesn't remember ever saying such a thing.

"That sounds like something I might say," he said to me. "But I don't know if I have ever said that particular thing."

I don't remember when I first learned of the quote. Did I read it in one of Simon's poems or stories? If so, then why doesn't Simon remember that he wrote it? Can a writer forget something that he's written in one of his own books? Yes, of course. I wrote my first novel over two decades ago, and fans often stump me by asking questions about passages that I don't remember writing. So perhaps I read that quote somewhere else and have mistakenly attributed it to

Simon. Or did I hear somebody else quote Simon? My college writing teacher, Alex Kuo, is a big fan of literary-inspired practical jokes and postmodern riddles, so maybe he's the one who quoted or misquoted Simon.

"Do you know this Simon Ortiz quote about fiction and truth?" I asked Alex. "Did you tell me he said it?"

"No," he said, "I don't remember that quote. But that doesn't mean I didn't tell you I knew it sometime in the past. I could have invented it. Or maybe you invented the quote and are giving me partial credit for citing the quote while fully crediting Simon for originally inventing the quote."

"So maybe I'm the one who thought it first?" I said. "And I want to honor you and Simon."

"Well," Alex said. "Crediting your thoughts to your mentors sounds more like you're honoring yourself."

"That's funny," I said. "And sad. Is my ego the source of all my deception and self-deception?"

"Perhaps," Alex said. "Since you've just invented this entire conversation about storytelling and truth that you and I never had, and put it in the first chapter of your memoir, then I'm just going to call you the unreliable narrator of your own life."

So, okay, maybe I am unreliable to some degree. But, despite what my teachers, parents, friends, siblings, and I say about my storytelling—about my labyrinthine fantasy life—I also know that I have an excellent memory.

To quote a song lyric I vaguely remember from a song and band I can't fully recall: *I remember everything.*

I remember that my mother and father hosted a New Year's Eve party in our HUD house on the Spokane Indian Reservation in 1973. Or 1972 or 1974.

I was only seven years old, but I knew, with a fundamentalist's fervor, that the party was potentially lethal. Not because of my mother and father's actions, but because of their inattentions. They were alcoholics who'd get what they laughingly called bottle-blind, as in "I was so bottle-blind that I didn't even realize I'd driven off the road until I woke up with a pine tree branch sticking through the car windshield about four inches from my nose." That's what my father said—or approximately what he said—after his eleventh or nineteenth or twenty-seventh drunken car wreck.

So, yes, my bottle-blind parents invited everybody on the reservation to that dangerous New Year's Eve party, including two Indian men who were widely believed—who were *known*—to have committed murders.

One of those murderers, a half-white little guy with a wicked temper and a silly-ass gunfighter's mustache, had supposedly buried his victim's body in Manito Park, in Spokane. An anonymous person had called into a secret witness phone line and claimed that my father, while not guilty of the murder, knew where the body was buried. My father had twice been in prison for burglary and forgery, so he was certainly known to the police. They must have taken that anonymous call seriously because they asked my father to come in and answer a few questions. And I still find it strange and hilarious that my father took me, only nine or ten years old, along on that little cold-case adventure.

As my father drove us from the reservation to the police station in Spokane, he told me that he'd only heard the same rumors about the murder as everybody else.

"They could talk to every Indian around here," my father said. "And we'd all tell the same story."

My father was a shy and gentle man, even when drunk, so I don't believe that he was capable of physically hurting anybody. But he was also an alcoholic who was exceedingly loyal to other indigenous folks and deeply suspicious of any authority figure. I knew that my father would protect any Indian against any investigation by white men. My father wouldn't throw a punch or pull a trigger or name names. Silence was his short bow and quiver of arrows.

I didn't witness that interview—or maybe I should call it a casual interrogation—and my father never shared any of the details. I just waited for hours in our family car outside the police station as he told the story—or did not tell the story—about his alleged role or nonrole in that murder. He must have been innocent of any wrongdoing because he was free to drive us back to the reservation that day and was never compelled to speak of the incident again.

But I still wonder if there is a body buried in Manito Park. I still wonder if my father knew where to find that body. I know exactly where my dead father is buried. Maybe I'll interrogate his tombstone the next time I visit that reservation cemetery.

"How many murderers did you know?" I will ask the tombstone again and again.

And the tombstone will never answer. Because the dead have only the voices we give to them.

The other murderer at that New Year's Eve party was a Vietnam War veteran. Not long after he'd been honorably discharged and returned to the reservation, he and some Indian friends attacked a white man. According to the stories, the war vet kicked that white man's eye clean out of his head and then dumped him to die in a roadside ditch. Today, some folks say the man survived the beating—and that cold night spent unconscious in the dirt—and moved to another state. Some say the beating wasn't that bad in the first place. It was just an ordinary fight—as ordinary as a fight can be when it's five or six Indian men assaulting one white man. Some say the white man did lose his eye but blamed himself for the fight and for his injury. Some say he became a better man because of his missing eye. Yes, some folks have turned that murder story into a mythical tale about redemption. Some folks—some creative storytellers—have changed a violent Indian man into the spiritual teacher of a one-eyed white wanderer.

We all justify our sins, venal or mortal.

There was also a third murderer at that New Year's Eve party, but that killing would take place a few years later. So maybe I should say there was a future murderer at the party. And that murder would take place in a convenience-store parking lot in Spokane. It would happen in an old car. One of my father's more distant friends would shoot and kill one of my father's closest cousins.

He served only five or eight years in prison for the murder and then vanished, either to escape the Indians intent on revenge or because those vengeful Indians had made him vanish.

But no, my little sister fact-checked me and said, "That guy got out of prison and lived in a HUD house on the rez until he died."

"What?" I said. "He lived in Wellpinit? No way. Did you ever talk to him?"

"He tried to talk to us," she said. "But I just walked past him."

"And nobody tried to get revenge on him?"

"No, he was just an outcast. People walked circles around him like he was a disease."

"That's all that happened to him?" I asked.

"Killers get away with killing," she said.

So, yes, I grew up with murderers. But, strangely enough, I wasn't all that worried about their presence at that New Year's Eve party. I wasn't afraid of being killed as much as I was afraid of being sexually abused. I knew there would be five or six party guests who'd sexually molested my friends and cousins. There would be guests who'd raped only adults. And guests who'd raped only children. And opportunists who had and would violate any vulnerable woman, man, or child. I'd been abused by one man. I knew he'd be at the party, so I assumed I'd have to specifically protect myself against him and generally protect myself against all of the other predators.

As an adult, I can look back at the violence on my reservation and logically trace it back to the horrific degradations, sexual and otherwise, committed against my tribe by generations of white American priests, nuns, soldiers, teachers, missionaries, and government officials. The abused can become abusers. It's a tragic progression. But, as a child, even a very bright child, I had little knowledge of Native American history. We Spokane Indian children weren't even taught about our own tribal history. I only knew my personal history. And, in my story, the villains were other Spokane Indians. My monsters had brown skin, with dark hair and eyes, and they looked like me.

So, as my mother and father prepared for that New Year's Eve party, I walked downstairs into my bedroom, reached far under my bed, and pulled out a clear plastic bag heavy with forty metal butter knives. I'd purchased the bag of used knives at Goodwill or Value Village or Salvation Army or some other secondhand store. Or maybe I bought them at Dutch's Pawnshop in downtown Spokane. I don't remember. But I do recall that the bag cost me two dollars. That was a significant amount of money for a poor reservation kid. I could have bought at least thirty pieces of penny candy at Irene's Grocery Store. But, even as a kid, I had more important uses for my money than sweets. I needed knives. And I shoved them, one by one, into the narrow gap between my bedroom door and the jamb. This locked the door in place. It could not be easily opened. That door looked armored with all of those knives. That door looked like a giant wood and metal porcupine, fierce and ready to defend me. But, alas, that door and jamb were actually hollow and thin. The knives were cheap and pliable. I still hoped their combined strength would be enough to keep the door shut against any monsters. Well, truthfully, I knew those knives were not strong enough to keep a dedicated monster from breaking into my room. But those forty knives would be strong enough to make a monster pause and reconsider. Those forty knives would make a monster worry that he was making too much noise as he beat at the door. He'd be scared that the noise would attract the attention of other adults—maybe my parents if they weren't too bottle-blind—who would then come downstairs to investigate the commotion. Those forty knives might make a monster wonder if I was armed with other, sharper knives. Maybe that monster would decide to search for an easier target. Do you know that old joke about how you don't have to run faster than a charging grizzly—you just have to run faster than your hiking companions? Well, I was using the same survivor logic. My bedroom fortress didn't need to be impenetrable. It just needed to be stronger than everybody else's defenses—stronger than all of the other Indian children who were as vulnerable as or more vulnerable than me.

Self-preservation was my religion.

Above all else, I knew those forty butter knives would delay the monster long enough for me to climb through my basement window and escape into the pine forest behind my house. I'd spent so much time in those woods that I'd memorized them. I could safely run and avoid all the trees, fallen and not. I could leap the small creek and hurdle the glacial boulders. It would not have mattered if the forest was barely lit by moonlight or not illuminated at all. I wasn't afraid of the dark nearly as much as I was afraid of the monsters who hunted by night and day.

But the monsters didn't come after me that night. Instead, it was my parents who terrified me the most.

I was still awake at midnight when the party went into full crazy mode, with singing and screaming and cursing and pistols and rifles fired into the night sky. Those reservation Indian parties felt less like celebrations and more like ceremonial preparation for a battle that never quite arrived.

But I was asleep when I heard my father curse and grunt and war-whoop. When I heard bodies slamming into walls. When I heard my father cry out in pain.

Stupidly, bravely, I crawled out of bed, pulled the forty butter knives from my door—keeping one as a dull weapon—and ran upstairs. I was only seven or eight or nine years old, but I was going to defend my father. I'd always been that foolish and brave. When I was four, I picked up a miniature wooden baseball bat and attacked the skulls, arms, and legs of three white boys who were picking on my big brother in a motel parking lot in Spokane. I chased those white boys away and then, still blind with rage, attacked my brother. And, as he often had to during our youth, he disarmed me, and bear-hugged me until I, exhausted and furious, passed out in his arms.

At that New Year's Eve party, I raced up the stairs, whipped open the door, expecting to stab the men attacking my father, but was surprised to see he was playing a rough version of rugby, wrestling, boxing, and one-on-one Nerf basketball against an Indian friend—one of those guys nicknamed Bug or Mouse or Poochie. My father and his friend were drunkenly laughing and bleeding from various cuts and scrapes. They were unholy clowns. Dozens of partygoers were cheering and making bets. Nobody noticed me. I wasn't scared as much as I was confused.

Then my father and his friend, locked in a violent embrace, wrestle-staggered toward me. I froze. And I would have likely been knocked over and maybe badly hurt, but some conscientious drunk pulled me out of the way. And I watched as my father and his friend pulled and pushed each other through the open basement door—the door I had left open—and tumbled down the thinly carpeted staircase.

Fearing they had killed themselves, I ran to the top of the staircase to see them, even more bloody and bruised, weakly laughing in a two-man pile on the basement floor. They were too drunk and injured to stand, so they soon fell asleep still wrapped in each other's arms.

Meanwhile, my mother was playing poker against a group of other Native women.

"You're cheating me," my mother screamed at Birdie, a Spokane Indian woman who was not much bigger than me.

"No, Lillian," Birdie said. "I don't know how to play. I'm not cheating. Teach me how to play."

My mother screamed again and punched Birdie in the mouth.

Birdie grabbed her face and wept.

My mother punched her in the forehead.

Then Birdie wailed like a rabbit being killed by a hawk. She was only bruised and bloody, but her pain still sounded like a death cry,

"Why did you hit me?" Birdie howled. "Why? Why? Why?"

I remember the blood ran between Birdie's teeth like water flowing around river rocks.

"Lillian, why did you hit me?" Birdie wailed. "Lillian. Lillian."

I was terrified and turned to run back downstairs. But somebody picked me up, carried me to the master bedroom, and threw me onto the bed, where a dozen other Indian kids were already wrapped around one another like a frightened litter of pups.

I found my little sisters in that dark scrum, and we held hands until we fell asleep.

At dawn, my mother woke my sisters and me. My big brother stood at her side. I don't know where he had slept that night. In his room? At our cousins' house? In a tree in the woods behind our house?

"Wake up, wake up," my mother said. "We're leaving and we're never coming back."

Exhausted, terrified, my siblings and I followed our mother outside to the car. We all piled into the backseat—without seat belts, kid seats, or any other kind of safety—as Mom started the engine and sped us away from our HUD house.

She cursed our father as she drove.

She also sang Christian hymns.

She sang ancient Spokane Indian songs that sounded like each note was filled with ten thousand years of grief.

Our mother drove us to Chewelah, Washington, the small white town north of the reservation where she was born. In her most desperate and lonesome moments, my mother often returned like a salmon to her place of birth, which had been a Spokane Indian gathering place in earlier centuries. Once in Chewelah, she pulled us out of the car and into a diner. We shuffled past white customers who stared at us with hate, pity, disgust, and anger—the Four Horsemen of the Anti-Indian Apocalypse.

Then my mother ordered us into a back booth and called for the waitress.

"Pancakes and bacon and orange juice," my mother ordered. "For everybody."

The white waitress looked at us four Indian kids still dressed in the clothes we'd slept in. And then she stared at me.

"Your nose is bleeding," she said.

I wiped my face and looked at the red glow on my fingers.

"His nose bleeds when he's heated up," my mother said.

It was true. But the waitress had her doubts.

"Did somebody hit you, baby?" the waitress asked me.

I thought about lying. I thought about blaming my mother. I thought about telling the waitress that my mother had slapped me. I thought about being rescued by white people.

But I was more afraid of any white people than I was of my Indian mother.

"My mom saved us," I said. "She saved us from drunks."

The waitress looked down at my bare and dirty feet. My mother had dragged her kids out of the house without putting socks and shoes on us. It was winter. But I don't remember if my bare feet felt cold. They had to be cold. But I don't trust this particular detail. I don't believe we left the house with bare feet. There's no way our mother made us walk with bare feet in the snow and ice. She would not have done that to us, right? I think my mind is adding a Dickensian detail to heighten the narrative punch. I hope our bare winter feet are only a metaphor or simile. I hope it means "Our cheap shoes weren't much better than bare feet."

"Did your daddy hit you?" the waitress asked me.

"No," I said. "It was the other men who hurt us. Mommy saved us from the other men."

The waitress knelt beside me.

"You can tell me the truth," the waitress said. "Do you need help, little sweetie?"

"I'm hungry," I said. "I'm thirsty."

The waitress brought us our breakfast. Then she said that she'd pay for it when my mother said she didn't have any money. And then, as we prepared to leave the diner, that kind waitress needed to help us even more.

"You take these kids somewhere safe," the waitress

told my mother. "Don't go back to the place you ran from."

I don't remember my mother's response to that waitress. I can only imagine my mother's desperation and fear. She'd wanted to escape. She'd wanted to rescue her kids. But where could she go? Was there a place where she and her kids could be safe? Has there ever been a place in the United States where a poor Native woman and her kids could be truly safe? She had no money. She had no knowledge of family shelters. Did those even exist in the early 1970s? She must have debated her options. She knew that Indian children were often taken from their families for the flimsiest of reasons—as a late twentieth-century continuation of official government assimilation and termination efforts. Split up, separated, we kids would be sent to foster homes, where we'd be in potential danger. We might be sent to the last Indian boarding schools, where we would definitely be in danger. Our mother had already lost us once to Social Services. A second time might mean she'd lose us for good. She couldn't risk it. She couldn't trust any white officials. She had to go home.

So my mother drove us back to the reservation. Back to our HUD house. Almost all of the partygoers were gone. My father, scratched and bloody and bruised, was asleep alone in his bed. My mother and my siblings and I crawled into bed with him.

We slept all day and long into the night.

At some point, my mother woke alone and cleaned the house. Then she woke us, her children, and promised us that she would stop drinking booze that very second and would never drink again.

My mother was a liar. She broke many promises over the coming decades. But she kept that greatest of vows. She was sober for the rest of her life.

And that's why I am still alive.

2.

Sacred Heart

IN MAY 2015, my mother, struggling to breathe, was rushed from the reservation to Sacred Heart Hospital in Spokane, where she was eventually diagnosed with Parkinson's disease. She was seventy-eight years old and had been suffering with major and minor health problems since her husband—my father—had died twelve years earlier. I knew Parkinson's wasn't fatal, but it can significantly reduce a person's life span and lead to severe physical and mental impairment, especially for older people. How quickly would it transform my elderly but mostly self-sufficient mother into an utter dependent? And what about the quality of her last years? How could I make sure she lived and died well?

I am not an organized person, but I suddenly felt

the need to make serious and complicated plans for my mother's life—for the end of her life. However, it felt more like formal duty than affection. My mother and I had often been estranged. We'd battled and exiled each other. And then, after my father's death, we'd settled into a relationship based on irregular phone calls and occasional visits. My mother and I loved each other—mostly or partly loved each other, I think—but I'd always felt the need to armor myself against her emotional excesses, and I imagine she felt the same about me.

But she needed me now—financially and spiritually—so I booked an immediate flight from Seattle to Spokane to visit her, and my siblings, in Sacred Heart Hospital. In my taxi to the airport, I researched senior care facilities in Seattle and Spokane. Some of them were quite beautiful and offered extensive programs for residents with Parkinson's. They also seemed to be legal pyramid schemes where elderly patients and their families poured money into end-of-life rent rivers that only flowed up toward the corporate owners and stockholders.

But if I were to be grifted, then let the grift be lovely.

I did the math on my book sales and expected royalties, and knew I could afford a great place for my mother in Spokane if I gave up my outside office and worked only at home. Maybe I could do more lucrative gigs speaking on college campuses. Maybe I could return to script doctoring in Hollywood. I had many financial opportunities, some more probable and profitable than others. I was the lucky Native American son—the fortunate writer—who could take good care of his dying Native American mother. Isn't that an oddly tribalistic and narcissistic realization? Then again, isn't tribalism a form of group narcissism?

"I can put Mom in a fancy place by the Little Spokane River," I said to my sister on the phone from my departure gate in Seattle–Tacoma International Airport.

"That's what she was worried about today," my sister said. "She thinks we're going to put her in an old folks' home and forget about her."

"Indians don't do that," I said, instantly romanticizing my race.

"Some Indians do," my sister said, immediately deromanticizing us.

"I can also rent a cheap studio apartment near the senior-citizen home," I said. "It's just a few blocks away. And you guys can stay there when you're visiting her. You can take turns seeing her every day."

I felt my back spasm and ache from the heavy burden of my messiah complex.

"She doesn't want to be in a place where everybody

is white," my sister said. "She thinks old white people will be racist toward her."

"I don't think she's wrong," I said. "I bet old white people are probably more racist in Spokane. Old people are probably more racist everywhere. Just look at Clint Eastwood."

I thought about my late father, a Coeur d'Alene Indian, who'd gradually grown more racist as he aged. But it was a passive form of racism—if there is such a thing—in which he would use a lesser racist epithet to describe a person after a relatively tense encounter. Aside from the time he called a white cop Custer, my father never insulted anybody to their face. He once came out of a 7-Eleven complaining about the "towel-head" who owned the place, so I called my father buffalo-head for the rest of the day to shame him for his racism. That wasn't quite a progressive move on my part. I wondered if my mother had also grown more racist in her elderly years. I hadn't spent concentrated time with her since my father's death, so I didn't know exactly how my mother's personality and politics might have changed. I knew she was a fan of the callow Sarah Palin only because that former vice-presidential candidate had married a dude with a Yu'pik great-grandmother.

But, strangely enough for an activist artist like me, I had never thought about how white privilege, or lack thereof, can extend even into the last few days of a person's life. I now had to worry about my mother being racially harassed as she was dying. So I researched senior-citizen homes that catered to more diverse populations—a difficult task in the very white cities of Spokane and Seattle—but I found a few reservation-based facilities that specialized in taking care of Native Americans.

"There is an elder-care place on the Colville Indian Rez," I said to my sister as I waited in the Seattle airport.

That rez-based nursing home was one hundred miles from my mother's home on the Spokane Indian Reservation.

"Is it Indian Health Service?" my sister asked.

"I think so," I said. "That's kind of worrisome, isn't it?"

I worried about the quality of a government facility that served only Indians. Scenes from *One Flew Over the Cuckoo's Nest* flashed through my head. I didn't want to turn my mother into Chief Broom. Or Randle P. McMurphy. I didn't want her shuffling through the hospital hallways, leaning on a walker made of elk bones and coyote spit. I also wondered if my mother would want to live out her last years on another tribe's reservation. I'd been an urban Indian for half my life and was often the only Indian in any gathering, but living on another tribe's reservation felt even more alienating to me. How would it feel to my reservation-bound mother?

"Maybe there will be some old Colville Indians who speak a little Spokane," I said. "Maybe Mom will get to gossip in the old language. Even if she's on somebody else's rez."

The Colvilles and Spokanes speak tribal languages that are related and share some words, but they are distinct dialects.

"I think Mom would be even lonelier around a bunch of old Indian strangers," my sister said. "I wouldn't want to live on somebody else's rez."

"How about senior housing in Wellpinit?" I asked. "Maybe I could hire a full-time nurse to live with Mom there."

"No way," my sister said. "Auntie Vi lives there. And they can't stand each other."

Despite living only a few miles apart, my mother and her eldest sister hadn't spoken in a decade. My mom had always been good at making enemies. Her sister, nicknamed Nasty Nanny, was even better at it.

"We can just take care of Mom at home," my sister said.

None of us knew how sick my mother might become—how difficult it could be to take care of her. We didn't know if she would eventually need help on a weekly or daily or hourly basis. My sisters were not physically well either. I worried they'd endanger their health by taking care of our mother.

"I want Mom to have expert care," I said.

"She just wants to be home," my sister said.

"Okay, I have to hang up now," I said. "My plane is boarding. I'll see you at the hospital in a couple of hours."

In 1966, I was born in Sacred Heart Hospital in Spokane.

My father died in Sacred Heart in 2003.

He'd wanted to die at home, but he was suffering and suffocating—drowning in his own fluids—so my mother and sisters had rushed him to the hospital. I'd seen him on his last night at home on the reservation but fled back to Seattle rather than be with him in his last moments.

He'd often abandoned me when I was a child. He'd often chosen to go on days- and weeks-long drinking binges instead of staying home with his wife and kids. So, to be blunt, I chose to leave him in the same way he had left me. In that difficult time, I chose to be with my wife and children—the family I had created—instead of the family I was born into.

Did that decision make me a bad son?

I suppose it did.

Do I feel guilty about it?

Yes.

But I don't regret my decision. Given the chance to travel back in time, I would have still abandoned my father so I could be a father to my sons.

So, yeah, if you close your eyes and listen hard, then you can hear a drum group singing a powwow version of "Cat's in the Cradle":

coffee spoon, way ya hi yo
Indian moon, way ya hi yo
daddy is drunk at noon
and won't be home soon
way ya way ya way ya ho

But my father wasn't alone in his hospital room— on his deathbed. My mother and sisters were at his side.

At home in Seattle, I called his room in Sacred Heart.

"How is Dad?" I asked my sister when she answered.

"He's leaving us," she said. "His breathing is really slowing down. He's not responding to us."

"Put the phone up to his ear," I said.

"Okay," my sister said.

"Dad," I said into the phone. "It's me."

I heard him sigh and move. I heard my mother and sisters gasp. Somewhere deep in his morphine coma, my father had recognized my voice and was trying to respond—had responded in the only way he could.

"Dad," I said. "It's okay. You can let go. I love you. You can let go. You can stop fighting. It's time to say good-bye. I love you. I love you. Good-bye."

Twelve hours later, as I walked through a Seattle toy store with my sons, ages two and six, my sister called to tell me that our father had died.

I paid for my sons' new toys, drove us home, and helped them into the house. Then, as my wife held our boys, I collapsed to the floor of our living room and wept.

On my flight to Spokane, I used the airplane Wi-Fi to do more research on Parkinson's disease. It would certainly make my mother's last years incredibly difficult—even torturous. She'd be taking multiple medications many times a day. I wondered if Indian Health Service would cover everything or if I would have to pay for some of the more expensive and experimental drugs.

I then vowed to finally finish the years-late sequel to my best-selling book *The Absolutely True Diary of a Part-Time Indian*. I needed that money. My mother needed that money. I hadn't been able to finish the book because of the pathological fear that my sequel would be *The Phantom Menace* instead of *The Empire Strikes Back*. But, on the airplane, I thought, "Okay,

okay, *Phantom* sucked, but it still made big cash. I'm gonna Yoda this book for my mother."

After landing in Spokane, I took a taxi to Sacred Heart Hospital and hurried to my mother's room. I leaned over and kissed her forehead. She wiped away tears and said hello.

I hugged my sisters and my niece. She was our second cousin, but my sisters had adopted her and raised her as their daughter. My family, despite all of our troubles, had temporarily or permanently taken care of various cousins and friends over the years. In adulthood, many of my childhood friends told me they'd felt safer in our house than they ever did in their own homes. My father's drunken kindness and my mother's angry sobriety had provided an unlikely refuge on our reservation.

"So what's the plan?" I asked my sister.

"The doctor said they'll get Mom stabilized here and then send her to a rehabilitation center to work on her Parkinson's."

"How long will she be there?" I asked.

"Six to eight weeks," my sister said.

"I can pay for a private room," I said.

"They want her to have a roommate. So she'll stay social."

"Okay," I said.

I sat on the bed next to Mom.

"Hey, Lillian," I said. "How are you?"

"I'm old," she said, and laughed. She was aware of her surroundings but also seemed confused, like she was two people, one much older than the other.

"How's your brain?" I asked her.

"I get tired," she said. "And I forget things."

"Are you getting senile on me?"

"I've been getting senile."

I realized I had not seen her in at least four months. She'd been her usual witty self the last time we'd been together. But now she seemed fragmented.

"Do you like your doctor?" I asked.

"Yes," she said. "She likes your books. She wants you to sign one for her."

That was one of the best privileges of my literary fame. My parents had both received more attentive health care because they had conceived me. My father and I had the same name, so he'd often been asked by medical professionals to sign my books instead of me.

"I'm going to take care of you, Mom," I said.

That wasn't a lie, not exactly, but it didn't turn out to be true.

During the early years of my writing career, my mother was afraid to tell me family stories.

"You're just going to put things out there for everybody to read," she said. "Ugly things."

But after I became more famous in the Indian world, after other Natives would learn her last name and ask if she was related to me, and then ask for her autograph and take photos with her, my mother began to tell me more and more about her personal history.

She was a storyteller, too.

So, diagnosed with Parkinson's, exhausted and afraid, she lay in her hospital bed in Sacred Heart Hospital and told me another story about that old and primitive house on the rez—about who we used to be and who we would always be. I'd heard all of her stories multiple times. She repeated them and repeated them until I learned how to repeat them.

When repeated enough times, the same story becomes a song.

"Okay," she said. "So your dad's cousins, Bill and Tinker and Johnny—they were brothers—and they always slept in the attic. It wasn't insulated, but I don't remember how they stayed warm. I guess we had a lot of blankets. I don't think we had any sleeping bags. And even if we did, they would have been army surplus. And they would have smelled too moldy to use. And sometimes there were mice in them.

"You and Johnny had the same birthday. You shared a cake once. You weren't happy about that at all. You cried and cried.

"Tinker fought in Vietnam. It took him a while to get okay with that.

"Eugene and Leonard and Sam were brothers, too, and your dad's cousins, and they lived in the attic sometimes, until Sam went hitchhiking that one day and disappeared. Leonard moved to New Mexico and went to college for twenty years. Eugene still visited all the time, but I don't think he ever slept in our house again. Not in that old house and not in the new one either. After Sam disappeared, Eugene never really lived anywhere again. And then he got murdered, remember? Shot in the parking lot of the liquor store. Imagine how Leonard feels with two brothers gone like that.

"Stubby—he was your father's great-uncle—he slept on that twin bed in the hallway. He was small so he fit. You remember him? He always pinched your face and made you mad. One time, when you were three, you called him a Japanese sniper. You were just trying to get him back for pinching you, but Stubby really did look Japanese.

"Lizzie Bee—your father's grandmother—she slept on an army cot in the kitchen. She had arthritis bad so she liked to sleep near that woodstove. We didn't have enough wood to keep the fire going every night, but it would stay warm for a while. She used to give you dollar bills. And you saved them all in an old coffee tin. You hid that tin in the rocks behind the house. Somebody found it, though, and stole your money. It was probably one of the attic boys who stole it. But it could have been your dad, too. He was drinking a lot when we lived in that old house.

"Your big sister, Mary, when she wasn't living with her father in Montana, or running around with some boy, she would sleep on the couch in the living room.

"Your little sisters, the twins, they shared a crib in the bedroom.

"Your dad and I slept in the bed.

"When Mary was home, you slept on the floor beside our bed. If she was gone, you slept on the couch. Sometimes, though, when you knew Mary was getting ready to leave again, you'd sleep on the floor by the couch. And then you'd cry for days after she was gone.

"Your big brother? He slept in the bedroom closet. He was too big for it. He had to sleep curled up like a dog. He always liked to sleep in places that squeezed him. I don't know why.

"And, oh, you had those night terrors when you were little. You'd wake up screaming and shake the whole house.

"And, yeah, we didn't have indoor plumbing until 'seventy-two.

"You remember the outhouse? It wasn't too bad to use it in daytime or in good weather. But it was pretty rugged if it was winter and three in the morning.

"Do you remember how I caught you peeing out the window one night?

"Yeah, you said your dad had taught you how to pee that way so you didn't have to go to the out-house in the dark.

"And then, a few days later, I found a bunch of pee stains in the snow under the window and I asked you about it, and you blamed your sisters. That was so funny.

"You didn't even know your sisters had different anatomy and couldn't have balanced on the win-dowsill and peed that far.

"And then that old house burned down. Do you re-member that?

"Yeah, I was sorry about leaving that old house. And I was happy when we moved into the new HUD house. But I loved that old house, too. Remember the pharmacist at the clinic—the white guy? French name, I think? Very handsome?

"He took a photo of the old house burning, but there was this optical illusion that made it look like the new house was burning, too?

"Yeah, two house fires at the same time. That was us."

Ten days after our mother was diagnosed with Parkinson's, we learned that she was also afflicted with small-cell lung cancer.

Terminal cancer, the doctor said. She had only weeks to live.

She had not smoked since she'd stopped drinking.

But our father had puffed on cigars for decades.

Can cigar smoke cause small-cell lung cancer?

Yes.

Can secondhand cigar smoke cause small-cell lung cancer?

Yes.

In 1987, while a senior in high school, my future college girlfriend, a white woman, measured radon levels in various reservation houses as part of a science project.

Our HUD house had moderately dangerous levels of radon, a colorless, odorless, tasteless, and radioactive noble gas.

Can radon cause small-cell lung cancer?

Yes.

My reservation is also home to two closed uranium mines and a closed uranium mill. One mine, the Sherwood, operated for only a few years and was shut down and cleaned with award-winning thoroughness. The other mine, Midnite, which operated from 1955 to 1981, was simply abandoned and never made safe on any level.

Can uranium cause cancer?

Yes, especially when inhaled as dust.

Gated, barbed-wired, the 350-acre Midnite Mine

is now dotted with massive mounds of radioactive waste rock and ore—over thirty million tons in total—and uncounted barrels of various and mysterious chemicals. For years, huge trucks hauled uranium ore through Wellpinit, passing less than a mile from my childhood home, on their way to the uranium mill located on the east side of the reservation. I remember those trucks shedding small rocks and dust as they rumbled past us Indian kids walking, running, and riding our bicycles. Many driveways and roads on our reservation were paved with those waste rocks.

Located only six miles from my childhood HUD house, the mine also contains massive covered and uncovered pits, some more than five hundred feet deep, that are filled with impossibly green and blue wastewater. According to the Environmental Protection Agency, the flora, fauna, and groundwater near the Midnite Mine are unsafe to eat and drink.

That radioactive groundwater has, for decades, drained down the hillside into Blue Creek, which then flows into the Spokane River. There is a beach at that place where the radioactive creek merges with the radioactive river.

Over the years, many Spokane Indians collected water and rocks from Blue Creek to use in our sacred sweat lodges. A sweat lodge is made by bending flexible wood branches into a dome shape that is draped with blankets and tarps. That flexible wood was sometimes collected from willows along Blue Creek. Other wood, like ponderosa pine, was sometimes gathered from trees felled near the mine. That wood was used to build campfires. Pots of Blue Creek's radioactive water were boiled on those campfires. Ladles of that water were poured onto the piles of radioactive rocks placed inside sweat lodges. That steam was meant to purify us. We sang and prayed in the superheated and closed spaces of our radioactive sweat lodges.

During my childhood, Blue Creek Beach was also our family's favorite place to picnic, play in the sand, and swim. Unlike the rest of our family, my mother and I had always been terribly afraid of water.

She and I had never learned how to swim.

But when I close my eyes, I can see her walking barefoot through that beach sand. I can see her kicking dust into the air. I can see her step into the creek up to her ankles. I can see her wade into the river up to her knees.

I can see her waving hello, hello, hello, and good-bye.

3.

The Call

IN LATE JUNE 2015, my sister called me.

"You better get here," she said. "The doctor said Mom is near the end."

"Okay," I said. "I'm on the way."

My wife, Diane, and I and our teenage sons drove from Seattle to the reservation and made our way to my childhood home.

As we pulled into the driveway, I saw my sister sitting on the front porch steps.

"Oh, God," I said to my wife. "Mom must have died already. Arlene wants to tell me before I go inside the house."

I hurried out of the car and ran to embrace my sister.

"When did she die?" I asked.

"Mom's not dead yet," my sister said.

I was confused. I couldn't recall a single time when any Indian in my life had formally greeted me at their front door.

"Then why were you waiting for us outside?" I asked.

"I have to warn you," my sister said.

"What?" I asked. "Is Mom deformed or something?"

I couldn't imagine how lung cancer, how any cancer other than skin cancer, might dramatically change a person's appearance.

"No," my sister said. "It's just—well, it's just—"

She hesitated and covered her face with her hands. I thought she was crying. But then I realized she was laughing.

"What?" I asked. "What's so funny?"

"I wanted to warn you," she said. "I wanted to prepare you. You see, Mom is being *affectionate*. She's, like, hugging people and telling us she loves us. It's *weird*."

My sister and I laughed together.

We hugged again.

And then we walked inside to greet my dying mother.

4.

Good Hair

ON HER DEATHBED, my mother reached up and touched my face. She touched my hair.

"Your hair is so curly," she said. "You have the curliest hair of any Indian ever."

"My sons have curlier hair than me," I said. "Look at them."

My mother looked at her grandsons and laughed.

"Everybody is curly," she said.

I said, "When Indians have curly hair, I call it the Geronifro."

My mother laughed.

"Don't cut your hair when I die," she said.

When my father died, I sliced off my long hair and buried it in a secret place.

"I don't have braids anymore," I said. "My hair is messy but it's short."

"Don't cut your curls," my mother said. "And don't let the boys cut their hair."

"Okay," I said.

"You should grow back your braids," she said. "Honor me by wearing your hair long again."

"Okay," I said.

I lied.

5.

Soda Can

NINETEEN SEVENTY-SEVEN. I was ten. My mother and I were arguing. I don't remember how the fight started. We, the bipolar mother and her bipolar son, fought so often that all of the arguments blended into a terrifying yet predictable ride. My mother and I were roller-coaster cars on parallel tracks.

During that argument in 1977, I remember the hatred I felt for my mother. It didn't feel like a temporary hatred. And it didn't feel like an adolescent rage. It felt like something more profound and permanent than youthful angst. My hatred felt as ancient as a cave painting. I didn't want to physically hurt my mother, but I certainly wanted my words to break her soul's back over my soul's knee. But, as

I screamed at her and she screamed back, she kept working on the damn quilt in her lap.

"I hate your quilts!" I screamed.

On the surface, those four words don't seem all that bad, but my mother's quilting wasn't a hobby. Quilting was her philosophy.

Fabric square ad infinitum.

"I hate your quilts!" I screamed again.

"Shut up!" she screamed.

And then I called her the worst thing possible. I know what word you think I used—the worst epithet an American man can throw at an American woman. But I've never used that particular word during any heated moment and can't recall ever saying it in even the most ironic sense. Instead, I called her something that had become my greatest personal weapon against her.

"Why don't you shut up!" I screamed. "You old bag!"

Yes, my mother vehemently hated to be called an old bag. It's an unpleasant thing to say to anybody, let alone your mother, but it's a slur that could play on Nickelodeon TV. Why did my mother hate that curse more than any other? I suppose it had to do more with the force of the emotion behind the insult than the insult itself.

But I must also note that a friend, after reading an early draft of this chapter, interpreted "old bag" as meaning "used condom." I was shocked by his observation. Did my mother think that I was calling her a used condom? I doubt it, but I wonder about her definition of "old bag." I'd always thought that I was just insulting her age and wrinkled skin—and her existential emptiness.

I wish I could ask my mother why she hated that particular insult so much. It makes me want to buy a Ouija board and ask her about the whole damn situation. Maybe her ghost would be honest with me.

So, yes, I'd insulted my mother's quilting and called her an old bag. She'd had enough of my disrespect. She reached over toward the end table, grabbed a mostly full can of Pepsi, and threw it at me.

I stood by the back door. She sat on the couch. We were at least fifteen feet apart. My mother did not have good hand-eye coordination. She was not athletic. And yet, as that Pepsi can flew toward me, seemingly in slow motion, I found myself thinking, *Shit, that thing is going to hit me in the face.*

I could have easily dodged the can. But I didn't. Instead, I watched it with amazement. I kept marveling that my extremely clumsy mother had thrown it with such force and accuracy. I worry now that I didn't duck because I *wanted* to get hit. In any case, I continued to be amazed and/or expectant as that can struck me in the forehead and knocked me unconscious.

Okay, I need to remind you that I was a hydrocephalic kid who had brain surgery at five months and then again at two years, and suffered epileptic seizures until I was seven. I still have four burr hole soft spots in my skull and a Frankenstein mess of head scars. So, yes, along with bipolar disorder, my brain damage might have also made me quick to rage.

But let's get back to that soda can. It would be dangerous to throw that projectile at anybody's face, but it was especially threatening to me.

I don't know how long I was unconscious. When I opened my eyes and looked at the water-stained ceiling, I was in shock. I wasn't bleeding very much but would have a huge bruise—a black eye of the forehead—for a week. I slowly sat up and saw that my mother was still quilting. I don't know if she'd even moved from the couch after she'd knocked me out. Maybe she'd thought I was faking it. That's the only way to justify the fact that she hadn't sought to help me.

I silently and slowly got to my feet.

I was dizzy, nauseated, and confused. It felt like my arms and legs had switched places and I would have to relearn how to walk again.

There was no concussion protocol in those days.

Carefully, I walked to the basement door, opened it, eased my way downstairs, shuffled to my room, slumped onto my bed, and slept for many dreamless hours.

I suppose I could have died from my head injury—from a clotted vein or subdural hematoma or brain bleed.

But I woke the next morning with a massive headache, slowly walked upstairs, and ate the hash browns and Spam that my mother had left for me on the dining table.

It was a greasy and unspoken apology.

And by eating her food, I guess I had accepted it.

6.

Prayer Animals

When I was ten or twelve, my late mother told
  me that,
When she was ten or twelve, she grabbed a
  stray cat
By the front legs while her little niece grabbed
Its rear legs, and they twisted and pulled that
  damned
And doomed animal until it split into bloody
  halves.

Would you be shocked to know that I wasn't
  shocked
By that story? On the reservation, violence is a
  clock,

Ordinary and relentless. Even stopped, it doesn't
  stop.
But, Jesus, as an adult in the city, I am rocked
By that story's implications. My mother was not

A sociopath, but animal torture is a common
  crime
For serial killers in training. So how and why
Did my mother and her niece commit an act so
  borderline?
Of course, being Native females, they were
  bull's-eyes
For every man—known or unknown, indigenous or white—

So which men hurt my mother and her niece so
  terribly
And so often that they would possess the need
To capture, torture, and murder something so
  weak?
How disconnected was my mother from her body
And her emotions? To survive, she had to be as
  mean

As those who would do her harm. So I guess I
  know
Why she was often distant, storm-hearted, and
  cold.

But my reluctant compassion does nothing to
    console
Me, as a middle-aged man who remembers, in
    whole,
The day an older and larger white boy named
    Mike cajoled

Five of us Indian boys into his trailer "for some
    fun."
At first, he let each of us marvel at his new pellet
    gun
And then he shot Gooch in the neck. There was
    blood.
It still felt ordinary, though. After all, we were
    young
And dumb. We laughed at Gooch. We didn't run.

And then Mike shot Gooch in the ear. He
    screamed
In pain. So Mike kicked him quiet. Gooch was
    weak.
But then Mike shot all of us. He shot me.
Terrified, we did not fight. We gave up so easily
As Mike roped us together into one fragile body.

I'd guess I was pellet-shot at least five times.
Punched in the face once, kicked in the balls
    twice.

Mike struck matches and flicked them at our
eyes.
And then he pulled out a huge hunting knife.
And made us beg for our "useless little lives."

After hours of this, we escaped when I broke
Through a window and ran. Everybody ran
without
Rhyme or reason. The five of us fled in five sep-
arate
Directions. I ran home and immediately told my
mother
What had just happened. And she did nothing.

"Oh," she said to me. "Mike was joking. You
take
Everything so seriously." My mother, so traumatized
By her own painful life, could not see the sharp
danger
Of anybody else's knife. I don't know if the other
boys
Were as traumatized as me. They've never
talked about Mike,

So maybe they are mute with post-traumatic
stress.
Maybe they don't know how to talk about Mike.

I often wonder why I'm the one who remembers
All the pain. Why am I the one who remains
    obsessed
By the bloody nose, but rarely remembers any
    joy?

Eight years after our faux kidnapping, I was
    watching TV
With my girlfriend when Mike's face appeared
    on-screen.
He'd been arrested in Spokane for kidnapping,
    raping,
And murdering two little girls. One of their
    bodies
Has never been found. And then he'd tried to
    hide

His crime by piling brush on the other girl's
    body
And setting her aflame. After seeing this news,
I turned to my girlfriend and said, "We were
    practice
For him. We were dress rehearsal for rape
And torture and murder. We were his game."

Growing up on the rez, I'd often felt like a prey
Animal, like a carnivore's easiest meal.
But that fear was more metaphor than real,

Except for the time, only a mile from my house,
When a killer played with me like I was his
   mouse.

I called my mother and asked her if she'd heard
About Mike. About the murders he had
   committed.
She said she'd forgotten about him, which
   meant
That she'd forgotten what he had done to me
And the other Indian boys. "Mom," I said.

"Mike *hurt* us. Don't you remember that?"
She denied that it had ever happened.
And that if it had happened, then it could not
Have been that bad. "If Mike had done that
To you for real," she said, "then he would've
   been

In trouble. He would have gone to jail."
I laughed. "Mom," I said. "Nothing happened
Because you didn't take me seriously."
"Well," my mother said. "He's in jail now.
So what's done is done." I was pissed

At my mother's dismissal. I hung up the
   phone
And remembered yet again that she, as a child,

Had once tortured, killed, and mutilated a cat.
Who does shit like that? Who can be that
    cruel?
It was my mother. It was my mother. That's
    who.

7.

Benediction

I only spent a few hours with my mother
As she lay dying in her rented hospital bed.
I kissed her, told her I loved her,
And then I fled.

8.

My Sister's Waltz

OUR MOTHER WAS on her deathbed. Dreaming morphine dreams. Speaking the tribal language in her sleep. And then she was awake. And she was thirsty. So she called out in English to my sister.

"Help me," she said. "My mouth is dry."

Using a bendy straw in a plastic cup, my sister tried to give our mother a sip of water.

But my sister wasn't wearing her glasses, so her depth perception was off. And she was exhausted. So she accidentally spilled the water on Mom.

"Oh, no," my sister said to our mother. "You're soaked now."

Our mother was too high on painkillers to care, but my sober sister was mortified.

For perhaps the tenth time that day, she cried.

"Here, Mom," my sister said. "Let me help you

into your wheelchair and then I can change your sheets first. And then I can change your clothes."

My sister and our mother had traded maternal responsibilities.

"Lift your arms," my sister said. "And I'll lift you."

My sister carefully pulled our mother to her feet and wrapped her in a hug.

"Okay," my sister said. "Now two steps forward and then we'll sit in your chair."

Ah, the slow-motion choreography of hospice ballet.

"Okay, Mom," my sister said, "take one step forward."

Our dying mother took that one step toward her wheelchair, but then she immediately took a step back. Our mother swayed.

"Mom, let me help you," my sister said.

"It's okay," our mother said. "I'm dancing on purpose. I want to dance. Dance with me."

It was three in the morning but our mother was awake, and she shuffled left and right.

"Oh," our mother said. "We are dancing. It's been so long since I danced. And I don't know why nobody asked me. I was a good dancer."

My sister laughed. She was alone in the night with our mother. There was no music. But my sister held our mother closely and shuffled with her. They moved in the smallest of circles.

"We only danced for a few seconds," my sister later said. "But, all the next day, whenever she was awake and had visitors, Mom kept bragging that she'd danced until sunrise."

O Mother! O Mother! Even in your last moments, you told beautiful lies.

9.

End of Life

My MOTHER WAS a tiny woman, just under five feet tall. But her mother, Etta Adams, was over six feet tall. Her matriarchal power matched her physical size, so everybody called her Big Mom. She was born in 1904 in Nespelem, Washington, and she and her parents were close friends with the Nez Perce leader Chief Joseph and his family.

Yes, my grandmother was babysat by the famous Chief Joseph, who in 1877 led his seven hundred followers on an epic eleven-hundred-mile flight from two thousand U.S. Cavalry soldiers. He was eventually captured and delivered his mournful promise that he would "fight no more forever." He and his followers were exiled to the Colville Indian Reservation, where Joseph died not long after my grandmother was born.

For Indians, loneliness is a natural cause of death.

In 1980, as she lay dying of lung cancer in her reservation home, Big Mom was visited daily by many Indians. She was famous in the Indian world for her spiritual power—for her ancient stories and songs. We still have a dozen photo albums of Big Mom, thin and bald from chemotherapy, posing with all of her indigenous visitors.

My grandmother wanted to say good-bye to everybody.

As she died, she wanted to be celebrated for her life.

She wanted to be remembered.

In 2015, as my mother lay dying of cancer in her reservation home, she asked my sisters to tell only her most trusted friends and relatives.

"I don't want to see people I don't want to see," our mother said.

So, while my grandmother was visited by hundreds of Indians, my mother said her official good-byes to maybe only thirty people. Most folks on the reservation didn't know she was terminally ill.

My mother was a spy who treated her own death like a top-secret mission.

Or maybe she was like a mad queen who believed only a few of her most loyal subjects deserved to know about her cancer.

Or maybe she was terrified.

Or maybe, as my wife thinks, my mother just wanted to leave this complicated world in the most uncomplicated way possible.

When I visited my mother for the last time, along with my wife and teenage sons, she asked for a photograph.

"Oh," my sister said. "Do you want to pose with Junior's family?"

"No," my mother said. "I just want a picture of Arnold and Junior and my grandsons. All the men. Put them right there."

She pointed at the plasma television located only three feet from her rented hospital bed.

"Don't you want to be in the picture with the men?" my sister asked my mother.

"No, no," she said. "Just them."

So, yes, there exists a photograph of my big brother, my sons, and I as we stand with our arms around one another in front of my late mother's big television that happened to be playing the reality show *Naked and Afraid*.

Death is always incongruous.

In that photo, you can see the foot of my mother's deathbed. But you don't see my mother.

She is located outside the frame. She is the unseen witness. She exists in that negative space.

10.

Valediction

After my sisters told me they had to contort
Themselves and my terminally ill mother

As they lifted her from her deathbed
And led her down the hallway

Into the narrow bathroom of my childhood
home,
Then bruised her hip when they lost their grip

And dropped her to the floor,
I texted my big brother that he could make

A greater space for everyone to navigate
If he removed the bathroom door.

He quickly did as he was asked,
But I should have done more

Than I did. I should have done
Something more. I've kept the score.

I keep on keeping the score.
When it comes to my mother's

Last days, I should have done more
Than ask my brother to fix that door.

I should have done more. I should
Have done more. I should have bought

My mother a new door. A new house.
I should have bargained with the gods

And given my mother a few more weeks.
A few more days. A few more minutes.

I should have forgiven her for all of her sins
Against me. I should have asked to be

Forgiven for my sins against her.
But I never spoke of forgiveness. I only

Talked about the door. I only asked
My brother to perform the minor work

That I didn't know how to do. I made it
Easier for my mother to use the restroom.

That's all I did. That's all I did. Jesus,
I should have done more than worry

About that goddamn door. I should have
Done more. I should have done more.

But, wait, what exactly should I have done?
How could I have made anything better?

I don't know, not exactly, but I'm inexactly
Ashamed that I was, until the end, a bitter son.

11.

Some Prophecies
Are More Obvious
than Others

LILLIAN ALEXIE DIED on the night of July 1, 2015.

Like our mother, my siblings and I will eventually get cancer. And some of us—maybe all of us—will be killed by that cancer.

"You will get sick," my wife often says to me.

My wife is a Hidatsa/Ho-Chunk/Potawatomi Indian. The daughter of a Bureau of Indian Affairs administrator, she lived on five different reservations before her high school and college years in the relatively big city of Riverside, California. Therefore, she is wise and wise-ass.

"I know I will get cancer," I say to her.

"You have to be vigilant," she says.

"I know, I know," I say.

But how do I kill the cancer cells that probably infiltrated my body decades ago? Aren't those microscopic and domestic terrorists just waiting to strike? How do I stop the process that probably started when I took my first breath on the Spokane Indian Reservation?

I cannot defeat cancer. Nobody defeats cancer. There is no winning or losing. There is no surviving or not surviving.

There are only coin flips: heads or tails; benign or malignant; weight loss or bloating; morphine or oxycodone; extreme rescue efforts or Do Not Resuscitate; live or die.

12.

Terminal Velocity

Fuck you, Small-Cell Cancer. Fuck you, Fission,
For splitting cells, for birthing the tumors
That killed my mother. Diagnosed and dead

In a few weeks, my mother was evacuated
From this world like it was on fire.
Fuck you, Small-Cell Cancer, for invading

My mother's lungs. She was not a smoker!
I want to choke you to death, Small-Cell Cancer,
And suffocate you, suffocate you, suffocate you

Like you suffocated my mother. Fuck you,
Small-Cell Cancer, I want to shoot you in the
    heart
And mount you on the hood of my truck.

I want to trophy you like you trophied my
    mother.
Fuck you, Cancer, fuck you, Cemetery Dancer,
I'm going to learn or invent a war anthem—
A song that will obliterate you when you attack.
Note by note, my song will kill you, atom by
    atom.
My song will protect cousins, nieces, nephews,
    sisters

And brothers. My song will protect everybody's
    fathers
And mothers. Fuck you, fuck you, fuck you,
    Cancer,
For making me wish that I could write a song

Powerful enough to banish you. Fuck you, God
Of Cancer, for killing my mother, for splitting
    her
Into many halves, for turning her blood and
    body

Into host. Fuck you, Small-Cell Cancer. Fuck
    you,
Mr. Death, for making me so grateful to be
    alive—
For making me count and write odes to each
    breath.

Fuck you, Cancer, for being as constant as
　gravity—
For being as necessary as food, shelter, and
　warmth.
Fuck you, fuck you, Cancer, fuck you for your
　immortality.

13.

Who Died on the First of July?

Great American actor turned recluse
Marlon Brando died of respiratory
failure. After twenty years in exile,
Juan Perón died of a heart attack

One year into his return to power.
Wilhelm Bach, composer and eldest son
Of Johann Sebastian Bach, never
Lived up to his father's fame and genius

And died in poverty. Wolfman Jack,
Disc jockey and rock 'n' roll pioneer,
Died only moments after he returned
Home from work and kissed his wife.

Oliver Plunkett, Irish saint, was hanged,
Drawn and quartered because of his
  faith.
Harriet Beecher Stowe, abolitionist
And author of *Uncle Tom's Cabin,*

The novel that, according to some,
Was the first shot fired in the Civil War,
Died of natural causes. Nostradamus,
A doctor who believed that he could see

The future. Though I don't know if he
  predicted
His own death. Luther Vandross, the Tenor
Of the Gods, was only fifty-four years old
When he died of diabetes and heart failure.

Lillian Alexie, my mother, died
Of small-cell cancer in a hospital bed
At her reservation home. She'd wanted
To die on the living room couch where she'd
  slept

For nearly forty years. It wasn't the same
  couch
All that time. Five previous couches died
Before my mother did. She is survived
By the living and the ghosts of her tribe.

To honor her legacy, light a fire
So that you smell like powwow campground
  smoke.
In lieu of flowers, please donate your time
To quilt work, basketball, and dirty jokes.

14.

Drive, She Said

Traveling 296 miles to my mother's wake and
    funeral,
My wife and sons and I drive past

Five roadkill deer, two squashed coyotes, and a
    porcupine
Roughly ripped in half. In another time,

If my mother had been a passenger, she'd have
    insisted
That we pull over the car and park

So she could carefully collect that porcupine
And take it home to harvest the sharp quills

For war-dance regalia. But my mother is dead,
And my wife and sons and I don't war-dance,

So we drive past that dead porcupine
And abandon its ceremonial possibilities.

But I know, for the rest of my life,
I will think of my mother and her knife

And the dozens of times
She gave extraordinary meaning

To ordinary porcupines and their quills.
Ah, listen closely

When you drive along a two-lane highway
Between the pines

And you'll hear a hundred war-dancers
Rattling their now-human quills

And thanking my mother, thanking
My mother, thanking my mother

For her beauty and will.

15.

The Viewing

As the story goes, my beautiful cousin was born
With deer legs, dropped from the womb, and
  sprinted

Out of the clinic and made it halfway home
Before the tribal cops pulled her over for
  speeding.

In kindergarten, she was faster than every adult.
I watched her, three feet tall, outrace my
  father up

A sand hill while dodging rattlesnakes at Blue
  Creek.
In sixth grade, racing in her first organized meet,

She looked back near the finish line
And was so far ahead that she burst into tears

Because she'd hurt her opponents' feelings.
And then she never raced again.
In 2015, a few days after my mother's death,
My quick cousin stood next to me as I stared

At my dead mother lying in her plain pine coffin
At the funeral home in Spokane.

The undertakers were white men
But they'd buried generation of local Indians

So they knew how to culturally comfort us,
And better, they knew how to leave us alone.

That was the private family-and-friends viewing,
So that meant thirty loud Indians had gathered

In the otherwise quiet funeral home.
"Lillian looks beautiful," my cousin said.

And I had to agree. My mother wore her
    favorite
Turquoise business suit and a multicolored
Beaded medallion that could have eclipsed
The sun or moon. My cousin took my hand,

Bumped me with her hip, and said, "Hey,
You and I used to be the skinny and pretty
  cousins.

And now we're old and fat and homely."
"Hey," I said. "I'm still pretty from the neck up."

My cousin laughed and said, "My soul's spirit animal is
The butterfly, but my ass's spirit animal is the
  buffalo."
And I said, "I eat food like my father used to
  drink booze.
I binge and binge." And my cousin said, "Oh,
  man! Me, too!"

And then my cousin began to weep. I didn't cry
  with her.
But I mourned. I don't know if I was mourning
  my mother

Or if I was mourning for myself or if I was
  mourning
For my cousin's mourning. Maybe I was mourning everything.

"Nothing makes me hungrier than sadness," I
  said.

"I could eat a TV dinner made out of apple
strudel,

Salisbury steak, carrots, and grief." My cousin
smiled.
We hugged and shared a half-lipped cousinly
kiss,

Then ambled over to the waiting room, where
My eternal cousin reached into her tote bag

And pulled out a bag of nacho cheese tortilla
chips
Like it was a relic worthy of worship—

Like we'd just returned from an ancient vault
Where the dead worshipped only crunch and
salt.

My cousin and I ate all those chips. We ate the
walls
And floors. We ate all of the coffins, jewelry, and
shawls.

We ate all of the flowers. And we ate all of the air.
Then, for dessert, we ate all of the prayers.

16.

Everything Costs

SITTING IN THE funeral home, with my mother's body lying in view in another room only twenty feet away, I paid for her coffin and burial and transportation with a credit card.

I had enough cash to pay for all the expenses, but I wanted to collect the Alaska Airlines miles.

The bureaucracy of death. The sacredness of death. The sacredness of bureaucracy. The beauty of frequent-flyer miles.

"Did you know my mother?" I asked the white undertaker.

And yes, of course, he did.

"I talked to Lillian at many wakes and funerals," the undertaker said. "She was a funny person."

I'd been to twenty or thirty funerals on my reservation, but I realized that the undertaker had probably been to a hundred or more—he'd buried so many of my fellow tribal members.

No matter how much you think you know about death, there is always somebody else who knows more.

As I signed the funeral home contracts, I thought about the last time I had talked to my mother—the last time I'd talked to her before she had become seriously, and then terminally, ill.

Before she'd gotten sick, I had not seen or e-mailed or texted or spoken to my mother for—I don't know—three or five months. After all of that silence on my part, not exactly intentional but not at all surprising, she called and left a weeping message on my phone.

"Junior," she said. "I know you blame me for everything, but please talk to me."

A week later, I called.

"What's happening on the rez?" I asked. I didn't ask her about the weepy message she'd left. I didn't want to encourage her dramatics. I knew her tears had been lures.

"Oh," she said. "We had a funeral yesterday."

"Who died?"

She said the name. I remembered him. An old Indian guy who used to work forestry. I knew him better thirty years ago. I knew his kids twenty years ago. Didn't know his grandkids at all.

"How'd he die?" I asked.

"Heart attack."

I remembered when my mother used to cook for almost every funeral and wake on the reservation. Some other folks took over that responsibility after my mother got too old.

"That other family cooks now, right?" I asked my mother. "Instead of you?"

"Yeah," she said. "They'll cook for my wake and funeral when I die."

"That'll be weird," I said. "They hate me."

"That's okay. They love your brothers and sisters."

I laughed.

"And besides," she said. "They'll feed you good anyway. You know that's how it works."

The unwritten rules of tribalism. The inherent responsibilities. The silent acceptance of duty. The endless social legacy of a people who've spent most of their existence living at a subsistence level.

Taking care of one is taking care of the many. And vice versa.

"Remember that time in high school," I asked my mother, "when I slid on ice and drove into the ditch?"

"Which time?" my mother asked.

Another truth: If you live in a wintry climate and are too poor to afford good tires, then you will often hit the ditch, hopefully at low speeds.

"That time by the dump," I said. "When I was day-dreaming about winning the lottery and just spaced out."

"Oh, right," my mother said. "That's when your cousin pulled you out. You were lucky he showed up."

My cousin did rescue me and I was grateful to him. But he disliked me so much that he never said a word as he stopped his truck, grabbed a rope out of the back, tied one end to his rig and one end to mine, and pulled me out of the snow. And then he continued to ignore me as he untied the rope, got back in his truck, and drove away.

I am greatly amused by the white folks who believe that being Indian means you automatically fit like a puzzle piece into the jigsaw of your family and tribe. I'm even more amused by the Indians who believe that, too.

"Is there anything else you need?" I asked my mother on the phone.

I wanted to hang up. I couldn't handle too much time talking to her. I needed to reclaim my separation from her.

"Can you send some money?" she said. "I spent my Social Security on the cable bill and the electricity."

"I'll send a check," I said.

"Don't forget," she said,

"I won't forget."

"Yes, you will."

I did forget for a week. Then my mother left another message on my phone.

"Junior," she said. "We need firewood."

Except the message was garbled, so I thought she said, "Junior, she breathes fire good."

So imagine my disappointment when I discovered the truth.

"Oh, man," I said to my wife. "I thought maybe some woman named She Breathes Fire Good had moved to the rez. That sounds like a Montana Indian name, right? Like maybe a new Crow Indian woman doctor started working at the clinic. Dr. She Breathes Fire Good. That name rocks. I'm gonna write a new short story about a Crow doctor named that. It'll be awesome."

I haven't yet written that short story. I often have ideas for stories I know that I will never write.

But there is a good story in everything.

My mother died of lung cancer even though she had not smoked a cigarette in forty years.

So let me now imagine Dr. She Breathes Fire Good. Let me imagine she somehow diagnoses my mother when the cancer is only one split cell. Let me imagine that Dr. She Breathes Fire Good gave my mother another five years of life. Another ten. Another twenty.

Let me imagine my one-hundred-year-old mother leaving a message for the seventy-year-old me.

"Junior," she says into the machine. "You better call me. I could die at any second."

"Mom," I say back. "I'm an old Indian man. Chances are good I will die before you do."

But, of course, my mother died first. And my father is dead, too. And, based on health statistics and lifestyles, I would bet that I'm going to outlive my reservation-based siblings as well.

It's a morbid thought.

But it's not inaccurate.

Dear brothers, dear sisters, if you die before me, then I will pay to put you in the ground. I will bury you near our parents.

And, once or twice a year, I will lug my old and battered self to your collective grave and apologize for winning the final spin of the Alexie Family Terminal Cancer Roulette Wheel.

17.

Reviewing

IN THE FUNERAL home, I told my sister that my mother looked better than she had in years—better than she had since our father had died, twelve years earlier.

"The undertaker did a great job with her makeup," I said.

"He didn't make her look pretty," my sister said. "I did that."

"Wow," I said. "What did that feel like?"

"I felt like a little girl," she said. "Like Mom was teaching me how to put on makeup again."

"I don't remember her teaching you that," I said.

"Why would you remember that?" she asked.

"It just seems like a normal thing for a mother to teach a daughter," I said. "And Mom rarely did normal things."

"Well," my sister said. "Mom taught us how to put on makeup by making us practice on Dad."

"What?" I asked, and laughed. "You put makeup on Dad?"

"Yeah," my sister said. "Lipstick, eye shadow, blush, and everything."

"No way," I said. "I don't believe you."

"It's true."

"Dad was okay with that?" I asked.

"He didn't say anything," my sister said. "But I think he wished he looked prettier in makeup."

"What?" I said, and laughed even harder.

"Yeah," my sister said. "This one time, he stared at his face in the mirror and said, 'All that work and I still look like myself.'"

"That's so funny," I said. "Maybe Mom and Dad are doing each other's makeup in Heaven."

"That would be beautiful," my sister said. "And silly."

"If Heaven ain't filled with gender-swapping Indians," I said, "then I don't want to go there."

18.

Scatological

AFTER EVERYBODY ELSE left the funeral home—after our closest friends and family had said their private good-byes to my mother—I stayed behind to use the restroom.

As I squatted on the old toilet, I wept for the first time since my mother died. And then I shat. I wept and shat. And, yes, I am famously gifted as a weeper and a shitter.

My Alcoholics Anonymous friend—who remains nameless, of course, as do many other folks in this book—calls me Thunder Tears.

My siblings call me Dairy Queen because I have always filled up toilets like a human soft-serve ice cream machine.

Well, on that grief-stricken day, as my mother's

body lay only two walls away, I took the largest shit of my life. I expelled *everything*.

After I was done, I stood and looked at that shit cobra floating in the toilet, and I said aloud, "I'm gonna need Rikki-tikki-tavi to kill that thing."

And then I noticed the handwritten sign on the wall above the toilet: *Please be gentle with our toilet. The pipes are old. Be judicious in your use of toilet paper.*

I was impressed with the undertaker's vocabulary. But it was too late. I'd certainly been judicious with the toilet paper, but my shit was so large—so audacious—that I knew it would clog up that toilet and flood the bathroom.

Nobody wants to be the guy who clogs the toilet, let alone the commode only two rooms removed from his mother's coffin.

I realized that I needed to break my own shit into pieces in order to make it easier to flush.

But I also knew that the toilet would still clog if I tried to flush all of the pieces at once.

So I wrapped my right hand in paper, reached into the toilet, and chopped my shit into four manageable fragments. Then, using my paper-wrapped right hand as a dam, I held three pieces out of the water as I flushed the toilet with my left hand.

And then I waited a few minutes for the old toilet to refill so I could flush the second piece of shit.

And then I waited for even more minutes so I could flush the third piece of shit.

And then, finally, after maybe five minutes, I was able to flush the last piece of shit.

And then I washed my hands with all the liquid soap in the world.

I walked out of the bathroom to see the undertaker waiting for me.

"Are you okay?" he asked.

I was embarrassed.

"Yes," I said.

"I just wanted to make sure you were okay," he said. "You were in there a long time."

He was genuinely concerned. I knew his empathy was real. I knew I could be honest with him.

I said, "I just took a grief poop like you wouldn't believe. You ever seen a grief poop? Thing was big as a walrus."

The undertaker touched my shoulder.

"Happens all the time," he said.

He wished me well and said he would see me at the tribal longhouse the next day for my mother's wake and funeral.

He walked me to the door.

He said another good-bye.

He wished me well again.

He patted me on the shoulder.

But he didn't shake my hand.

19.

The Procession

THE UNDERTAKER DROVE my mother's body to the reservation. But he didn't use a hearse. No, he drove a black minivan converted into a more contemporary and fuel-efficient funeral carriage.

I guess death now has a smaller carbon footprint.

Behind the undertaker was the procession of seventeen cars filled with family and friends.

It took less than an hour to deliver my mother's body back to our reservation.

I thought it would feel more epic.

But it only felt like a sad and brief commute.

20.

Nonfiction

WE BURIED LILLIAN Alexie on July 6, 2015.

We'd thought about burying her on the Fourth of July, but the funeral expenses would have doubled and tripled because of the holiday.

Yes, saying good-bye to a Native American woman would have cost us more on Independence Day.

21.

Blood

At my mother's wake,
A mosquito alights
On my knuckle

And sucks and fattens
On my blood.
I ponder smashing

The damn thing
So I can pretend to read
My fortune

In the broken
Insect pieces.
But instead, I allow

That mosquito to fly
Away, fat and drunk.
I don't know if
I loved my mother.
I don't know
If she loved me.

At my mother's wake,
Another mosquito alights
On another knuckle

And sucks and fattens
On my blood.
When it reaches

Maximum density,
I smash
The damn thing

And read my fortune
In the broken
Insect pieces.

One wing says, "Yes,
You did love your mother."
And another wing says,

"And, yes, yes, of course,
Your mother loved you."
But the dismembered

Proboscis shouts,
"You don't have to forgive
Her sins or your sins

But it's probably best
If you give it a try,
You blood bag of a son."

At my mother's wake,
A third mosquito buzzes
My ear. And a fourth

And a fifth and a dozen more.
They're singing
For my mother.

It is only the female mosquitoes
Who know how to speak,
Who know how to sing,

Who know how to grieve.
So I stand at three in the morning
In the tribal longhouse

And I hum and hum
And hum along
Because I'm only a man

Who doesn't know
Any of the words or music
To this death song.

22.

Needle & Thread

My brother wanted to bury
My mother with the necklace

Gifted to her by her late husband—
Our late father—but my sister says,

"You want us to bury her
With all of her jewelry?
Like she's Cleopatra?"

We gave away that necklace
To a granddaughter instead.

We gave away other necklaces
And rings and beaded medallions
To cousins and friends.

We gave it away
Because an Indian's wealth

Is determined by what they lose
And not by what they save.

We gave away her clothes
To secondhand stores

And we give her deathbed
Back to the hospice.

But we keep her TV
Because that thing is HD

And epic and awesome.
But we don't know what to do

With the mounds of loose fabric
That my mother kept for quilting.

"There must be five hundred pounds
Of blue jeans," says my sister.

She says, "The only people who need
That much denim are Mr. Levi

And Mr. Wrangler themselves."
I tell my sister we should stitch

Random pieces together
And make five hundred scarecrows.
Then we'll round up wild bison
And tie those scarecrows

Onto the bisons' backs
Like angry denim and calico warriors.

And then we'll herd those scarecrowed bison
Into big trucks, drive them into Spokane

Or even into Washington, D.C., and release
  them
Into the streets and turn it all

Into a huge political installation art
  thing
That we'll call *Honor Our Treaty*
  Rights,
You Criminal White Motherfuckers from
  Hell.

My sister laughs
And ponders that for a bit.

Then she says, "You've got a lot of crafty
    ambition
For an Indian boy who can't sew for shit."

23.

How to Be an Atheist at a Spokane Indian Christian Funeral

We stay awake
For 29 hours—
We sisters

And brothers—
To guide our
Dead mother

As she transitions
Into something else.
If we are not here,

Near her coffin,
She might rise
And wander from

Sweat lodge to trading post
To post office to church
In search of us,

And maybe miss the last bus
To whatever happens
Next. I don't believe

In the afterlife
But I stay awake
To honor my siblings' grief

And our mother's theology.
I don't believe in God
But I pray anyway.

And when it is time
To throw dirt
Onto my mother's coffin,

I say good-bye
Only in my head.
I don't believe

I will see her again,
But I know I will see
My siblings because

We are still alive.
So I try to remain
Respectfully silent

Even when the Evangelical
Indian preacher delivers
A graveside tangent

About the Rapture
And how true believers
Will be lifted into Heaven

At 186,000 miles per minute,
At 186,000 miles per minute,
At 186,000 miles per minute.

"Oh, you dumb-ass
Fundamentalist," I think.
"The speed of light

Is 186,000 miles *per second*."
And then I laugh and laugh
Because I imagine

My mother in charge
Of her own damn story
As she slowly, slowly ascends

Into her Personal Glory.
"Dear God," she texts.
"I'll get there when I get there.

I know the path.
Just leave a key
Under the welcome mat."

24.

Brother Man

I have seen my big brother cry
Only twice in my life. The first,
In 1977, when our mother gathered us
In my brother's basement bedroom

To tell us that Arthur Tulee—
My brother's best friend who'd,
The previous year, moved
From our reservation to another—

Had drowned in the Yakima River.
Upon hearing the news,
My brother fell to the floor
Like a skinny stick and wept so hard

That I feared he would aspirate
His pain and dry-drown.
The second time I saw my brother cry
Was at our mother's funeral.

As we adult siblings stood together
At my mother's open coffin,
With our arms wrapped around
One another in a grief-scrum—

Collectively, we five siblings must
  weigh
Sixteen hundred pounds. Shit,
We're a defensive line
Of hunger and insatiable sorrow.

At our mother's coffin,
My brother shook so violently
That I thought he might fall again,
A much more dangerous thing now

That he was over fifty years old
With gout, arthritis, and fragile hips.
But he leaned against the coffin,
Supported by our mother one last time,

And kept his balance. But oh,
He cried into his fists

And I cried, too, but more
For my brother's loss

Than for the loss of our mother.
Truth be told, I had only seen her
Three or four times a year
Over the last decade of her life,
And talked to her on the phone
Maybe twice a month. I had become
The farthest planet orbiting her
But my brother had lived his entire life

Never more than ten minutes away
From our mother's star.
He loved her far more than I did
So I knew his grief was larger

And more pure than mine.
I grieved that I hadn't been loved
   enough
By our cold mother
While my brother mourned her.

I am the brother with money and fame
But he is the brother who possesses
The most kindness and pain.
I wonder if I will ever see him weep
   again.

I wonder if I want to see
My brother weep again,
I have never known how to comfort
   him.
I don't even know how to take his joy,

As when, moments after we'd
   learned
About Arthur Tulee's death,
We got a phone call from Arthur's
   mother
To tell us that it was a different

Arthur Tulee who had drowned.
My brother's best friend was alive!
Oh, my brother rose to his feet
And slammed himself against

His bedroom door. Laughing,
He shadowboxed the air.
Laughing, he punched
As if he wanted to push

The house from its foundation.
Laughing, he thanked God
And he thanked our mother.
And then he stopped

Laughing, threw one last punch
Against the air, wiped the tears
From his face, and went searching
And searching and searching for lunch.

25.

Silence

FROM WINTER 1987 until summer 1990, my mother and I didn't say a word to each other, not through letters, not on the phone, not through intermediaries, and not in person. She and I didn't speak to each other when we were in the same house. Not when we were in the same room. Not when we were in the same car.

I tried to break the silence in 1989 when my parents drove to Pullman, Washington, to give me cash to pay the rent for my college apartment.

My father chatted in the living room with Kari, my white girlfriend, while I walked outside to make peace with my mother, sitting in the car.

"You have to talk to her," Kari had said a few moments before my parents arrived. "She's your mother."

That particular argument didn't quite convince

me. After all, Gertrude was Hamlet's mother, and look how that ended up.

"My mom is crazy," I said.

"She reminds me of Zsa Zsa Gabor," Kari said.

I remembered that Zsa Zsa was a Hungarian-born actress and socialite. I'd never seen any of her movies or TV shows, and I'd certainly never attended any of her society parties, but I still knew so many details about her life. As they say, she was famous for being famous. Zsa Zsa was charismatic in the banal and voracious way that reality stars like Kim Kardashian are charismatic now.

"Why does my mom remind you of Zsa Zsa?" I asked Kari.

"Because your mom gets all the attention like a beautiful actress," she said. "And she has a fancy accent."

"My mom is from the rez," I said, and laughed. "Rez accents are the opposite of fancy."

"You just say that because you don't like the sound of your voice," Kari said. "But rez accents make everything sound like music."

I waved away the compliment.

"Should I marry a man who doesn't talk to his mother?" Kari asked. "You think I want a mother-in-law who treats her son this way, too? Maybe you two should marry each other. Or marry yourselves. You're like the same person anyway."

Kari often said insightful and funny shit like that. She was an eccentric small-town empath. So, because I respected Kari and her opinions, and because I missed talking to my mother, I tried to end the silence, to make amends, to restart our relationship, to do *something*.

I was desperate.

As I walked toward my mother, sitting alone in the car, I knew she was aware of me. She knew I was walking toward her. She knew I was going to use my words. It was a strangely religious experience, like I was a pilgrim searching for wisdom from a monk who had not spoken in one hundred years.

"Hey, Mom," I said.

She didn't respond. She was making a scarf or baby blanket or some rectangular object of beauty. All I could hear was the *click-click* of her knitting needles.

"Mom," I said. "Talk to me."

Knitting needles.

"Mom, please."

Click-click.

Furious, I spun and rushed back to my apartment. I passed my father along the way.

"'Bye, Dad," I said. We were poor Indians. It was always a struggle to find enough money to enjoy a decent life, let alone pay for college. I was grateful to him for paying that month's rent, but I was too mad to properly show my appreciation.

I was an asshole.

Back in the apartment, I yelled at Kari.

"You told me to talk to her! You made me do it! And she just ignored me! It was embarrassing!"

Like I said, I was an asshole.

I screamed, ran at the living room wall, and slammed into it like I was trying to tackle the apartment building. Then I punched the wall once, twice, three times.

I left a shoulder-shaped dent in the cheap plasterboard. And three fist-shaped holes. I was lucky I only punched through the hollow plasterboard and didn't break my hand on a wooden or metal wall stud.

Now, after years of good mental health care, I can look back and see that my rage—my assholery—was mostly the product of undiagnosed and untreated post-traumatic stress disorder and bipolar emotional swings. But, in my youth, I only knew that I needed to physically, if irrationally, express my rage. I didn't want to hit my mother or my father or Kari, or anybody else, so I punched objects. I punched metaphors. So, at that moment, I would have certainly kicked our metaphorical God in his even more metaphorical nuts if I'd been given the chance.

Kari, bored and scared by my self-righteous and self-pitying temper, gathered up her things and walked back to her apartment. We'd flirted in high school and had kissed a few times. And then we dated in college

121

until a year after she graduated. She didn't want to marry a writer, she said, especially one who was probably going to be famous. Yes, she believed in my artistry if not my marriageability. I used her manual typewriter to write my first two or three hundred poems and stories. You want to know the identity of my first muse and benefactor? She was a math- and science-minded white woman with an auto-mechanic father. Kari fed me when I had no money.

I loved her. She loved me.

But I don't know how much joy she experienced while loving me. I don't know much joy I was capable of feeling or providing.

So, after my mother ignored me again, and after I made holes in the walls, and after Kari walked home, I rounded up some poet friends—none of whom write anymore—and we pooled our meager resources and got drunk in the cocktail bar of a Chinese restaurant. We drunkenly vowed to start our own literary magazine, like all drunken student poets do, but we'd publish only "the good shit," which meant that we'd print only our poems and any poems that sounded exactly like ours.

Then we argued about naming the magazine.

"Let's call it *The Silent Mother*," I said.

I remember that one of my friends—it was probably Old John—said *The Silent Mother* sounded more like a Bette Davis movie than a poetry magazine.

Zsa Zsa Gabor. Bette Davis. Lillian Alexie. It might sound ludicrous to think of my mother as being a part of that grandiose trinity. But she really did loom that large for me. And she loomed that large in our tribe. She was wildly intelligent, arrogant, opinionated, intimidating, and generous with her time and spirit. She was a contradictory person. She was, all by herself, an entire tribe of contradictions.

What do you call a gathering of women like Lillian? A contradiction of mothers.

At her funeral, half of the mourners talked about being kindly rescued by my mother. For many years, she was the drug and addiction treatment counselor for our tribe. She helped at least a dozen addicts get clean and stay clean. She helped many other addicts get clean once, twice, three, four times and more in that endless cycle of sobriety and relapse.

"She never gave up on me," said one mourner. "She helped me get my kids back after I lost them to foster care. I raised my own kids because of Lillian."

Three other mourners also praised my mother for helping them get back their kids.

My mother was a lifeguard on the shores of Lake Fucked.

But hey, my mother's eldest daughter died in an alcoholic-fueled trailer fire. Two of her other children are active alcoholics. One is a recovering drug addict. And then there's me, the dry-drunk poet with a Scrabble board full of mental illness acronyms. Only one of my mother's children is a nondrinker and nonsmoker and nonpill swallower.

Her husband, our father, died of alcoholism.

My mother, the healer, could not heal the people closest to her. I don't know if she tried to help us.

At my mother's funeral, many other mourners talked about being publicly rebuked and shamed by her.

"At the powwow," a mourner said, "I sat in a folding chair and Lillian yelled at me and told me I should let an elder have that chair. Made me cry. I was just a kid. But she was right. Lillian was always right about stuff like that. I have never sat in a folding chair at any powwow ever again. I probably won't sit in a folding chair even when I'm old."

"I was at the post office," said another mourner. "This was when I was a senior in high school and we lost that big game to Selkirk. Anyway, Lillian comes walking up to me and she yells at me for being a ball hog. For shooting too much. And I yell back, saying I pass the ball all the time, and then she yells at me about one play. At the end of the third quarter, on a fast break, I went up for a jump shot. And I was in midair when I saw Greg was open in the key. I knew I should pass to him, but I wanted to make a buzzer beater. I wanted to pass and I wanted to shoot. Anyway, I ended up shooting but was so distracted by everything that I threw up an air ball. I missed everything. And Lillian is yelling at me in the post office. She yells about that air ball. She tells me I shot an air ball because I felt guilty about not passing. She tells me Greg was open. She saw that Greg was open. And she was right. Man, Lillian knew basketball."

Yes, my mother had vision. She had glare. So imagine how it felt to grow up under her surveillance.

At her wake and funeral, after hours of listening to other Indians talk about my mother's life and death, I stood to deliver my eulogy. I'd wanted to say something epic and honest. But epics are rarely honest, and honesty should never be epic.

I said, "My mother and I had a difficult relationship. We weren't always kind to each other. So it's good to hear how kind she was to some of you. But it hurts, too, to hear that she mothered some of you better than she mothered me. And it was also good to hear how mean she was to some of you, too. I knew the mean Lillian maybe better than all of you, maybe even better than my brothers and sisters. My mother was good to people and she was mean to people. And sometimes, she was good and mean to the same person at the same time. Anyway, that's all I really have to say. I am not a traditional Indian. You all know that. I don't sing or dance or do the ceremonies. I don't pray like other people pray. I just talk. So I am really going to miss talking to my mother. I am really going to miss her voice."

My mother is buried next to my father. They share a tombstone. My reservation is a very quiet place. You can hear the wind whistling through the pine trees from miles away.

Hush, hush, hush, the wind says to the trees.

Hush, hush, hush, the trees say to the wind.

Yes, there was a three-year span when my mother and I did not speak to each other.

But I cannot remember exactly why we stopped talking to each other.

And I do not remember the moment when we forgave each other and resumed our lifelong conversation.

How could I have forgotten important shit like that? I have no answers for that question. And my mother has no answers, either, because she is dead.

26.

Your Multiverse
or Mine?

AT MY MOTHER'S funeral, my smartest Indian friend—the one who never went to college—corners me to deliver a metaphysical lecture.

He says, "In an alternate universe, exploding next to this one, you are the creator of your mother. You are her mad scientist and she is your monster.

"In another universe, you are the man who gives birth to his own mother. I know that sounds crazy but, speaking outside of biology, it's possible.

"And in the universe next to that, your mother and you are strangers who ride the same train to work every day and are always unsettled by the sense of having met before. You stare at each other all the time.

"And in that universe after that—well, I just

blanked and can't think of any other universes—but physics teaches us that all kinds of crazy shit is theoretically possible.

"I mean, in another universe, maybe I'm your mother.

"Maybe there are ninety-nine people, totally unknown to you in this universe, who are your mother in other universes. And you spend all your time, in this universe, trying to find the ninety-nine people who retain a bit of that other-universe maternity and can maybe give you the love and attention you ache for.

"Maybe there are ninety-nine women in the world who you could have happily married because they are your mother in other universes.

"Maybe your wife is your mother in another universe.

"Or maybe I'm full of shit. Maybe I'm just trying to assuage your grief. Maybe I'm just trying to find some way to help you believe in a world beyond this one.

"I'm sorry I sound so crazy.

"I just want you to believe in something. If you won't let religion help ease your pain, Junior, then maybe you'll let science comfort you."

I hugged my friend because I love him and because I didn't know how to respond in that moment and because I wanted him to shut up.

But, now, let me respond to my smart and eccentric friend with a little poem:

Ah, friend, this world—this one universe—
Is already too expansive for me.
When I die, let my mourners know
That I shrugged at the possibility
Of other universes. Hire a choir—
Let them tell the truth
But tell it choral—
Let the assembled voices sing
About my theology:
I'm the fragile and finite mortal
Who wanted no part of immortality.

27.

Clotheshorse

DURING MY MOTHER'S funeral, one of her friends—a man I'll call Xavier because I grew up vaguely Catholic—walked up to me and said, "Your shirt is wrinkled."

I felt the urge to punch him. But Xavier is a tiny man. I probably would've broken his face and ended up in jail.

I also felt the urge to say, "Xavier, you've been a jerk your whole damn life. I have my theories about why you've been so angry since puberty. But I ain't judging you for having those theoretical fears and doubts. I'm judging you because you've let your fears and doubts turn you into a judgmental little monster."

But I didn't say any of that. I just smiled and said, "I'm always wrinkled."

The smug bastard walked away. I suppose he thought that he'd burned me with his quick wit. We Spokane Indians are famous for our verbal cruelty. I'd been trained from an early age to fire insults like arrows. Hell, I've made a lucrative career out of being a smart-ass who can cuss you out in free verse or in rhyme and meter. But I wasn't interested in insulting Xavier back.

Well, I didn't want to dishonor my mother by insulting her friend during the funeral. And maybe I had the slightest bit of compassion for him. After all, he'd been my mother's friend for years. He was in pain.

But, regardless of that pain, I am perfectly content to give him hell now that the funeral is only a memory.

Hey, Xavier, at my mother's funeral, did you notice that I am at least a foot taller than my sisters, nieces, and female cousins? Did you also notice that all of them were crying? So maybe, if you had noticed those things and put the clues together, Xavier, you could have solved the sartorial crime. My shirt was wrinkled because a few dozen short women had pressed their weepy faces into my chest when they hugged me. Did you also notice that my shirt was damp with tears and makeup?

Dear Xavier, my shirt was wrinkled because of our family's collective grief.

And, okay, okay, okay, I had also pulled the imperfectly folded shirt from the suitcase that morning, and had briefly considered ironing it, but then thought, *Rez funerals are way casual and 90 percent of the Indians will be in T-shirts and jean shorts anyway, so it doesn't really matter.*

So, yeah, honestly speaking, my shirt wasn't exactly crisp when I arrived at my mother's funeral, but my sisters and cousins had wrinkled it even more with their grief.

So, yeah, honestly speaking, fuck you, Xavier, and the farm-raised salmon you rode in on.

28.

Eulogize Rhymes with *Disguise*

When I was four and weeping
For my father, gone
On another binge-drinking
Sabbatical, my mother tore

Me from my bed at 4 a.m.
On a December night
And pushed me outside
Onto the porch.

"You can come back in when
You stop crying!" she screamed
And slammed and locked
The door. It wasn't a freezing night

And the porch was covered
So I wasn't completely exposed.
And, for more warmth, I crawled
Into the doghouse with our mutts.

Three minutes or three hours later—
I don't know which—my mother
 opened
The door and called me back inside.
But I refused. I told her I would sleep

With the dogs. And I did, I did,
Like some prehistoric Indian boy
Learning how to survive
Any weather or wilderness.

At my mother's funeral,
I heard other tribal members
Remember her as someone better
Than I had ever known—

I briefly wondered if I was at a funeral
For a stranger who only resembled
My mother. Then my cousin,
Wearing a ribbon shirt and moccasins

Made by my mother, said, "Lillian was
Our last connection to the ancient

Stories and songs. Lillian was
Also a mean and foulmouthed

Woman who scolded everybody.
Right now, I bet you Lillian just arrived
In Heaven and is scolding Jesus
For playing the wrong welcoming song."
We all laughed and laughed
Because, yes, my mother was
Exactly the kind of mortal
Who challenged the Gods.

She was the reservation Medea.
She was the indigenous Antigone.
But just imagine how it felt to be
Her fragile child. I never stopped

Being afraid of her. I never left
That dark porch. I am still
Sleeping with those dogs.
Yes, I am always cold and curled

Like a question mark
Among those animal bodies.
As I wait for the glorious
Warmth of the rising sun.

29.

The Undertaking

Five days after our mother's death,
We bury her next to our father,
And as I stare at their shared
Gravestone, I see our mother's date

Of birth carved into the granite
And realize belatedly that we'd
Forgotten to hire somebody
To carve her date of death.

I also realize that it was odd—
And equally fatalistic
And romantic—to have carved,
At our mother's request, her name

Into this gravestone twelve years ago
When we buried our father—her husband.
So, yes, our mother lived for over
A decade with her name etched above

Her grave-to-be. And now, as we lower her
Into the grave-that-is, she doesn't have
An official date of expiration.
Does this make her potentially immortal?

If we never hire a carver
To finish the gravestone then maybe
We can pretend that this funeral
Is yet another one of her spectacular lies.

Dear Mother, you bipolar necromancer,
I fully expect you to rise like a shawl dancer
Out of your false coffin and cry,
"Surprise, surprise, I am still alive!"

30.

The Urban Indian Boy
Sings a Death Song

How does one deliver an honest eulogy?
I mean—shit, shit, shit—I lied when my mother
    died
And said nothing forceful about her cruelty

Or her kindness. I could have said she was crazy
And dead-salmon cold and pathologically lied,
But who wants such honesty in a eulogy?

I could have celebrated her sobriety
And chastised drunk cousins for their various
    crimes
Against our tribe or their specific cruelty—

With their fists and cocks—against me and my
    body.
But I would have been speaking out of angry
    pride.
My narcissism could have turned my eulogy

Into *Law & Order* courtroom testimony.
I could've said, "I felt safe almost half the time
With Mom. She protected me against cruelty

Three days a week." And, yes, I know my
    scrutiny
Is dead-salmon cold and probably misapplied,
But I want this to be an honest eulogy
About how I learned to receive and deliver
    cruelty.

31.

Downtown

AT MY MOTHER'S funeral, my sister said, "When she was really sick, Mom was talking about the time she lost custody of us."

"They only lost us once?" I asked.

"She only talked about one time," my sister said.

I'd heard stories about Social Service visits to our various childhood homes—and knew we'd been taken away once—but I didn't know the details.

"When did this happen?" I asked.

"Arlene and I were just a few months old," my sister said. "And you were still just a baby. And Arnold was a toddler."

"Why'd they lose us?" I asked. "What did they do?"

"Drinking, I'm sure," my sister said.

"And probably one of the times we were living in Spokane," I said.

"Probably."

I have only impressionistic memories of living with my parents in a series of sad-ass residential hotels in downtown Spokane. And I've likely created those memories by blending old photographs I've seen firsthand with old stories I've heard secondhand.

So I remember my father pulling three empty drawers out of a dresser to use as cribs for my two sisters and me.

I remember the smell of cigarette smoke and body odor.

I remember the old black man who worked the manual elevator in one of those places.

I remember ratty area rugs and sticky wood floors.

I remember a lot of Indians, familiar and strange, staring at me.

But I don't have any memories, impressionistic or not, about becoming wards of the state.

"You think Mom was telling the truth about losing us?" I asked my sister.

"You think she'd lie when she knew she was dying?" my sister asked me.

"Yes," I said.

My mother was a fabulist. Wouldn't her deathbed have been her greatest stage? Wouldn't the people at her bedside have been her most captive audience?

Sometimes, my mother was such a gifted liar that she would fool even us children—her most ardent skeptics. But she sometimes lied so obviously that it shocked us, too. After my older son was born with meconium aspiration that collapsed his lungs, he was put on a blood transfer machine for a week. Then he was in neonatal intensive care for another two weeks. He was critically ill. He'd crashed twice—he'd died—and had to be resuscitated. He had a stroke. And even after he'd made it through those difficult early days, he still had major struggles with eating, walking, and talking. He has since grown into a vibrant adult—an actual Eagle Scout—but for the first year of his life, my mother told every Indian she could that my son had been born *without a brain.*

I usually let her falsehoods go unchallenged—it was too exhausting to police all of them—but I eventually called her on the phone about that particular lie.

"Mom," I said. "Why are you telling people my son doesn't have a brain?"

"Isn't that what's wrong with him?" she asked.

"You know it's his lungs," I said. "You know his brain was oxygen-starved and damaged. But he still has a brain. And a good one, too. He has spoken to you on the phone."

"Okay," she said.

I thought the issue had been resolved, but then my mother told people that my son *didn't have lungs.*

So, yes, I knew that my mother was capable of slinging bullshit even as she lay dying.

"Mom didn't give you any details about why they lost custody of us?" I asked my sister.

"She just said they lost us and we were put in a foster home," my sister said.

I wondered what terrible shit might have happened to four Indian kids in four foster homes.

"She said all of us stayed together," my sister said. "With that redhead white woman. She became our babysitter later. Remember her?"

I couldn't remember her name but, yes, I remembered that redhead. I think I remember a photograph of her visiting our house at Christmas.

"Are you sure Mom didn't give you more details?" I asked my sister again.

"That's it," my sister said. "This is all I know."

I can only imagine how my parents might have lost us.

I imagine we were living in a Spokane hotel and that my father had gone drinking at one of the nearby Indian bars—probably the Buck & Doe—and left my mother and us in the hotel room. And my mother was probably pissed to be left behind with three babies and a toddler. And since she was constantly drinking in those days, she was probably boozing it up in the room. Or maybe she was suffering from a minor case of alcohol withdrawal. Maybe she was beer-thirsty and going crazy in that little room. So I imagine she sang us to sleep. She had a beautiful voice and could always sing us to sleep. And then I bet she left us children sleeping in that hotel room and went to have a few drinks. I can imagine her saying to herself: "Okay, Lillian, you're going to have three beers and then you're coming back to the room to your babies."

So maybe a few swallows became a lot of drinks. And I would imagine that she eventually met up with our father. They probably drank until closing time, and then they probably went to an after-hours party at somebody's house or apartment. Maybe they even came back to the hotel and partied in a nearby room. Maybe they both passed out some-where and completely forgot about us.

So I imagine that, sometime during that drunken night, one of us children woke in our dark hotel room and cried. I imagine the first of us to cry woke the second baby and the third and the fourth.

I imagine us as a small chorus. I Imagine us crying so loud and strong that our weeping became a tribal song.

I imagine us waking our hotel neighbors with our syncopated fear.

I imagine hotel staff being summoned.

I imagine the night manager knocking on our door.

I imagine a passkey being used.

I imagine the shock and disgust of discovering four abandoned Indian babies weeping and weeping and weeping and weeping.

I imagine the policemen arriving.

I imagine them carrying us to a county shelter with donated cribs and beds.

I imagine four white women holding four sleeping Indian babies and rocking them to sleep.

So, yes, this seems like a plausible version of how we were lost. And it makes me sad and angry as an adult to imagine my mother returning to the hotel to discover that her babies had been officially taken away.

But I cannot imagine how much shame she must have felt.

"You know," I said to my sister later at the funeral. "I think Mom is telling the truth about losing us. We're never going to know the exact details. But there's too much real pain in this story for it to be a lie."

My sister nodded. She agreed. But what did we agree to? Jesus, we as adults were grateful that our mother had probably told the truth about endangering us as children.

How fucked is that?

32.

Dear Dylan Thomas, Dear Dr. Extreme, Dear Rage

Hey, climber, you fell from such a great height.
Does that mean your death was somehow better
Than my mom's? She was in bed when she died.

Hey, hiker, you fought a courageous fight,
But did not survive that winter weather
And were found frozen at such a great height.

Hey, pilot, on your experimental flight,
You shattered like a ceramic feather.
My mom was wholly in bed when she died.

She never base-jumped or surfed in the night
Or walked across glacier gaps on ladders.
She never touched sea floors or great heights.

She was female, poor, indigenous, bright,
Commodified, hunted, and tape-measured.
She survived one hundred deaths before she
    died,

But was never thrilled by her endangered life.
So death became her gentle endeavor.
We raised her last bed to a modest height,
Then she sighed, sighed, closed her eyes, and
    died.

33.

Lasting Rites

I was not
At my mother's side
When she took
Her last breath.

I was home
in Seattle
Waiting for word
Of her death.

My sister
Texted, "She's gone."
I collapsed
With grief,

But to tell
The difficult truth:
I also collapsed
With relief.

I assumed
I'd be freed
From my mother
And her endless

Accusations,
Falsehoods,
Exaggerations,
And deceptions.

But looking
At this book,
I was obviously
Mistaken,

because my mother continues to scare the shit out of me. On a morning soon after her death, my phone rang. The caller ID announced it was "MOM." For a moment, I believed it was her calling from the afterlife. So I pondered what I would say. And I decided that I'd go with "Hey, Lillian, gotta say I'm impressed with your resurrection, but is it a Jesus thing or a zombie fling?" Of course, it wasn't my mother. It was my sister calling me from our mother's house. "Dang," I said to my sister. "I really thought you were Mom come back to life." And my sister said, "I know what you mean. This morning, I made her a cup of coffee and set it on the table and wondered why she hadn't drunk it yet."

Dear Mother,
My jury,
As you travel
Into the nocturnal,

As you continue
To make me hold
My breath
Even after your death,

Could it be
That you've finally
And strangely
Become maternal?

34.

Equine

At my mother's funeral, I learned the three
   horses
Who'd escaped their barn years ago have transformed—

Have lightninged and thundered—
Into a wild herd of 400.

O wild horses, O wild horses, as you run,
I hope that my mother has become 401.

35.

Feast

AFTER WE BURIED my mother, we feasted. Dozens of people sat in the tribal longhouse and ate venison stew, salmon, and fry bread. Hot dogs and hamburgers. Kool-Aid and soda pop. Apple and cherry pie.

My cousin the logger said, "Junior, I wish I saw you somewhere except funerals."

I smiled. He was right. I was a stranger to him.

"Did you kill this deer I'm eating?" I asked.

"Yes," he said.

"Thank you for hunting," I said.

"Thank the deer," he said.

"Yes," I said. "Bless you. And bless the deer."

"You should come hunting with us next time."

I thought he was serious—and tried to imagine

hobbling with my bad back through the pine forests in search of a deer or elk—but then my cousin laughed and laughed.

"Little Sherm the Great Indian Hunter!" he proclaimed.

I laughed and laughed with him and ate two more bowls of venison stew.

36.

U t e n s i l

While feasting
On venison stew
After we buried my mother,
I recognized my spoon

And realized my family
Had been using it
For at least forty-two years.
How does one commemorate

The ordinary? I thanked
The spoon for being a spoon

And finished my stew.
How does one get through

A difficult time? How does
A son properly mourn his mother?
It helps to run the errands—
To get shit done. I washed

That spoon, dried it,
And put it back
In the drawer,
But I did it consciously,

Paying attention
To my hands, my wrists,
And the feel of steel
Against my fingertips.

Then my wife drove us back
Home to Seattle, where I wrote
This poem about ordinary
Grief. Thank you, poem,

For being a poem. Thank you,
Paper and ink, for being paper
And ink. Thank you, desk,
For being a desk. Thank you,

Mother, for being my mother.
Thank you for your imperfect love.
It almost worked. It mostly worked.
Or partly worked. It was almost enough.

37.

Sibling Rivalry

Yes, my mother was a better mother
To my sisters and brothers,

But they were better children

Than me, the prodigal who yearned
And spurned and never returned.

38.

Eulogy

My mother was a dictionary.

She was one of the last fluent speakers of our tribal language.

She knew dozens of words that nobody else knew.

When she died, we buried all of those words with her.

My mother was a dictionary.

She knew words that had been spoken for thousands of years.

She knew words that will never be spoken again.

She knew songs that will never be sung again.

She knew stories that will never be told again.

My mother was a dictionary.

My mother was a thesaurus,

My mother was an encyclopedia.

My mother never taught her children the tribal language.

Oh, she taught us how to count to ten.

Oh, she taught us how to say "I love you."

Oh, she taught us how to say "Listen to me."

And, of course, she taught us how to curse.

My mother was a dictionary.

She was one of the last four speakers of the tribal language.

In a few years, the last surviving speakers, all elderly, will also be gone.

There are younger Indians who speak a new version of the tribal language.

But the last old-time speakers will be gone.

My mother was a dictionary.

But she never taught me the tribal language.

And I never demanded to learn.

My mother always said to me, "English will be your best weapon."

She was right, she was right, she was right.

My mother was a dictionary.

When she died, her children mourned her in English.

My mother knew words that had been spoken for thousands of years.

Sometimes, late at night, she would sing one of the old songs.

She would lullaby us with ancient songs.

We were lullabied by our ancestors.

My mother was a dictionary.

I own a cassette tape, recorded in 1974.

On that cassette, my mother speaks the tribal language.

She's speaking the tribal language with her mother, Big Mom.

And then they sing an ancient song.

I haven't listened to that cassette tape in two decades.

I don't want to risk snapping the tape in some old cassette player.

And I don't want to risk letting anybody else transfer that tape to digital.

My mother and grandmother's conversation doesn't belong in the cloud.

That old song is too sacred for the Internet.

So, as that cassette tape deteriorates, I know that it will soon be dead.

Maybe I will bury it near my mother's grave.

Maybe I will bury it at the base of the tombstone she shares with my father.

Of course, I'm lying.

I would never bury it where somebody might find it.

Stay away, archaeologists! Begone, begone!

My mother was a dictionary.

She knew words that have been spoken for thousands of years.

She knew words that will never be spoken again.

I wish I could build tombstones for each of those words.

Maybe this poem is a tombstone.

My mother was a dictionary.

She spoke the old language.

But she never taught me how to say those ancient words.

She always said to me, "English will be your best weapon."

She was right, she was right, she was right.

39.

Drum

AM I DANCING on my mother's grave?

Well, my mother would have loved to be the subject of a memoir, no matter how laudatory and/or critical. Or rather, if the memoir were equally positive and negative. She would have loved all of the attention. She would have sat beside me in bookstores and signed copies of this book.

And, if she could do it from the afterlife, my mother would schedule a giant powwow on her grave.

"Okay, folks, welcome to the Seventeenth Annual Lillian Alexie Gravesite Powwow. Every song at this powwow will be a Special for Lillian. Every Grand Entry, Owl Dance, Blanket Dance, and Happy Dance will be for Lillian. And, yes, the venerable

Prairie Chicken Dance will also be for Lillian. Okay, next drum is the Lillian Alexie Memorial Singers. This song will be an Intertribal. That means everybody gets to dance. Even you white people. Yes, that means all of you white people will also be dancing for Lillian. So, okay, Lillian Alexie Memorial Singers, whenever you're ready, you can take it away!"

Am I dancing on my mother's grave?

Of course I am!

Now shut up and listen to the song.

You need to two-step, two-step, two-step, two-step with the drum's rhythm. But ain't nobody gonna judge you if you miss a beat.

Ah, listen to the singers drumming and them drummers singing.

Ain't they celebratory? Ain't they mournful? Ain't they angry? Ain't they sweet?

Listen to the drum, the drum, the drum, the drum, the drum.

Hey, grave-dancers, I'm calling all of you grave-dancers, come and grave-dance with me.

40.

Rebel Without a Clause

I AM Sherman Joseph Alexie, Jr., and I have always struggled with being the second of my name. Everybody on the reservation called me Junior. Most of my family and childhood friends still call me Junior. During my youth, there were at least five or six other men and boys who were also called Junior. A couple of guys, named John and Joseph after their father, went by John-John and JoJo, which makes me wonder if things like this have ever been said:

"Hey, my name is Joseph, and this is my son, JoJo, and that's my grandson, JoJoJo, and his best friend, John-John-Johnny."

There are a lot of Juniors in the Indian world. That might seem like a product of patriarchal European colonial culture, and maybe it is, but we Indians have also created patriarchal systems of our own. My tribe has elected only two women to Tribal Council in 122 years. Even Crazy Horse, the famous Oglala warrior, was named for his father. But nobody called him Junior, for rather logical reasons.

"Look! There's the most feared and mysterious Indian of all time! Behold! It is Junior!"

So, yeah, as a name, Junior lacks a certain gravitas. And Crazy Horse, Jr., isn't all that much better. It seems oddly formal and carnivalesque at the same time:

"Hello, my name is Crazy Horse, Jr., attorney at law, and I am here to fight for your tribal rights!"

I never hated my father, but I didn't want to share his moniker. This personal struggle is the reason I wrote a picture book, *Thunder Boy Jr.,* about a Native boy's rather innocent and ultimately successful quest for a new name.

My quest wasn't as innocent and it wasn't all that successful either.

At age three, when I was first taught how to spell my name—my nickname—I immediately added a *u* and wrote "Juniour."

"That's wrong," the preschool teacher said. He was an eccentric white man who did double duty as my speech therapist. He was also an ex-Catholic priest and would later be the publisher, editor, writer, and photographer for an alternative rag that directly competed with the tribe's official newspaper. So, yes, that white man was the *Village Voice* of the Spokane Indian Reservation. He was the White Fallen Holy Man with a Mimeograph Machine. Years later, he would take my first official author photo. But in 1969, he was just trying to teach a rez boy how to spell his own damn name.

"There is only one *u* in Junior," he said.

"I know it's wrong," I said. "But that's how I'm going to spell it. That's my name."

Many of you doubt that a three-year-old could speak like that. Some of you are probably worried that your doubt is racist and classist. After all, how could a poor reservation Indian kid be that self-possessed and radical? Well, that was me. I was the UnChild.

I said, "I will spell my name the way I want to spell my name."

I vividly remember the expression on the ex–holy man's face. I have seen that expression on many faces. I have often caused that expression. That expression means "I might win this one fight with Junior, a.k.a. Sherman Two, the son of Lillian the Cruel, but he will immediately start another fight. And another. And another."

For the next three years, in my own handwriting and in official school reports, I was Juniour, pronounced the same as Junior, yes, but it carried a whole different meaning.

I think the *u* in Juniour was short for "Fuck you and you and you and you and especially you. Yeah, you, the one who still thinks I am going to obey you."

41.

Unsaved

ABU GHRAIB.

Abu Ghraib.

Abu Ghraib.

Do you remember Abu Ghraib?

Do you remember that American soldiers tortured detainees at the Abu Ghraib prison during the Iraq War?

Has Abu Ghraib already become a historical footnote? Is it mentioned in the history textbooks? Do the tortured prisoners have names? I didn't remember any of their names until I Googled them. I don't remember if I had ever heard any of their names. But I certainly remember some of the names of the American torturers. I don't want to use their names here. Naming them gives them more respect than

they deserve. They were convicted of relatively minor crimes. They were sentenced to short prison
terms. They are free back here in the United States.
Two of the torturers—a man and woman—married
each other. I don't know if they are still married. I
don't know if they have children. I don't want to
know. Or maybe I'm lying. I imagine that moment
when their children go online and find those images of torture, when they see their mother and
father posing—*smiling*—with naked, humiliated,
wounded, and helpless prisoners. And when I imagine that moment, I feel like it might be a form of
justice. I feel a slight sense of satisfaction. Or maybe
it just feels like revenge for a crime that wasn't even
committed against me. Maybe this just reveals my
own cruelty. But I feel something mostly grim and
partly good when I imagine that painful conversation between those torturer parents and their children. I realize those parents—if they have any sense
of decency—would be forced to reveal their crimes
to their children before they discovered them
themselves.

"Mom, Dad, how could you do that to another human being?"

Jesus, how do you explain that evil shit to your
own kids?

But then I imagine those Abu Ghraib torturers
have long ago forgiven themselves, have repeated

their self-justifications so often that they have become personal scripture.

I imagine those torturers have exonerated themselves. I imagine they'd be able to persuade their children toward forgiveness, understanding, empathy, and agreement. Maybe those torturers have become good parents. Maybe they have become good people, better than could possibly be expected. Maybe they have earned the forgiveness of their children. But will they ever deserve the forgiveness of their prisoners? Have those torturers ever apologized to the tortured?

One of the tortured prisoners was named Satar Jabar.

Do you remember the photo of Mr. Jabar, hooded, standing on a box, arms eagle-spread, with electrical wires connected to his hands and penis?

He was told, repeatedly, that he'd be electrocuted if he fell off that box. Mr. Jabar testified that he was indeed electrocuted many times. His torturers claim he wasn't. Whom do you believe? Whom do you want to believe?

If you fall off that box, you will be electrocuted.
Say it aloud.
If you fall off that box, you will be electrocuted.
Say it louder.
If you fall off that box, you will be electrocuted.

Scream it at the sky. Scream it for hours. Do you think it will ever sound like a prayer?

Do you remember the photos of other prisoners, naked and handcuffed, hanging upside down from their bunk beds? Do you remember other prisoners crouched and blindfolded with their arms tied and extended at acute angles behind their backs? Do you remember other prisoners being attacked by dogs?

When I first saw those photographs on television, I vomited on our living room carpet. At first, I was confused by my extreme reaction. Any compassionate person would be distressed by such terrible images. But my reaction felt more personal. Frankly speaking, it felt selfish.

And then I heard the news reporter say "stress positions."

What are stress positions? According to the Collins English Dictionary, they are "an enforced body position, applied especially in the interrogation of detainees, which causes the victim pain by concentrating a large amount of his or her weight on a small number of muscles, joints, etc." According to Amnesty International, Human Rights Watch, and the Geneva Conventions, stress positions are a form of torture—illegal, immoral, and inhumane.

I didn't vomit because I saw photographs of other human beings placed in stress positions. I didn't vomit because of their pain. I vomited because I finally had a name for my pain, for the torture that my classmates and I endured at the hands of a second-grade teacher on the Spokane Indian Reservation.

To discipline us Indian kids, that teacher would push and pinch us. She'd scream in our face until our ears rang. An ex-nun, white-skinned and red-haired, she called us sinners and threatened us with eternal damnation.

Worse, she would make us stand eagle-armed in front of the classroom with a book in each hand. I don't remember how long she made us hold those books aloft. But seconds must have felt like minutes; minutes must have felt like hours. Even now, over four decades later, I can feel the pain in my arms—the memory of pain—and the terror.

Don't you drop those books.

Don't you drop those books.

Don't you drop those books.

That was a stress position. That was torture. That was a crime. A felony, don't you think?

But that wasn't the most painful thing she did to us.

Sitting at our desks, we were ordered to clasp our hands behind our back, extend them at an acute angle, and lean forward until only the tip of our nose touched the desktop.

She walked among us, screaming at those of us who couldn't hold our arms high enough or who tried to rest our head on our desk. We cried in pain. Tears and snot dripped onto the desks, pooled, and rolled down off the edge and onto our lap. Some of us peed our pants from pain and fear.

Keep those arms up.

Nose on your desk.

Keep those arms up.

Nose on your desk.

Keep those arms up.

Nose on your desk.

That was a stress position. That was torture. That was a crime. A felony, don't you think?

Abu Ghraib.

What does it mean to those American torturers?

Abu Ghraib.

What does it mean to those tortured prisoners?

Abu Ghraib.

What does it mean to you and me?

I vomited because I realized that we Indian kids, at seven years of age, had been treated like prisoners of war. We were guilty of the crime of being Indian.

I remember coming home from school one day, weeping, and telling my mother that I was afraid of that teacher. I remember telling my mother what that teacher was doing to us. I remember that my mother demanded a meeting with that teacher.

After the meeting, my mother told me everything was going to be okay.

I told my mother that I was still scared.

My mother promised me that teacher wouldn't scare me anymore.

I believed my mother.

The next morning, when I walked into class, that teacher called my name.

"Hey, Junior," she said.

"What?" I asked.

"Boo," she said with her hands curled into claws.

I recoiled.

"Boo," she said, and laughed.

I was only seven years old when I first realized that my mother was powerless against white teachers. She was powerless against white schools. She was powerless against white government. She was powerless against whiteness in all of its forms.

My mother and father were so powerless against that teacher that she was able to torture my younger sisters, the twins, and their classmates the next year.

My sister remembers how, on the playground, that teacher grabbed her by the ponytail and pulled her to the ground.

"My neck hurt so bad," my sister told me. "Hurt for days."

Whiplash.

"When she got mad at the whole class," my sister told me, "she made us draw circles on the chalkboard. Then we'd have to put our hands behind our back and lean forward until just our nose touched inside that circle."

Stress position.

"But that wasn't even the worst," my sister said. "After tests, she would walk around the classroom and say out loud the names of the kids who got Ds and Fs. She'd call them the dumbest kids in the class. And say they were just going to be dumb Indians all their lives."

"Boo," that white teacher said, wanting to hurt and shame us.

I wanted to cry.

But I did not cry.

I wanted to cry.

But I did not cry.

I wanted to cry.

But I did not cry.

I never cried in front of that teacher again, even when she forced us into stress positions, even when she pulled out scissors and cut the long hair and braids of us Indian boys.

Don't cry, I told myself.

Don't cry.

Don't cry.

Years later, long after that teacher had retired and left the reservation, I heard she'd been bragging about me. She told other folks how proud she was of me, how she had to take a little credit for my literary success.

Okay, Miss Teacher.

Okay, Miss Torturer.

I give you full credit for the pain you caused all of us. I give you full credit for my scars. And I give you full credit for making me realize that my mother could not protect me from the likes of you. I give you full credit for making me wonder why my mother was so powerless.

Dear Mother, were you also tortured as a child?

Dear Mother, were you also a prisoner of war?

Dear Mother, did you also look into the eyes of your mother and see only pain and fear?

Dear Mother, were you broken in the same places where I am broken, too?

42.

God Damn, God Dam

IN JULY 1933, construction began on the Grand Coulee Dam. Still one of the largest concrete structures in the world, that dam submerged ancient villages and falls and eventually killed all of the wild salmon in the upper Columbia and Spokane rivers.

My mother once told me, "When I was just a toddler, before the dam was finished, I walked from one side of the Spokane River to the other on the backs of wild salmon."

"Hey, wait," I said. "Big Mom said she did that same walk when she was a little girl."

"She did it and I did it," my mother said. "We both did it."

"You're lying," I said.

"It's not a lie," my mother said.

During the tumultuous course of her life, my mother told many clever and clumsy lies. As I have said, I think she was an undiagnosed bipolar grandiose fabulist. But, as an adult and indigenous half-assed intellectual, I also realize that she wasn't lying about walking across the river on the backs of salmon. Well, let's get it straight. Speaking in terms of history and physics, my mother absolutely did not make that walk across the river. And Big Mom certainly never made that walk either. But they weren't lying when they claimed to have made that walk. They were telling a story—a fable, if you must— about how the Spokane River once was home to an epic number of wild salmon. If you insist that my mother and grandmother lied about making a foot-bridge of salmon, then it's a lie in service of scientific and spiritual truth.

Scientifically speaking, there were endless numbers of wild salmon in the Spokane and upper Columbia rivers before the Grand Coulee Dam was built.

Spiritually speaking, the Spokane Indians and all other Salish tribes worshipped the salmon as passionately as any other people in the world worship their deities.

So, scientifically and spiritually, the Grand Coulee Dam murdered my tribe's history. Murdered my tribe's relationship with its deity. And murdered my tribe's relationship with its future.

For us, the Grand Coulee Dam is an epic gravestone. And we Salish people have been mourning the death of our wild salmon for over seven decades.

What is it like to be a Spokane Indian without wild salmon? It is like being a Christian if Jesus had never rolled back the stone and risen from his tomb.

43

I Turn My Mother Into a Salmon, I Turn Salmon Into My Mother

This fiery summer, my mother is
    dying
Because the streams are too shallow
And warm. There is nowhere
For my mother to rest and hide

From the sun and heat and predators.
Experts warn that my mother
Will go extinct in certain bodies of
    water
As the earth grows hotter and hotter.

Yes, my mother will soon be the last
Mother to perish in this sacred river.

My mother will be mourned by the
   trees,
And diver birds and hungry grizzlies.

There will be nothing left to deliver
Other than centuries of eulogies.

44.

Communion

we worship
the salmon

because we
eat salmon

45.

Storm

It rained salmon
On the day my mother was buried.

The salmon fell to the grass
Among headstones

And struggled to breathe.
They wanted to survive.

My siblings and I gathered
As many salmon

As we could fit in the baskets
Of our arms, in our pockets,

And ran for the river
That suddenly flowed through the cemetery.

The salmon were dying.
The river was dead.

But we children dove into the water because
We needed the salmon to survive.

46.

C Is for Clan

IN 1938, FIVE years after construction began on the Grand Coulee Dam, a wild salmon made its way to the face of that monolith and could not pass. That was the last wild salmon that attempted to find a way around, over, or through the dam into the upper Columbia and Spokane rivers. That was the last wild salmon that *remembered*.

The Interior Salish, my people, had worshipped the wild salmon since our beginnings. That sacred fish had been our primary source of physical and spiritual sustenance for thousands of years.

And then, over the course of five short years— after only eighteen hundred days—the endless and ancient wild salmon were gone from our waters.

My mother was two years old when that last wild salmon appeared at the face of the Grand Coulee Dam. My father was in his mother's womb.

In 1945, when my father was six years old, his father died in World War II. Killed in action on Okinawa Island. Then, six months later, my father's mother died of tuberculosis, a death as invasive and violent as war.

My mother and father were members of the first generation of Interior Salish people who lived entirely without wild salmon.

My mother and father, without wild salmon, were spiritual orphans.

My father was also orphaned by war and contagious disease.

My siblings and I were conceived, birthed, and nurtured by orphans—by the salmonless and parentless and non-immune.

And now, as I think of my mother's and father's salmon-grief, as I think of mourning the wild salmon I had never known, and of mourning the grandparents who died two decades before I was born, I remember a Navajo woman who hated me.

Many years ago, I was the visiting writer at her college, mostly populated by Natives of the Southwest.

"It's weird to be a salmon boy in the desert," I said to the students. "I feel extra thirsty."

Because of my early success, I was younger than most of the students. I was not comfortable being introduced as a possible mentor to older Indians. But I was happy to be among Indians who saw the world through artistic eyes. I thought I fully belonged. I was wrong.

"What's your clan? What's your Indian name?" that Navajo woman asked. I had not met her previously. I have not seen her since. She was obviously angry at me. Ready to argue. I think she saw herself as being a real Indian artist and saw me, the world-traveling writer, as something less than artful and also something less than indigenous. I was suddenly involved in an Indian-versus-Indian cultural battle—a fight that I have faced again and again and again and again. Yep, that shit has come at me from all four directions. To paraphrase that tribal elder named Shakespeare, we Native folks are "more than kin and less than kind."

"What's your clan? What's your Indian name?" she asked again. But she was actually asking me to prove how Indian I am. She was the full-blood Navajo. She was a 4/4 Indian. She'd proudly included that fraction in her bio and in her art. I had a Scottish grandparent, so I am a 7/8. I'd also included my fraction in my art, but with far more amusement and discernment. After all, I have grown so much chest hair in my middle age that I suspect my fraction is wrong. I suspect every Native's fraction is wrong. That Navajo and I were suddenly in an Aboriginal Blood Quantum Test of Wills. She was trying to embarrass me in front of her Indian classmates. And in front of her Indian teacher. And that teacher just sat back and watched. She wasn't a fan of mine either.

Arggh, I thought. *Why do so many Indians do this fucking shit to one another? Why this need to become enemies?*

That Navajo was trying to bully me. And my natural instinct was to fight back. I leaned toward her and prepared to verbally attack her—to use my forensic debate and stand-up comedy skills to dismantle and mock her fundamentalism. She was my literary heckler. And hecklers, indigenous or not, need to be embarrassed into silence. *It's the law.*

"Okay—," I said as a dozen improvised insults synapsed through my brain.

But then I relaxed. Breathed deep. Cleaned my teeth with my tongue. I didn't want to be the indigenous man arguing with an indigenous woman—didn't want to re-create the domestic strife that had existed in my childhood home— didn't want to replay what had likely happened in many of those students' lives. *I didn't want to turn that Navajo woman into an avatar for my mother.* No, I could not teach the class anything by arguing. But maybe I could teach them how to disarm—how to mitigate—how to step away with grace. That Navajo artist had likely targeted other people in the room. And I'm sure some of the other men and women were also anger-junkies. And, yes, I'm an anger-junkie, too.

But not that day. Not that day.

So I smiled, leaned back in my chair, and said, "I was not raised inside a clan structure. My parents are from different tribes and raised us to be powwow-goers and basketball players. My sisters know how to jingle. And my brothers and I know how to dribble."

The other Indians in the class laughed. I assumed some of them came from powwow and basketball families like me. And, of course, they all knew, like all Natives know, a thousand powwow nomads and Indian basketball players. And, sure, in most ways, powwows and basketball are pop culture for Indians, but it's pop culture with applied sacredness. Or something like that.

I just tried to be funny, okay, okay, okay?

But that angry Navajo woman didn't laugh. She wanted none of it. She stood and left the room.

I regret that I did not directly and seriously

challenge that other artist's aesthetic—her working definition of indigenous art—with my own.

"What's your clan? What's your Indian name?" the Navajo woman had asked me.

So, please, let me properly answer her question now.

My name is Sherman Alexie.

Yes, I have an Indian name. But I ain't going to share it with you. I learned a long time ago that the only way to keep something sacred is to keep it private. So, yeah, you might think I reveal everything, but I keep plenty of good and bad stuff all to myself.

On my mother's side, I was born into the Clan of Busted Promises and Dynamite and White Man's Hydroelectric Concrete.

On my father's side, I was born into the Clan of Sniper and Head Shot and Posthumous Bronze Star and Purple Heart.

On my mother's side, I was born into the Clan of Rivers Flowing with Wild Salmon Ghosts.

On my father's side, I was born into the Clan of Bloody and Broken Lungs.

And all of us Spokanes and Coeur d'Alenes, after the Grand Coulee Dam, have been born into the Clan of Doing Our Best to Re-create and Replicate the Sacred Things That Were Brutally Stolen from Us.

My name is Sherman Alexie and I was born from loss and loss and loss and loss and loss and loss and loss and loss and loss and loss and loss and loss and loss.

And loss.

47.

Apocalypse

There is a salmon swimming from star to star.
Some name it Comet. Some name it Distant
  Light.

There is a salmon returning to our sky.
Some name it Constellation. Some name it
  Moon.

There is a salmon swallowing the earth.
Some name it Black Hole. Some name it God.

48

Creation Story

I catch the salmon
With my bare hands

And offer it
To my mother.

She opens the fish
And finds

A city of Indians
Living among the thin bones.

49.

The Loss Extends in All Directions

AFTER WE BURIED our mother, my big brother, little brother, and me and our cousins sat in the tribal longhouse and ate salmon.

"Hey," my big brother said. "What's the Spokane word for *salmon?*"

We all looked at one another and were embarrassed to realize none of us knew.

"Man," my cousin said. "If there's any Spokane word we should know, it's the word for *salmon.*"

It wasn't funny. But we laughed anyway.

50.

Revision

AT SOME POINT in my childhood—in my early teens—my mother, Lillian, told me the most painful secret of her life.

"Junior," she said. "I am the daughter of a rape."

"What?" I asked, unsure that I'd heard her correctly.

"A man raped my mother. And she got pregnant with me."

"Oh, my God," I said. "When did this happen? Are you okay? Did he go to jail? Who was the rapist?"

My mother said his name. He was a man from another tribe who'd died years earlier. I'd never known him, but I knew his children and his grand-children. They were tall kids. Unlike my siblings and parents, I was tall, too. I'd always wondered

197

why I was so much taller than the rest of my family. Why I was darker. I'd sometimes worried that perhaps I wasn't my father's biological child. But I have the same widow's-peak cowlick—a rebellious lock of black hair that defies styling—as my father. My biological older brother and my younger twin sisters have that cowlick, too. Plus, as I've aged from a skinny dark kid into a chubby paler man—having lived in sunless Seattle for twenty-three years—I have come to more strongly resemble my father and my siblings.

But not in height.

"The man who raped your mother," I said. "Your father—"

"He's not my father," my mother said. She was understandably angry. "My father is James Cox, the man who raised me."

I was always afraid of her anger. Everybody was afraid of Lillian's anger. We were always trying to mollify her.

"I'm sorry," I said. "The rapist. Was he tall?"

My mother immediately understood what I was asking.

"Yes," she said. "That's where you get your height."

I didn't ask my mother anything else. I didn't have the emotional vocabulary. And I'm not sure she had the emotional vocabulary either. I would eventually talk about my mother's story, but that would be years after I'd first learned of her violent conception.

Rape was common on my reservation. But it was rarely discussed. And even more rarely prosecuted. In that way, my reservation is sadly like the rest of the world. But I think there are specific cultural reasons for the injustice on my reservation. I would guess it has something to do with the strict social rules of a tribe. White folks love to think that Native American culture is progressive and liberal. But it is often repressive. Indians are quick to socially judge one another. And even quicker to publicly condemn and ostracize. I wouldn't realize it until I read more widely in college, but living on an Indian reservation was like living inside an Edith Wharton novel—a place where good and bad manners were weaponized. One could choose to abide by social rules or flaunt them, but there would be serious repercussions for any social misstep. But why was this the case? For thousands of years, we Spokanes had endured and enjoyed subsistence lives. We'd lived communally. Every member of the tribe had a job. And each job was equally vital. So, inside a subsistence culture, a socially disruptive tribal member would have been mortally dangerous to everybody else.

But there is a logical problem with that, isn't there? First of all, we were living in the twentieth century and not the fourteenth or fifteenth. And if that were still true—if socially disruptive tribal members were traditionally punished, no matter the century—then wouldn't it make more sense for the tribe to ostracize and even expel rapists? Not if the rapist was a culturally significant figure. Not if the rapist, however economically poor, was socially rich and powerful. Not if the rapist could put on an eagle-feather headdress and make a beautiful and powerful entrance into the powwow arena.

In many ways, a powerful Native American leader can operate inside his tribe and reservation like the repressive dictator of a Third World country.

And, in any case, what would happen inside a small tribe if every minor or major crime, if every small or large transgression, was made public? Could a small tribe survive that unveiling of secrets? What if we Natives practiced the same kind of justice inside our own communities as the justice that we demand from white society? Of course, centuries of genocidal acts by white Americans have certainly helped teach us Natives how to commit genocidal acts against one another. But at what point do we Native American victims start demanding more justice and freedom from our Native American oppressors?

And what happens if those indigenous oppressors happen to be our fathers and mothers?

51.

Bullet Point

IJOKE THAT I could be blindfolded in a room filled with strangers and I'd still be able to sniff out the people who have the same mental, emotional, and physical ailments as I do.

"Bad-back people smell like hot ointments," I say. "Bipolar people smell like that grease they put on the wheels of roller-coaster cars."

It's not true. At least, I don't think it's true. Well, bad-back people certainly smell of liniment, but bipolar people smell like every other person—that same bouquet of hairless groomed primate. But, then again, each of us has our own scent, right?

"If you hung forty dirty shirts on a line," my sister said once, "I could smell which ones had been worn by my brothers and sisters and mother and father. By everybody I love."

"That's a fairly useless superhero skill," I said.

My sister laughed.

"Might be useless in saving the world," she said. "But it means I know my people are close before they turn the corner."

"Your superhero name is Psychic Nose," I said.

"Or maybe," my sister said. "Maybe it just means you guys don't use enough soap."

I don't think I could recognize my friends by scent, not even the dudes I have played basketball with for two decades. Not even though I've been heavily marked by their sweat. I have arrived home in hoops gear smelling so heavily of athletic endeavor—like an odiferous sonnet of fourteen men—that I've undressed on the front porch and left my shirt and trunks draped over a railing. Maybe you think that's sexy—and I suppose it would be for folks with a very particular kink—but, for me, it's just the smelliest part of the game.

But could I find my wife and sons in a crowded room using only my nose? Yes, yes, I believe I could perform that trick.

But that's all subterranean, right? That is all about the animals we truly are and not the civilized people we pretend to be, correct?

Do we choose our friends based on primal shit we don't even understand?

I knew a woman who smelled exactly like Campbell's vegetable soup. It was hilarious and maddeningly erotic. I couldn't stand next to her for any longer than a few moments before I went dumb with sexual arousal. So, yeah, that meant I was always walking away from that platonic friend. She probably thought I didn't like her. I haven't seen her in fifteen years. I am okay with that.

Or, hey, let's get really weird. Do I choose my friends because they smell like my mother or father? Have I chosen friends because they smell like *absence*?

More specifically, do I choose female friends who are like my mother? Or do I choose women who are the opposite of my mother? Do I choose the anti-mothers?

I asked some of my friends to write about their mother—to let me publish their words and my responses. A highly unscientific experiment. "Tell me about your mother," I said. "Good or bad memories. Just tell me what you remember most. Tell me something that you think defines your mother. Curate your memories."

I also told my friends that I'd keep them anonymous. I told them that I hoped I'd gain some deeper insight into the process by which I have chosen friends.

"Maybe it will bring us closer," I e-mailed one friend.

"Or maybe it will drive us apart," he wrote back.

"You pessimistic fucker," I wrote.

"I talk pessimism," he wrote. "You live pessimism."

"Fuck you."

"Fuck you, too."

"We need to get coffee soon," I wrote. "You fucker."

"Not until school starts back up," he wrote. "Summer is fucked for parents of young kids. I love my kids, but sometimes I just go sit in my car in the driveway, turn on the air conditioner, and take a nap."

"Okay, see you in September, October, or November," I wrote. "Or never."

But, wait, I got distracted. That busy dude is funny—and was too harried to send me a memory of his mother. And I had been wondering if I have chosen my female friends based on how much they subconsciously remind me of my mother. And it would have to be subconscious because I have never met a person who reminded me of my mother. Well, that's not exactly true. I had a therapist for six years who distinctly reminded me of my mother. But that therapist wasn't my friend. She was a mental health professional who helped me understand some of my behavior.

"I don't know that I'm like your mother," my therapist said. "Or if I'm just a woman of your mother's age who pays close attention to you."

So I wrote a female friend. I will call her Miss Orange. I already knew she'd had a difficult relationship with her mother, but I was surprised by her e-mail back to me:

Sherman,

I used to let my dad off the hook for being a drunk,
for raging, for forgetting to come home and leaving
me and my brother with no electricity or burst
pipes. I can't let my mom off the hook for her focused
cruelty.

Miss Orange's e-mail spun me around in my chair. Oh, shit, I have done that, too!

My father was a failure. Worse, he was a brilliant boy—a star athlete, classical pianist, and jitterbug dance champion—who turned into an inert man—into inertia itself. He died broke. He died young, at age sixty-four of alcoholism. He hadn't had a job in thirty years or more. He couldn't keep a job. He once pretended to have a job. He'd pack a lunch in the morning and walk to his road crew job—to the garage a half mile away, where he'd meet up with his co-workers to take care of the reservation highways and byways. Then, at five, he'd walk home and let me eat whatever was left of his lunch. I loved those half-sandwiches more than any food I've ever had in my entire life. I mean—my father finally had a job. I was ecstatic at the thought of my father's regular paycheck. We'd have cash at predictable intervals. Glory! Glory! Those partly eaten baloney sandwiches and that half-filled coffee thermos became my Eucharist. And, yes, my dad did work that job for maybe a week but then quit and pretended to go to work for another two weeks. So what did he do with all that real time spent at his imaginary job? He'd sit in one of the permanently broken trucks near the road crew garage and...do nothing.

Of course, I can now amateur-ass diagnose my father as being *incredibly fucking depressed.* When sober, that depressed man sat in his bedroom watching TV for eighteen hours a day. Then, at predictable intervals, he'd leave the house for days or weeks on drinking binges and leave his family—his young children—scrambling for money and food.

When he was gone on his drinking binges, I would sometimes cry myself, dehydrated and irrational, into the emergency room. When he was drunk, my father would drive and get arrested. He was once court-ordered into a ninety-day residential treatment program. Nine or ten years old, I was a useless wreck—a car fire—for three months. If my father had served his time during the academic year, I would have probably flunked out of grade school. Or maybe I could have anesthetized myself with homework and extra credit and binge-reading. In any case, I made it through those ninety days of loneliness and celebrated as I waited with my mother and siblings in the hospital parking lot. There's a photograph of me throwing a fake karate punch at the camera. Yeah, I was star student of the Dragon Dojo of Indian Boys Who Don't Know Fuck-All About Martial Arts. I had crooked poverty teeth. I wore government glasses. My hair was uncombed and unwashed. I was ecstatic.

My father was coming home! My father was going to be sober! My father was going to get a job and take care of us!

My mother had packed a celebratory picnic of baloney sandwiches, potato chips, and Pepsi. She'd been a single mother for three months. She had good reason to celebrate.

My big brother and little sisters and I played on the grass.

We were *almost a normal family.*

But then, only moments after that photo of me was taken, we learned that our father would have to spend another thirty days in treatment.

We were crushed. We wept. Our beleaguered

mother drove us back to the reservation. Along the way, we kids ate those sandwiches and chips. And drank those Pepsis. No matter how sad we were. No matter how much we just wanted to cry. We were too poor to waste the food. And we'd gone without meals enough times to learn that you absolutely devour any food placed before you. That's one of the ways in which hunger and loneliness can become inextricably linked.

Along the way, I also screamed at my mother.

I blamed her for my father's alcoholism.

I blamed her for our poverty.

I blamed her for everything wrong in our world.

Other days, she would have fought back. But, on that day, she remained silent as she drove us home. That day, she absorbed my rage and didn't respond with any rage of her own.

Throughout our lives, our mother had been the dependable one. After I was seven, she never went on drinking binges. She never opened up a canyon in her soul and silently disappeared into the dark recesses. She was always present for us. She made money by selling her handmade quilts and blankets. She worked regular jobs, too. Youth counselor, senior-citizen companion, trading post cashier, drug and alcohol treatment therapist. She rarely broke the material promises she made to us. She was *industrious.*

And yet, I have spent my literary career writing loving odes to my drunken and unreliable father. I have, in a spectacular show of hypocrisy, let my father off the hook for his lifetime of carelessness.

That is completely unfair to my mother. I know it is. And it must have caused her pain. But she never said anything. She never asked me why I didn't write much about her. And if she had asked, I'm sure I would have evaded the question.

But I can answer it now.

I wrote so many loving poems and stories about my father because I never once doubted his love for me. He rarely expressed his love. He was not affectionate. But he was shy and soft-spoken and obviously wounded and childlike and exuded kindness. He was never mean, not once, not to me or my siblings, and not directly to anyone else on the planet. You will not find a person who remembers a negative interaction with my father.

I know that my unreliable father loved me. I can say that without the need to present you with further evidence.

But my mother? And her love? How do I define that? Well, damn, the world is filled with people who can tell you stories about my mother's cruelty— about her arrogance and spite. And, sure, other folks, including my siblings, can tell you stories about her love and compassion.

But, as her son and as perhaps her most regular opponent, I remember only a little bit of my mother's kindness and almost everything about her coldness.

Did she love me? Did my mother love me? When I gather up all the available evidence, I have to say, "Yes, Lillian Alexie loved Sherman Alexie, Jr." But I can only render that verdict with reasonable doubts.

In 1983, when our cousin Eugene was shot and killed in a stupid alcohol-fueled tiff with his friend, I wept. And I say "tiff" because it was over the minor issue of who got to take the last drink from a bottle of fortified wine. My cousin died arguing over backwash. How could I not weep for that death and for the utter inanity of the way it happened? I sat on the bed in my basement bedroom and cried for hours. I loved Eugene.

"Junior, you're a weird kid," he once said to me. "But you're weird in a good way. Nobody gets you yet. I don't get you. But people are gonna get you someday."

After Eugene was shot and killed, my father took me to the outdoor basketball court on the rez. We silently shot hoops for hours. That was how my father mourned with me. I felt so much pain that I thought I might shoot basketballs forever, and I think my father would have kept shooting forever, too.

As I sat in my basement bedroom, it felt like I might weep forever. And, after I had wept for hours, my mother opened my bedroom door and said, "Shut up, Junior. That's enough crying."

I stopped weeping.

My mother went back upstairs and sat on her couch directly above me.

I stopped weeping. But I stood on my bed and I screamed and punched the ceiling.

My mother sat directly above me. I stopped weeping. But I stood on my bed and I screamed and punched the ceiling.

My mother sat directly above me.

I punched that ceiling until my knuckles bled.

I think my mother still sits directly above me.

I think my knuckles are still bleeding.

I think I am still screaming.

52.

The Quilting

My mother made quilts.
She would sew instead of sleep
And laugh at sunrise.

Cotton, denim, wool,
Needle, thread, scissors, thimble,
Blister, callus, cut.

Square by square by square,
My mother constructed quilts
And sold them for food.

My mother made quilts
With rheumatoid arthritis
In her neck and hands.

A memory quilt
Contains pieces of your past
Rejoined and renewed.
My mother made quilts.
She would sew instead of sleep
And rage at sunrise.

When Elvis perished,
My mom wept and wrapped herself
Inside a dark quilt.

Two hundred babies
Have slept beneath my mom's quilts.
Ah, such tenderness!

How many babies
Were conceived on my mom's quilts?
No one knows for sure.

My mother's hands ached
As she punched needles through
    wool,
Denim, canvas, jute.

I own fourteen quilts
That were built by my mother.
I use all of them.

My mom made a denim quilt
That was too heavy to lift.
She cut it in half!

Quilt by quilt by quilt,
My mom made enough money
To pay the mortgage.

My mom's arthritis
Turned her hands into cages
That captured ten birds.

My mother made quilts.
She would sew instead of sleep
And weep at sunrise.

We buried our mom
With a quilt she didn't make.
We gave her a break!

She made her last quilt
To honor a Native boy
Heading to college.

If you want a quilt
Constructed by my mother
Then you're out of luck.

My mom never slept
Beneath a quilt that she made.
Or maybe she did!

A memory quilt
Is designed to remind you
Of what you have lost.

I never sewed quilts.
My sisters made many quilts
Alongside our mom.

My mother started
To make a quilt from my poems,
But never finished.

As she made her quilts,
My mother sang Christian hymns
And old tribal songs.

My mother made quilts.
She would sew instead of sleep
And sigh at sunrise.

She once made a quilt
With thirty Jesus faces—
The Shroud of Too Much.

My wife doesn't quilt
So we don't have old fabric
Piled in the garage.

I miss my mother.
I miss watching her make quilts.
Sewing was her art.

My dad only slept
On top of sheets and blankets
Layered on his bed.

My mom only slept
Under many heavy quilts
On the front room couch.

When Mom and Dad slept,
They rarely shared the same bed
Or the same warm quilt.

My mom's arthritis
Turned her hands into fires
Fed by ten dry twigs.

How long do quilts last?
I think they've discovered quilts
In a pharaoh's tomb.

My mother made quilts.
She would sew instead of sleep
And mourn at sunrise.

How many coffins
Have been draped with my mom's quilts?
Too many to count.

When old quilts tattered,
My mother would repair them—
The Quilt Whisperer!

Square by square by square,
My mother constructed quilts
And sold them for wood.

Always cold, my mom
Often walked around the house
Quilted like a queen.

Even wrapped in quilts,
My mother kept our small house
Burning like the sun.

In flames, we kids kicked
Aside our quilts and thirsted
And desiccated.

Square by square by square,
My mom also abandoned
And ignored her quilts.

Ah, that poor half-quilt
Can only make a half-ghost
That haunts half of us.

A memory quilt
Is constructed with dark things
You'd rather forget.

I think I was raped
On one of my mother's quilts.
But my eyes were closed.

Wrapped in my mom's quilts,
I wept after funerals
For so many friends.

When my big sister died,
I wanted to gather quilts
And burn all of them.

My mother made quilts.
She would sew instead of sleep
And collapse at dawn.

Square by square by square,
She punched anger through our skin
And turned us into quilts.

Wrapped around our mom,
We quilts absorbed her anger
And her fear and pain.

Wrapped around our mom,
We quilts absorbed her courage
And her love and grace.

Square by square by square,
We quilts honor our mother
And her strange genius.

She taught us survival
With needle, thread, and thimble
All stained with her blood.

53.

Three Days

1.

Why is it that I never remember
How to spell "resurrection"?
I have to Internet search
For the correct spelling every time.

2.

Three days after my mother's death,
She rolls the stone from her tomb
And walks into my dreams.
Most people would insist that it's actually her

Or her soul reaching out to me.
But I'm not a literalist. I know,
Even as I'm dreaming,
That my subconscious is only
   fucking

With my conscious, or vice versa.
And, yet, as I dream of an ordinary day
Where I take my sons to school,
Grocery shop, drive through

For fast food, and browse a bookstore,
My mother feels shockingly real
As she follows me everywhere.
She doesn't speak. She doesn't touch.

She just follows me and follows me.
She's in the backseat, smiling at me
In the rearview mirror. She's knocking
Oranges and apples from the displays

In supermarkets. She's the barista
Making my coffee. She's the hum
Of the refrigerator. She's that tree
Heavy with crows. She follows me

Until the simple act of dropping
Ice cubes into an empty glass

Sounds like a thousand angels
Screaming with grief and rage.

3.

Dear Mother, I am sorry
That I don't believe
In your ghost. I am sorry
That you are a ghost.

Dear Mother, I would call out
Your name, but I'm not the one
Who made "resurrection" more
Difficult to spell than "doubt."

54.

Navigation

Hey, Smartphone, I'm lost. What am I supposed to do next?

—*Dear Sherman, you must eventually
  forgive your mother. Don't forget.*

Wow, Smartphone, I don't have the inner resources for that. Not yet.

—*You better hurry. I've scheduled you
  for increasing amounts of regret.*

Damn, Smartphone, that seems rather mean.

—*Well, pal, just like me,*
    Grief is a relentless machine.

**So, Smartphone, does this journey have an ulti-
mate destination?**

—*You might get somewhere, but it*
    won't be cause for celebration.

**Okay, Smartphone, how do I take the first step?
Then another?**

—*I already told you, asshole.*
    You gotta forgive your mother.

55.

Sedated

AND THEN, ONE summer night, when I was seventeen, my mother asked me to go find my father. He'd left home a week earlier on a drinking binge. And he had diabetes. After seven days, we had to go looking for him. It was a family rule. We had arbitrarily decided that my father would only begin to seriously endanger his health after a week of booze and bad food. Plus, we'd get lonely for him. So I got into my car and drove from our home on the Spokane Indian Reservation to the Coeur d'Alene Reservation. My father, a supposedly full-blood Coeur d'Alene who had a suspiciously full mustache, had not lived on his reservation since he was a child, but that's usually where he went to drink. He was always trying to fill some indigenous absence.

There were five or six party houses where I would search for him. And then, once I found him, I would have to persuade him to come home. My mother used to exclusively perform this family chore. But once I earned my driver's license, it was something I was often asked to do. My mother never commanded it, but she also knew I was unlikely to refuse the mission.

So, on that particular summer night, I discovered my father asleep in a chair in our cousin's house in the little town of Worley, Idaho. He was barely conscious and smelled of beer, vomit, urine, and shit. I didn't want him to stink up my upholstery, so I walked back out to my car, grabbed the old army surplus blanket out of the trunk, and covered the passenger seat. Then I walked back into the house and tried to fully rouse my father.

Most times, he'd argue with me. He was never a violent man, drunk or sober, but he often deployed a drunk's persistent, if incoherent, logic that I'd have to overcome in order to get him home.

But that time, when I woke him, my father was so hungover and exhausted that he got into my car without protest. And then, as I rolled down the car windows because of my father's stench, he tried to drunkenly explain our family history.

"That was the year your mother was addicted to Valium," he said.

"Wait," I said. "What?"

My mother was a recovering alcoholic who'd sobered up when I was seven years old.

"Don't you remember when she was chewing her lips and tongue all the time?" my father asked. "That was the Valium."

"I don't remember that," I said.

But I think I didn't want to remember it. My mother was often verbally cruel and emotionally unpredictable, but she was sober. I would only later learn that even a sober alcoholic can go on dry-drunk rages and sprees. But, in any case, I preferred my angry sober mother to my angry drunk mother. And I hated to think that my mother's sobriety extended only to alcohol.

"You were little when it happened," my father said.

"That was when she started sleeping on the couch all the time, right?" I asked.

"No, that was a different year."

As we traveled through the pine forest, I desperately tried to remember my stoned mother. But I could not. I could not. And then I did.

"Oh, wait," I said. "I remember when she thought she had MS and she was slurring her words."

"That wasn't MS," my drunk father said. "That was Valium."

"And didn't she have a mini-stroke once?"

"Valium."

"And didn't she use to wear a blindfold because of migraine headaches?"

"Valium," my father and I said together.

I drove us into Wellpinit, the center of our world.

"Where did she get the Valium?" I asked.

"I think that white doctor at the clinic was in love with her," my father said.

"So instead of flowers," I said, "he gave her drugs."

"She was in real pain, though."

"What kind of pain?" I asked

"The pain of being Indian," he said.

"Oh, come on, Dad."

"That's why I drink so much."

"You drink so much because you're a drunk."

"No," my father said. "I drink because I'm an Indian. I'm an Indian because I drink."

I laughed at my father's bullshit. When I was younger, during my father's extended alcoholic absences, I would become inconsolable. But, in my teen years, I had come to accept that my father would never stop drinking and would always leave home on binges. In order to survive, I think I'd learned how to love him a little less. I don't know what my mother did to survive his boozy sojourns but, hey, maybe Valium had been her temporary escape pod.

"How did Mom quit the Valium?" I asked.

"One day, she said she was done with it," my father said. "And she was. Never took them again."

"Maybe you should follow her example," I said. I was never mean to my father when he was sober. But I'd often insult and challenge him when he was drunk. So maybe I never did learn how to love him less. I don't know anything about my mother's strategies for loving him. I do know this sad fact: My father was at his most emotionally engaged with the world when he was somewhere between pretty-damn drunk and all-the-way drunk.

"How am I supposed to follow your mother's example?" my father asked, playing dumb.

"You're going to have to sober up someday," I said.

"That's never going to happen," he said.

He was telling the truth. My father died of alcoholism when he was sixty-four.

When I turn sixty-five, I'm going to throw the biggest birthday party of my life.

"Daddy, Daddy," I'll sing, "I lived longer than you."

56.

At the Diabetic River

Salmon disappear.
My father goes blind.

He kneels on the bank
Close to the river

So I can wash his face
With the sacred water.

O the ghosts of salmon.
O the ghosts of my father's eyes.

57.

Reunion

I release these salmon
I release

I release my father and mother
I release

I release these salmon
Into their personal rivers

The river of bitterroot
The river of broken bone

The river of stone
The river of sweet smoke

The river of blood and salt
The river of semen and sap

The river diverted
The river damned

I release these salmon
I release

I release these salmon
I release

O salmon, I release you
O salmon, I pray

O Father and Mother
O Father and Mother

return to me
return to me

58.

The Spokane Indian
Manual of Style

AFTER THE GRAND Coulee Dam murdered our
wild salmon, we stopped being Spokane Indians and
became a Paraphrase of Spokane Indians.

Our identity has been clarified for us.

We are the Unsalmon People.

We are Unsalmon.

We are Un.

59.

Testimony

TWENTY YEARS AGO, I sat in a room with more than fifty indigenous men from all over North America as they, one by one, stood and testified about being raped by white priests, white teachers, white coaches, and white security guards and soldiers. These rapes happened in residential boarding schools all across the United States and Canada. And they happened from the late nineteenth century into the late twentieth.

I had learned about the epidemic violence in Indian boarding schools, and I'd heard and read the countless stories of sexually abused women, but I had never seen so many male victims gathered together.

One elder, over seventy years old, stood and said,

"We were beaten for speaking our tribal languages. We were beaten for dancing and singing in traditional ways. We were beaten for resisting the beatings. Sometimes, we would escape and run away. The white men would catch us and beat us for running away. They'd beat us for wanting to go home. They'd beat us for crying. So, more than anything, we learned not to cry. Our tears were the only thing we could control. So not crying felt like we had won something."

He said, "Sometimes, white men would take you into private rooms and they would beat you. And you'd be happy to only get slapped and punched. Because, sometimes, those white men would take you into those private rooms and rape you. Sometimes, it was one white man. Sometimes, it was more."

The elder stopped speaking. He could not continue. He stood, without crying, and trembled.

I watched him.

That Indian man, over seventy years old, trembled like a frightened boy—like the boy he used to be and the boy he remained, trapped in time by his torture.

That trembling man—that trembling boy—stood in silence for many minutes. And we other Indian men sat in silence and waited. We all knew, collectively, that we would silently wait for that man— that boy—to resume speaking or to remain silent or to sing or dance or to cry or to leave the room.

We would have waited for hours. Maybe for days. I think some of those Indian men would have let themselves die while waiting in that room.

But that elder—that frozen child—smiled, placed his hand on his chest, and sat so he could listen to other Indian men tell their stories. And those men told their stories for hours.

When people consider the meaning of genocide, they might only think of corpses being pushed into mass graves.

But a person can be genocided—can have every connection to his past severed—and live to be an old man whose rib cage is a haunted house built around his heart.

I know this because I once sat in a room and listened to dozens of Indian men desperately try to speak louder than their howling, howling, howling, howling ghosts.

60.

Pack Behavior

NINETEEN SEVENTY-FIVE. Night on the reservation. Summer. Mosquitoes and moths following heat and light.

In the treehouse, five boy cousins pass three porn magazines from hand to hand, their version of the Internet.

This is the USA. Deny it, if you must, but nearly every American boy has been in a treehouse like that with cousins and magazines like that. There is nothing wrong with it.

Three of the cousins pulled out their penises and masturbated—performed—for the others.

Deny it if you need, but that kind of performance has happened in many an American treehouse.

There's nothing necessarily wrong with it. But,

depending on circumstances, there might be something wrong with it.

The other two cousins—who were brothers—did not perform. Instead, they shyly climbed down from the treehouse and walked home.

Why were two brothers, who grew up in a town of only fifteen hundred people, so unlike the three cousins who grew up in that same town?

There are no provable answers. Only psychological guesswork.

Those brothers who went home? One of them has spent time in jail for DUI and unpaid fines, but the other brother has only been in jails to visit his brother.

As for those other cousins, the ones who remained in the treehouse? All three grew up to be rapists. Two of them have spent years in prison for their crimes. The third cousin has never been convicted of any felony, though he has raped more people than the other two combined.

How has that third cousin escaped justice? Because he mimics proper human behavior better than the others. Because he speaks a little bit of the tribal language. Because he genuflects and prays in front of large crowds. Because he wears beads and feathers every day of the year. Because he plays the role of traditional Indian better than most. Because he proclaims himself holy and is superficially believed.

Because his victims have learned, on the reservation and everywhere else, that it is more painful and dangerous to testify than it is to silently grieve.

On the reservation, testifiers are shunned and exiled.

On the reservation, the silent are honored with more silence. In that way, silence becomes sacred. Silence becomes the tribal ceremony that everybody performs.

Perhaps everybody, indigenous and not, lives on their own kind of reservation.

If those five cousins were transformed into animals—into three wolves and two dogs—then this story might sound more like a parable, like a familiar fable, like an ancient lesson taught around the campfire.

This story would teach us that dogs and wolves are alike. But the story would also teach us that, in most ways, dogs and wolves are nothing alike.

Dogs and wolves might have the same ancestors, but they long ago became members of different tribes.

But how did dogs and wolves become so different from each other?

Dogs are wolves that were loved by humans. Dogs were created by human tenderness.

But wolves have always walked slow circles around humans. Wolves have seen humans only as potential prey and potential predators.

But, wait, you might say, there has never been a recorded instance of a healthy wolf attacking a human.

But, ah, the storyteller replies, did you hear me claim that those wolves, those three cousins, were ever healthy? Did you know that wolves will hunt other wolves? Did you know that wolves will eat their young? Did you know that wolves teach other wolves how to be wolves? Did you know that wolves *beget* wolves?

Did you know that some wolves will dress up as Indians and dance and sing and dance and hunt and sing and dance and hunt and sing and dance and hunt and hunt and hunt and hunt all night long?

Do you understand how one small dog—afraid of the wolves who had attacked him and those who would attack him anew—might stand on his hind legs, might evolve in a moment, so he could run away and never return?

61.

Prophecy

the salmon have built mansions
at the bottom of every ocean

thousands of rooms
thousands of rooms

the salmon have sent ambassadors
to live among Indians

thousands of salmon
thousands of salmon

those ambassadors are teaching us
how to breathe water

62.

Welcome to the Middle-Aged Orphans Club

One week after we buried my mother,
And four years after we buried hers, my wife and
  I went
To see *Wicked*, the musical, for the third time.
But that was the first time that my whole body
  ached
As the Wicked and Good Witches sang their
  final duet.

"Why am I hurting like this?" I asked my wife
  later.
And she said, "Um, your mother, who was
  wicked
Most of the time and good some of the time—

She just died. And you've only begun to
    reconcile
The two mothers who lived inside your one
    mother."

"Oh," I said, amused at my emotional blindness.
"My mom wasn't even that sick when I bought
The tickets," I said. "I wasn't thinking about her
    then."
"We're always thinking about our mothers," my
    wife said,
"Because, when it comes to death, you and I are
    up next."

63

Performance

ONSTAGE, IN BELLINGHAM, Washington, during a fund-raiser for salmon restoration, I pointed out to an audience of eight hundred that salmon go on their epic journey from the ocean into the insane mouths of rivers and up those rivers against the current, over dams, dodging bears and fishermen—and a lot of those fishermen are Indians, by the way— and then through and over and around trees and rocks and pollution and garbage—swimming hundreds, even thousands of miles—in order to *fuck*.

"Salmon," I said, "are the most epic *fuckers* in the animal kingdom."

The audience, crunchy-assed liberals one and all, laughed but not with the abandon I wanted to hear. Maybe they were socially and politically progressive, but I could feel their sexual repression, too. I could sense that shitloads of them were offended. I was being inappropriate. After all, man, we had gathered to save the salmon, not to talk about sex.

"So, honestly," I said, unafraid of being even more inappropriate. "When we celebrate salmon, we are celebrating *fucking*. And I don't think we celebrate fucking enough. In fact, forget salmon for a minute. Let's talk about our mothers and fathers. I mean—have any of you ever thanked your parents for fucking and conceiving you? And I don't mean thank them all cute and poetic like, 'Oh, I light this ancestral fire in tribute to you for my human creation.' No, I mean have you ever looked your mother and father in the eye and said, 'Thank you for fucking me into existence.'"

The audience laughed louder. I knew I'd won over a few more of them. But I wanted to win *all of them*. So I went stuntman.

"In fact," I said as I pulled out my cell phone and held it close to the microphone. "My father is dead. But I'm going to call my mother right now."

I heard gasps in the audience. Some woman shouted, "No!" The moment was hugely uncomfortable, very funny, and comedically dangerous. It was dangerous because I didn't know if my mother was home to answer the phone.

One ring.

Please be home, Mom.

Two rings.

Please don't be the machine.

Three rings.

What am I going to do if it's the machine? If I leave a message, will it be funny?

"Hello," my mother answered.

Thank God.

"Hey, Mom," I said. "I'm onstage in front of about eight hundred people in Bellingham, and we're trying to save the salmon, and I just wanted to thank you for fucking Dad and conceiving me."

The audience laughed.

My mother laughed.

"So what do you think about that?" I asked her.

She said, "I think you sound like you're drunk. Have you been going to your AA meetings?"

The audience laughed and laughed. I held the cell phone in the air as they laughed. That laughter was a celebration of my mother. She had won everybody in the room.

64.

Electrolux

FOUR IN THE morning and our mother was vacuuming. That was one of her ceremonies. She often stayed awake all night to make quilts or to bead powwow regalia or just to watch TV. On those sleepless nights, she was usually content to be alone. To keep the peace. But on other nights, she needed to disturb all of us. So she'd plug in that old wheezing vacuum and slam and clunk around the living room. We lived in a small house, so there was no escape from the goddamn racket of her loneliness.

Whir, whir, whir, whir.
Fuck you, vacuum.
Whir, whir, whir, whir.
Fuck you, Mom.

She knew my siblings and our father would stay in bed and pretend to be asleep. Maybe they'd even learned how to sleep through all of the forms of our mother's mania. Most of the time they passively accepted our mother's contempt. They rarely confronted her about any of her bullshit. But she knew that I would stand up to her. She knew that I would storm up the stairs to curse at her. Once, I unplugged the vacuum, opened the door, and threw it as far as I could into the dark. It smashed to the ground. I hoped I'd broken it. But I'd only knocked loose a rib or something structural because the vacuum kept working but thereafter rattled like a snake made out of tin cans.

Whir, whir, whir, whir.
Don't take the fucking bait.
Whir, whir, whir, whir.
She wins if you engage with her madness.

How many times had she woken us that way? Thirty or forty times over twenty years? Not nearly enough for it to be predictable. No, she always surprised us with that shit. And I would furiously react.

But, one night, I didn't react. I covered my head with my pillows and tried to fall back asleep. She kept vacuuming. I refused to fight; she refused to turn off the vacuum. A stalemate that lasted until dawn.

Later that morning, as we all ate breakfast, dark-eyed from lack of sleep, we all joked around as if it were another normal day in the Alexie household. But we didn't make jokes about our mother's vacuuming. We didn't address that at all.

Whir, whir, whir, whir.
Don't talk about the shit that is troubling you.
Whir, whir, whir, whir.
Swallow every indignity, small and large, without editorial comment.

I don't know what happened to that vacuum. I imagine it finally broke for good. It's probably buried deep in the reservation landfill. Maybe some twenty-seventh-century archaeologists will find it. They'll think it was just a primitive cleaning device. They won't know it was a nonlethal weapon in a domestic war.

65.

L o v e   P a r a d e

My mother married a war
Orphan. For the ceremony,

He sported a three-piece
Grief. She was lovely

In a white dress—a former child
Bride now marrying again

As a woman. They wed
On impulse in City Hall

After being witnesses
To their friends' equally

Impulsive marriage
That only lasted months.

But my mother and her war
Orphan were married

For nearly four decades,
Conceived four children

Together, raised another
Only biologically hers,

Sheltered a dozen cousins
For days and weeks

And sometimes years,
And officially adopted

One cousin and raised him
As their son. All of us—

We brothers and sisters
And cousins—were parented,

Well and not well,
By my mother

And her war orphan.
We were raised by two kinds

Of loneliness: One was silent
And solitary and depressed

While the other rehearsed lines,
Sought out the crowd,

And confessed to everything.
So, yes, I am the child

Of those two opposing forces.
I am the one

Who is half monk
And half clown.

Look at me pray!
Look at me pratfall!

I will beg, I will beg
For your devotion

Then do my best
To lead you astray.

66.

The Urban Indian Boy Enjoys Good Health Insurance

Though I drove to the rez and back, and sat in
   bad chairs
For three days straight, my chronically injured
   back
Somehow didn't collapse, so I made it through
My mother's funeral and wake. But, eleven days
   later,
My back spasms when I open our front door in
   Seattle

And I have to lower myself to the floor. Hello,
Mr. Grief, I was wondering when you would
   find
Where I am weakest. Look at me push myself

Across the floor with one leg extended like
An eccentric baby. At first, I crawl for the pain

Pills, then remember that I'm the recovering
Drunk who threw them away, so I force myself
To my feet and slowly pace the breadth and
  length
Of the hallway because using my re-torn muscles
Is the best way to regain their strength.

67.

The Raid

In the thirteen days and twelve hours since
We waked and honored and buried my mother,
I've murdered sixty-five carpenter ants—

In my now-invaded home—with spray, traps,
Magazines, books, spoons, and all of my shoes.
I stomp, I stomp, I stomp, I stomp and stomp

On those three-segmented Gods, and see,
With each death, that "retribute" is a verb
That's terse, lovely, and sadly underused.

68.

Ursine

Driving my son to camp, I saw a black bear
Rise on its hind legs to watch us roll by.
A few hours later, after dropping off my son,
I drove past that same spot and realized

That black bear was a small tree—burned, split,
And twisted by lightning. How had I confused
A tree for a bear? I didn't need to see a bear.
Minutes later, in a little town, I was bemused

To see my mother strolling on the sidewalk.
She'd been dead for a month. Oh! Hello, ghost!
I waved. She waved back. And then she tripped
And fell hard. Oh, shit! I pulled off the road,

Jumped out of my car, and ran back to help
My mother. But, wait, it wasn't my mother.
It was a white woman who fell. She smiled
As I helped her to her feet. And I wondered

What other ghosts might appear. "Are you okay?"
I asked. And the woman said, "I mostly fell
On the grass. Yes, I am good." She thanked me
And strolled away. *Another story to tell,*

I thought as I walked back to my car, *about how*
Everything I see and believe is contradicted
By everything else. But I am okay with my lack
Of faith. I don't feel sacred or afflicted.

I mean—hey, I get why people are desperate
To fit this copious world into one prayer.
But as for me? I'll be the secular clown
Happy to mistake his late mother for a bear.

69.

Persistence

ON A SATURDAY afternoon, sometime in the mid-1970s, I walked home from my friend's house to discover my mother, in our kitchen, loading canned food into a cardboard box. My mother often cooked for funerals, but I hadn't heard of anybody dying. And I wasn't sure how a few cans of baked beans and evaporated milk would feed dozens of mourners anyway.

"What are you doing?" I asked.

"I'm giving food to the O'Neal family," she said.

"But not the cling peaches," I said, worried. I *loved* the cling peaches.

The O'Neals were a poor white family who'd moved to the reservation a few months earlier. It wasn't unusual for Indians to marry white folks and create biracial families on our reservation. But the O'Neals—a mother, father, and approximately seven sons and daughters—weren't friends or family with anybody on the rez. They were an entirely white family who had suddenly appeared like a magician's rabbits. Why would a family choose to live on a strange reservation among Indian strangers? I would guess it had something to do with the O'Neals' extreme poverty. There were lots of poor Indians on our reservation. I'd say the poverty was almost universal—save for the few dozen people who worked for the tribe or the Bureau of Indian Affairs—but the O'Neals were so poor that it boggled our poor Indian minds. They wore the same gingham dresses and denim overalls to school every day, and their shoes and boots were repaired with generations of tape, string, and pieces of random fabric. I don't know how much time John Steinbeck had spent on Indian reservations, but he could have written the O'Neals into existence.

At school, a few days after their arrival, the O'Neal kid in my class, Bobby, sat beside me at lunch and attacked the food. He open-mouth-chewed, choked a few times because he was eating so fast, and finished his tray in seconds. I'd been hungry many times in my life. When I was seven years old, I once went thirty-two hours without eating as my parents were out looking for money like subsistence hunters scouting for deer. Thirty-two hours is certainly not a physically dangerous amount of time to go without food, but it was scary. I hadn't known when I would get to eat again. And as my hunger grew, I'd wondered if I would ever eat again. But I'd experienced only a hint of what it truly means to be hungry. I had never felt as ravenous in my life as Bobby O'Neal appeared to be on that bright afternoon. He must not have eaten *for days and days*. And I would later learn that the five school lunches that he received were often the only food he'd eat that week.

"Can I have more?" he asked me after he'd licked his tray clean.

"Yes," I said. "If they have extra."

"Really?" he said.

I nodded.

He started crying. From gratitude, I guess. He was sitting in the lunchroom of one of the poorest schools in the state and he was sobbing because there was a chance of getting a second helping of Tater Tots and mysterious gravy. If I'd had the literary vocabulary, I would have recognized the situation as a tragic comedy.

He stood and picked up his empty tray.

"You have to wait until they give the signal," I said. "And then you get in the line again. But be nice, or they won't serve you."

Bobby crouched with his tray, as if he were in

the starting blocks preparing for the hundred-meter dash. I remember looking at his legs, tensed in anticipation, and marveling at his muscular calves. He was a skinny, malnourished kid, but even at his most hungry, he ran faster than everybody in the school. And, as he ran, Bobby would slap his ass and neigh like he was the jockey and the horse. I wonder now what kind of amazing athlete he might have been if coached and parented and fed properly.

I don't remember much about the other O'Neal kids—one of the girls was shockingly beautiful even in her ragged clothes and kitchen-table haircut—but Bobby was treated like shit by us Indians. I suppose you'd like to believe that I, as a severely bullied kid who grew up into a reflexively compassionate adult, would have befriended Bobby. That was not the case. I wasn't physically mean. I never slapped, punched, or kicked Bobby, and I don't recall ever taunting him. But, after talking to him a few times during his first week at school, I learned to flee whenever he approached. I ostracized him as completely as everybody else did.

So, on that day when my mother packed canned goods into a box meant for the O'Neals, I didn't join in while singing work-camp songs. Instead, I was angry. It's not like our family enjoyed a surplus of nutrition.

"Why are you giving them the cling peaches?" I

said. "Those are my favorites." To reiterate, I *adored* the cling peaches.

In response, my mother quoted a Bible verse. I don't remember which one. Throughout my childhood, we'd all endured our mother's periodic Evangelical Christian fervors. She'd quoted hundreds of Bible verses at us, so they all blur together in my memory. If I had to guess at what she'd quoted while packing canned food for the O'Neals, I'd go with Matthew 7:12. And now, since I realize those canned goods had probably been given to us as charity, it seems that, on the reservation, the Golden Rule could be translated as "Hey, let's pass this same unopened can of shitty-ass chipped beef around like it's contagious."

After my mother finished packing the food, she made me drive with her to the O'Neals' house, a dilapidated shack that had been abandoned at least twenty years earlier. Half of the roof had collapsed, so the O'Neals had rigged and roped old plywood boards to act as some kind of semi-roof. It certainly wouldn't be roof enough when the rain and snow arrived.

"What are they going to do for winter?" I asked my mother.

"The pastor will fix it," she said.

Pastor Rod, the Assembly of God minister on the reservation, also had some serious carpentry skills. Talk about Jesus-like, right?

"Stay in the car," my mother said.

She carried that box of canned goods to their front door and kick-knocked with her right foot. I was nervous. In those days, I was wary of white people. Hell, I'm still wary of white people. But I have physical strength and money now.

After a few moments, a white man opened the door, Bobby O'Neal's father, I assume. I wish that I could describe him. But, in my memory of that day, I can see only a pale blur talking to my mother.

I do remember that he yelled and cursed at my mother. I do remember that he pushed the box of food that my mother was holding. He didn't push violently, but it was enough to make her step back. Then he slammed the door shut and left my mother standing shocked and silent.

She took a deep breath, then walked back to our car. She set the box of canned goods in the backseat, sat behind the steering wheel, and stared into the distance.

"What's wrong?" I asked.

"He doesn't want charity," she said.

We silently sat for another minute or two. I watched my mother making a decision. I wonder what Bible passages she was quoting to herself. Then she got out of the car, grabbed the food from the backseat, and walked toward the house again.

I was terrified. What would I do if the O'Neal man

got even more angry? What if he become more violent? I opened my car door a few inches. On the reservation, I'd been conditioned to throw the first punch, regardless of the enemy's size and strength. So I was ready to fight to protect my mother. I was, like all of the kids on the reservation, a child warrior.

Holding that box of food, my mother stood at the front door.

In the car, I was almost crying from fear.

My mother lifted her leg as if she were going to kick-knock again.

I opened the car door a little wider to give me more room to quickly exit the vehicle.

Then, without knocking or making a sound, my mother set down that box of food at the O'Neals' front door and walked back to me.

We didn't say a word as we drove away. But my mother must have been terrified, too, when she'd approached the O'Neal house for the second time—when she'd decided that she would risk the fact that the white man's pride and shame might turn into absolute rage.

She tried to find some music on the radio, but reception was even more random in those days than it is now, so we rode in silence for a while.

Then my mother sang.

But she didn't sing a Christian hymn.

No, she sang her favorite song of the moment, a

country ballad by Jessi Colter: *"I'm not Lisa / My name is Julie / Lisa left you years ago."*

My mother had a beautiful voice.

I loved it when she sang.

She kept singing all the way home.

And, yes, I am still pissed that she gave away the cling peaches.

70.

Ode in Reverse

This poem is for everyone in my life—
My sons, friends, mother, siblings, and my wife.
It's a cuff to the head—a self-rebuff.
Dear ones, I have not loved you well enough.

71.

Construction

SHERMAN," MY WIFE said after reading this memoir for the first time in its entirety. "Your book is constructed in fabric squares like one of your mom's quilts."

"I meant it that way," I said, but that's a half-truth.

I realized I had constructed a quilt of words only after I'd read my own damn book for the first time in its entirety.

And then I saw the patterns and repetition of patterns. I saw the stitches and knots. I saw that hands had worked in the same way that my mother's hands had worked.

Fabric square ad infinitum.

My mother, the quilter, will always haunt me.

72.

Freedom

IN FEBRUARY 1979, I came home from the reservation school and told my mother and father that I needed to leave. I wanted to go to college and become a pediatrician. And that would never happen if I stayed in the reservation school system.

I'd been trying to escape the rez for years. After all, Indian reservations were created by white men to serve as rural concentration camps, and I think that's still their primary purpose. So, of course, I ran away from home in third grade. I packed a small bag with comic books, peanut butter sandwiches, and my eyeglasses, and made it almost two miles down the road before my mother found me.

After that incident, she often said, "Junior, you were born with a suitcase in your hand." That might have been a complimentary thing to say to a nomad. But my tribe hadn't been nomadic in more than a century.

So when I came home that cold winter day in 1979 and asked my parents to let me leave the rez school, I wouldn't have been shocked if they had denied me. I was only twelve years old and I was asking them to let me abandon the tribe and become an indigenous refugee in the little farm town of Reardan.

"Can I leave?" I asked them.

And my parents, knowing that I was betraying thousands of years of tribal traditions to go live among white people, said, "Yes."

My parents, as wounded and fragile as they were, had the strength and courage to set me free.

I think they knew I would never return, not in body or spirit, but they loved me too much to make me stay.

73.

Chronology

IN EARLY SEPTEMBER 1980, my father drove my big brother, Arnold, and me from our home on the Spokane Indian Reservation twenty miles south for my first day of eighth grade and my big brother's first day of eleventh grade in Reardan, Washington. My brother and I became the only Spokane Indians in the Reardan school district, which was 99 percent white. We were brown kids in a sea of white kids inside an ocean of wheat fields. I'd made the decision on my own to leave Wellpinit. But I don't remember why my big brother had followed my lead. He was a great basketball player, and Reardan had a legendary sports program, so I can only assume he transferred for athletic reasons. He and I were brothers, but I think he'd always been emotionally closer to his reservation Indian friends and cousins than he'd ever been to me, which explains why he dropped out of Reardan before Thanksgiving and returned to the rez school. I love my brother. And I didn't want to be alone in a white town. I didn't want to be *the only one.* So I almost followed him back to the rez. But then I didn't. Because the thing you learn as a hugely ambitious Indian is that you're often going to be *the only Indian in the room,* so you'd better get used to it.

A couple of weeks before school started, my mother's brother, Leonard Cox, had died of cirrhosis. He was a gregarious alcoholic and gave me one-dollar bills whenever he saw me. At the end, his belly was so distended and black that my mother said, "He looked like an orca."

So I walked into that new school with multiple griefs. As I lost my uncle, I had also untethered myself from my tribe. I was terrified. And then it got worse.

On October 22, 1980, only a few weeks into school, my mother's mother, Etta Adams, Big Mom, died of cancer.

Big Mom's funeral was so crowded with Indian family, friends, and strangers that I was able to sneak out and walk home to mourn alone. Before she'd died, Big Mom had given me a battery-powered wall clock that didn't work even with batteries. Yes, my dying grandmother had gifted me a hell of a metaphor. But I wasn't thinking about metaphors on that day. I lay on my bed, held that stopped clock against my chest, and mourned.

Like my mother, I would often turn sleep into a weapon of self-defense. Or, if unable to sleep, I would throw the blankets over my face, turn toward the nearest wall, and pretend to sleep. Like my mother, I would turn my insomnia—my inability to sleep—into a weapon.

After her mother's funeral, my mother stayed in bed for two days.

Then, early in January 1981, less than three months after Big Mom's death, we learned that my big sister, Mary McCoy, and her husband, Steve McCoy, had died in a trailer-house fire in St. Ignatius, Montana. The fire started during a party. My sister and my brother-in-law were drunkenly passed out in the back bedroom and had no chance to escape. Mary was my half sister. We shared our mother, Lillian. Mary was only twenty-seven years old when she died.

In six months, my mother had lost her mother, daughter, and brother. I was not a superstitious kid but I worried that I had jinxed our family when I'd left the rez school. But then I reasoned, "Hey, I still live on the rez. I just go to a different school. There's no reason for our family to be cursed."

Today, as a nonsuperstitious adult, I still worry

that I'm at fault. It's a ridiculous narcissistic worry, but real nonetheless.

At my sister's funeral, my mother tried to climb into her coffin. My mother screamed in the tribal language. She wailed in English.

My mother screamed, "Mother!"

My mother screamed, "Brother!"

My mother screamed, "Daughter!"

My mother collapsed and said my sister's name.

She said, "Mary. O Mary, Mary, O my daughter, O Mary."

Of course, it was a prayer. That prayer sounded so powerful that I wondered if my mother might bring my sister back to life.

But she didn't.

Nobody has that kind of power.

Even God has brought back only a fistful of people.

And my mother was not God.

Then my mother wailed so loudly that I thought she'd snapped her ribs. I think something broke inside her. But not something anatomical. I believe that she broke her capacity to fully love the rest of her children. Or maybe to fully love me. Or maybe to fully love herself. That audible snap I heard—that crack of bone—was maybe her soul snapping in half.

That night, I traveled back to Reardan to play in a basketball game. I scored seventeen first-quarter points in a frenzied, irrational burst as I dribbled end to end without sense, fired up impossible shots that went in, and shoved my opponents and teammates into walls and to the floor. At the end of the quarter, I was enraged and exhausted. And I screamed at my teammates. My coach benched me after my outburst and I became a spectator for the rest of the game.

Afterward, in the locker room, my coach said, "I'm sorry I sat you. But you were playing too hard. You were going to hurt yourself. Or somebody else."

"It's okay, Coach," I said. "You were right."

"You didn't have to play tonight," he said.

"Yes, I did," I said. "This is my team now. These are my teammates."

I was talking in sports metaphors. But I was also talking about my tribal allegiances. My brilliant sister had died drunk in a fire. I feared—I knew—that I would die violently like that if I ever returned to my rez. I would die in a fire. In a car wreck. In a brawl. By my own hand. At that moment, sitting in that white-school locker room with my white coach and white teammates, I knew I would never again fully be a part of my reservation. I knew I was going to be a nomad.

I decided to live.

Later, after the game, when I returned home to the rez, my mother was sedated and asleep in the back bedroom.

I stood in the doorway and listened to her breathe.

I mourned with her and for her. She'd lost her mother, brother, and daughter to the next world.

And I understood that she'd also lost me.

She didn't cry out my name. She didn't whisper it.

I was now a ghost in her world. She was already haunted by who I might have become. Awake, I wept. My mother, still asleep, reached her hand toward somebody only she could see.

I whispered, "I love you," and walked, grief-drunk and afraid, into the rest of my life.

74.

Unsaved

AT REARDAN, I became something of a boarding school student. After late-night events, I would often stay over with friends rather than drive in the dark back to the reservation. I slept a few times in the high school locker room on piles of laundered towels. If my car was running and the weather was good, I might sleep in the backseat.

During winter, when the road between my reservation and Reardan was unnavigable, I would sometimes sleep on a couch in the basement of the Lutheran church.

Yeah, I was the Indian taking refuge with the Christians.

Rather ironic, enit?

And cinematic, too, in a Frank Capra dark-subtext sort of way.

But it wasn't completely cinematic because, if it had been a movie, I would have kissed the Lutheran minister's daughter—I would have made out with *the preacher's kid*.

But I never did kiss her.

She'd already graduated high school and was off to college by the time I was sleeping on that Lutheran couch.

I never enjoyed the spiritually ironic privilege of kissing any preacher's daughter.

But I did marry a Native American woman with a master's in theology. So, you know, I have made babies with a Christian. Yep, some ironies can be tender sacraments that feel great in the dark. And in the light.

75.

Skin

I DON'T REMEMBER my first pimple. But I do remember, at age seventeen, when I stood at the bathroom mirror and counted forty-seven zits on my face.

Who knows how much body dysmorphia I was experiencing at that moment—I've never read a scientific study about the psychological effects of having extensive acne—but I do remember feeling freakish and ugly. I felt *disfigured*.

At age fifty, I still have to use a variety of acne-treatment soaps and moisturizers. There's something poetic about one of my crow's-feet wrinkles reaching toward a zit as if it were a raspberry dropped on a brown dirt road.

My face doesn't appear to be acne-scarred, not at first or second glance. My brown skin seems to camouflage a lot of the damage. But in certain lights and at certain angles, and especially in black-and-white photos, my acne scars become more evident.

Or maybe they don't. Maybe I am hyperaware of them. After reading early drafts of this chapter, many friends told me that they'd never noticed my scars. So do I still have the scars? Am I seeing something that is not there? Maybe I have never stopped being that poor Indian teenager, staring into the mirror at his ravaged face.

I am especially self-conscious of the acne scars on my back.

A decade ago, my younger son saw my back as I was changing my shirt in the laundry room. I hadn't realized he was there. He later asked his mother, my wife, if my back had been burned.

"No," my wife said. "Your father had really bad acne. And those are his scars."

"Why didn't he use medicine?" my son asked.

"Your dad was too poor to get good health care," my wife said. "Nobody ever gave him the right medicine."

"Is that why Dad gets after us about washing our faces?" my son asked.

"Yes," she said.

It's true. I have been diligent about my sons' complexions. I've been paranoid. Thank God they have both inherited their mother's clear and lovely skin. But I started buying my sons the most scientifically effective acne soap and lotions as soon as they entered puberty.

For me, "Wash your face" is another way to say "I love you."

My mother and father had clear skin. My siblings all have clear skin. I don't know why I was the only one marked by acne. But sometimes I wonder if I was scarred by evil forces, or if I am the evil one who was scarred as a warning to others. Well, I don't actually believe in that kind of superstitious bullshit.

And yet. And yet.

When I was in sixth grade on the reservation, I witnessed an Indian girl getting bullied by an Indian boy. He was a tall and handsome star athlete from one of the more socially powerful families on the reservation. She was a member of a pow-wow family, not ostracized but not popular. Her family were all dancers, singers, drummers, and stick-game players. They were, to use a Native idiom, "traditional." And they were also rumored to possess *suumesh*, a Salish word that translates most simply as "magic," but is best understood by non-Salish people as the equivalent of the Force in *Star Wars* mythology.

So, yes, that bullied girl was a Spokane Indian Jedi.

Or maybe, given her age, she was only a Padawan, a Jedi apprentice, a beginner at *suumesh*.

But I wasn't thinking about magic when I witnessed that popular kid stand over that traditional girl's desk and whisper, "You're ugly."

"Leave me alone," she said.

"You're the ugliest girl in the whole school," he whispered.

"Shut up," she said.

Tears welled in her eyes. She was trying not to cry. There was nothing worse than crying. If you cried on my reservation, then even your best friends would make fun of you.

"You are the ugliest girl on the whole rez," he whispered.

She wept. Tears rolled down her face and dropped onto her desk. Other Indians laughed at her. I'd like to say I didn't laugh at her, but I don't remember. I was among the most bullied kids, and defending other bullied kids only earned you another beating. So I probably laughed at her.

"You are the ugliest Indian girl in the world," he whispered.

That was all she could endure. Only twelve years old, she rose from her desk, pointed at that bully, and said, "I curse you. I curse you. I curse you. You are going to be the ugly one. You are always going to be the ugly one."

Almost everybody laughed. But she scared the shit out of me. Her little-girl voice had sounded so adult, so old and scratchy, so grandmotherly.

Or maybe I only imagined it sounded like that.

A week later, the bully, so handsome and clean, came to school with a zit on his face. Within a month, his face was more ravaged by acne than even mine would be later. He would be acne-scarred until he died of cancer, in his late thirties.

That girl had cursed him. And, well, fuck me, it seemed like the curse was real. The curse had *worked*.

Of course, that popular kid had just entered his teen years—the age of acne—and he had to suffer through the same shitty health care as the rest of us. So there are logical, economic, and banal reasons for the sudden onset of his acne.

And yet. And yet.

My skin started to go bad when I left the reservation to attend the farm-town high school twenty-two miles away. So I have often wondered, irrationally, if I had been cursed for leaving my people. I wondered if I was the victim of dark *suumesh*.

It's more bullshit, right? I was just another kid with acne, yes? And, okay, my acne was more extensive and long-lasting than most other people's acne. But that is all scientifically explainable, isn't it? After all, I was a poor Indian teenager who had left his tribe for a town full of white strangers so HORMONES + STRESS + POOR HEALTH CARE = HORRIFIC ACNE.

When I was a kid, I once asked my mother if *suumesh* was real. And she said, "It's real if you believe it's real." As an adult, I once asked my mother why she didn't get me better health care for my skin. And she said, "I didn't think there was anything that could be done."

If my mother were still alive, I think I would ask her if there was ever a time when she felt powerful.

As for me? Well, my life is miraculous. I tell stories for a living. How amazing is that? As a storyteller, I sometimes feel like the most traditional kind of Indian. And, once in a great while, I feel like I possess a shard of that good *suumesh*.

But I have rarely allowed anybody to touch the most sensitive skin on my back. I've ordered massage and physical therapists to avoid my scars. I have never allowed myself to be that vulnerable, not even to my wife of twenty-four years.

I don't believe that I was cursed by an enemy—I don't actually believe in *suumesh*—but I still wouldn't be shocked to learn that I've been continually cursing myself for leaving my reservation, for fleeing from my tribe, for abandoning the place where my mother was born and where she died.

So, yes, sometimes, I stand at my mirror and I

strain my neck and turn my head so I can see the full of my back. And, yes, I still feel disfigured.

Look at those scars, the mirror whispers.

Look at those scars.

Look at those scars.

That is the skin of the boy who changed his destiny.

76.

Missionary Position

IN MY RURAL conservative Christian public high school, twenty-two miles from my reservation, I was the only Indian except for the mascot.

That's the one-line joke about my racial isolation.

Truthfully, by the time I graduated, I was one of five Indians in that high school. Two of them were my sisters.

Despite this racial isolation, I was, at various times, the captain of the basketball team, president of the Future Farmers of America, and prom royalty.

During my sophomore year, as I shared a table at the local pizza place with five white friends, we watched a drunk and disheveled Indian stagger inside and slump at the bar. He yelled unintelligibly, then sang and finger-drummed a powwow rhythm on the bar top. I didn't know him. He wasn't a member of my small tribe. But I was deeply embarrassed. We were the only Indians in the place. We were connected by race and culture if not by tribe and blood.

My white friends were visibly distressed by that loud singer and drummer. One of my friends, whom I shall call Tara, leaned forward and whispered, "I hate Indians."

My four other white friends gasped, but it took Tara a few moments to remember that she was sitting beside me, her Indian friend. She burst into tears and spent the rest of the night apologizing.

"It's okay," I kept saying. But it wasn't. I was hurt, ashamed, and angry.

If I'd had parents I trusted, I might have hurried home and shared that experience with them. I might have learned about all of the times they'd dealt with overt and covert racism. They might have taught me strategies for how to emotionally and physically deal with racism. But I didn't have parents like that. I didn't believe then, and I don't believe now, that my father and mother would have offered useful advice to me. I had to live as an Indian in the anti-Indian world without proper training. I had to teach myself how to practice racial self-defense, and I made some profound, amateurish mistakes.

Tara and I eventually dated for nearly three years. We talked about marriage. We lived together. She was always kind. I gave her a promise ring that I bought for twenty dollars in a pawnshop. When we broke up for the last time, she gave me back that promise ring. And I sold it for ten dollars back to that pawnshop.

That pawnshop is closed now.

What happens to the inventory of a closing pawnshop?

I would guess it is sold to another pawnshop.

A pawnshop buys a pawnshop.

I imagine that a poor man—as poor or poorer than I was—eventually bought that promise ring and gave it to the woman he loved.

That promise ring, small and lovely and inexpensive, is probably now buried in the jewelry box of that woman, who received a better ring when her husband could afford it later in their life together. But she keeps that first ring as a reminder of who she used to be.

I was once an Indian boy who was once in love with a white girl who once hated Indians.

This is a love story, I think.

77.

Shush

DURING HIGH SCHOOL, my white girlfriend's mother warned her to never go to the reservation with me.

"Why not?" I asked my girlfriend.

"My mom said that Indians are too angry."

Laughing at the casual racism, I later told my mother what my girlfriend had said.

"What your girlfriend's mother doesn't know," my mother said, "is that you're the Indian around here who has the worst temper."

Because of my childhood hydrocephalus and resultant brain surgery and seven years of seizures, petit and grand, along with addiction to several painkillers and sedatives, I was prone to blackout rages where somebody bigger had to sit on me to keep me from running through walls.

I once spent hours repeatedly crashing into a smallish pine tree until it broke and fell.

That was me, the lumberjack of irrational anger, the ax of self-destructive wounding, the sharp blade of get-me-the-fuck-out-of-here.

That white girlfriend never did visit my reservation home.

But I married a Native American woman, a powerful Hidatsa, who'd spent time on my reservation before I met her.

"Before I went to your rez," my wife said, "all the Indians in Spokane—all the Indians who weren't Spokane—said you Spokanes were mean."

"And?" I asked.

"You Spokanes *are* mean," my wife said. "Not with fists. But with words. I never met Indians so good at teasing each other—at burning people with insults."

"What about me?" I asked. "Am I mean?"

"You aren't mean to me with words," she said. "You're mean to me with your silences."

"Wow," I said, feeling *seen*. "You know, there was a three-year period in college when my mother and I didn't say a word to each other, even if we were in the same room. Even if we were in the same car."

"Why did you guys stop talking?"

"I don't remember," I said.

"What made you start talking again?"

"I don't remember that either."

"You should ask your mom," my wife said. "Maybe she remembers."

"Asking my mom about a fight," I said, "is like asking my mom to fight again. We probably stopped talking to each other because I reminded her of some other time when we weren't talking to each other."

"You're scared of your mother, aren't you?" my wife asked.

"Yes," I said.

"So am I," my wife said.

And we laughed.

78.

Harvest

THE DAY AFTER my big sister's burial on the reservation—after my mother had collapsed in grief five or six times—I returned to my farm-town school. The white kids, my friends and fellow eighth-graders, shook my hand, patted me on the back, said awkward and graceful things. They were reticent in the presence of grief. They were polite about my pain. I didn't understand it. I'd been raised by a mother who was so emotionally expansive. She often wildly expressed the wrong emotion, but at least she was always emotive. I'd seen my drunken father weeping and incoherently singing love songs while pissing his pants. So, yeah, I had no relation-ship with reticence.

A year after my sister's death, one of my white

classmates died in a car wreck. His name was Donny Piper. He was a farm kid who wore western shirts and cowboy boots every day. A constant smiler, he had a locker always filled with cans of Pepsi and bags of Nacho Cheese Doritos. And he generously shared his junk food. On certain days, when there'd been no money for breakfast or lunch, Donny's soda and chips were my only meal. Nobody at Reardan knew I was that poor. I never let any of them know when I was hungry. Though I qualified for free lunch, I never went to the cafeteria. I worried that being poor would negatively affect my social standing. Poverty kids are never popular kids, right?

My entire class, all fifty of us, went to Donny's funeral. I sat in a back pew and cried for a while. I liked Donny. I would miss him. He died so young. And because I'd already been to a few dozen wakes and funerals, it felt as if all of the separate grief had become one ever-growing grief, as if each grief was worse than the previous grief because of exponential math. So it felt like my grief for Donny was the same size as all the rest of my grief combined, plus one. But I stopped crying when I noticed that very few people were being openly emotional. I'd never seen that many stoic people at a funeral. I'd never experienced a silent and polite funeral. My tribe doesn't bury our dead that way. We wail, weep, and tell dirty jokes at graveside.

I was completely shocked to see that Donny's immediate family—little brother, mother, father, and grandparents—were sitting off to the side behind a black mesh screen. I could barely make out their features. They were grieving separately from the rest of us. I was boggled. How do people grieve if they're not grieving with the entire community? How do they grieve in a separate room? I didn't doubt the epic size of their pain. I didn't judge the quality of their grief. I was simply baffled by their ceremonies. That was the first time I truly understood that I was a foreigner. I might have been indigenous to the land itself, but I was a first-generation cultural immigrant to the United States. I was now living in a place where people did not grieve like me. Later, back at school, I was even more shocked to learn that it was the first funeral that most of my classmates had ever attended. Donny Piper was their first death. I thought they were kidding. But, no, it was true. My white classmates knew very little about death. We didn't keep a tally, but based on the stories I remember from that day, I think I might have attended more funerals than all of my white classmates put together.

Later that week, the teacher asked me to take attendance while she left the room for other business.

I quickly ran through the names, *A* through *O*, and then I said, "Donny Piper."

The room was so quiet.

"Donny Piper?" I asked. "Donny?"

I was oblivious to my mistake.

"Donny?" I asked. "Are you here?"

And then I realized that I'd been waiting for a response from my dead friend. So ashamed, so hurt, I put my head down on my desk and wept. Nobody said a word. Not then or later. None of the people in that classroom ever mentioned that incident to me. I was not reprimanded, teased, or consoled. I was left alone to feel my own emotions. So I cried for a few minutes, sat up, and finished taking roll.

A year earlier, on that day after my sister's burial, I sat at my desk and wondered how I would ever be happy without my sister in my life. She was the only one who'd ever thought I'd be a writer. I scoffed at the notion.

"Indians don't write books," I said. And, as far as I knew, Indians did not write books. I wasn't handed a book written by an Indian until a decade after my sister died.

In fourth grade, I wrote a Halloween story for my sister. I don't have a copy of that story, but I remember one line: "As the skeletons boned up the stairs, their bones sounded like powwow bells." Yes, I repeated "bones." Yes, I used "bones" as a noun and verb. My sister screamed when she read that.

"Junior," she said to me. "How do you think of shit like that?"

"I don't know," I said. "I just close my eyes and I see things with my brain."

"You should write a whole book," she said.

I laughed at that crazy idea.

I was surely not thinking about a writing career as I sat in that eighth-grade classroom a day after my sister's burial. I was probably wondering why the hell I was going to school with so many white kids, so many strangers.

And then Barb walked into the room, saw me sitting at my desk, and gasped. She ran to me, hugged me so tightly that I coughed, and then knelt in front of me.

"You're alive," she said.

"What?" I asked, confused.

"I heard you died."

"No," I said. "My sister died."

"I didn't hear 'Sherman's sister died,'" she said. "I only heard 'Sherman died.'"

I didn't know what to say.

Barb grabbed my hand and said, "I am so sad your sister died. And I am so happy you are alive. I like you. Everybody likes you."

She hugged me again. Then other girls—Pam, Rachel, Tiffany, and both Lisas—also hugged me.

I had only known those girls for a few months. I

think I was probably too shy to hug them back. But they hugged me. And Barb's words echoed in my ears.

Barb's words still echo.

My sister was dead. I was mostly a stranger in that school. I would become good friends with most of those kids. And most of those friendships went into suspended animation when we graduated from high school. I remain lifelong friends with a few of those kids, who are now middle-aged adults like me.

But I think I have only seen Barb twice in the last thirty-one years. And yet I often think of her. She was the first person to ever look at me—to sincerely make eye contact—and say, "I like you."

And I am still flabbergasted that she also said, "Everybody likes you."

That next year, on our first day as freshmen, I was unanimously elected class president. Donny Piper would die later that school year. But, on that day, he raised his hand and voted for me.

I am weeping now as I write this, as I remember that morning.

I was sitting at a desk and watched all of my classmates—white people—raise their hands to vote for me.

Those forty-nine raised arms turned that classroom into an odd garden. And I proudly stood. And I bloomed.

79.

The Game

BUT, THIRTY-SIX years after those white conservative kids in Reardan unanimously elected me
freshman-class president, I wonder how many of
them voted for the racist, sexist, homophobic, and
immoral Donald Trump to be United States president. How many of their parents and siblings voted
for Trump? How many of my former teachers
voted for Trump?

Reardan High School is located in Lincoln County,
the whitest and most conservative county in Washington. Trump won 72 percent of the Lincoln
County vote, so I assume that percentage holds true
among my former Reardan classmates and their
families who still live in the area. Based on my
anonymous looks at their social-media postings, I

also assume that percentage holds true, or close to true, for those people who moved away from Reardan to Spokane, Seattle, Alaska, Arizona, Montana, Idaho, Oregon, New York, and various other places.

Of the dozens of Reardan folks I still know, I am aware of only five who are vocal and active Democrats.

How do I make sense of this? How is it possible that I, the lifelong indigenous liberal, became so popular—so loved and loving—in that conservative community? How did I become captain of the basketball team, prom royalty, and president of the Future Farmers of America?

Was it because I had a killer jump shot and spin move on the basketball court?

Was it because I was once handsome and slender enough to be called pretty despite all my real and perceived scars?

Was it because I could publicly speak my mind with quick wit and honesty?

Was it because I was so book-smart?

Was it because I was mostly kind and egalitarian and made friends with stoners, jocks, musicians, geeks, brainiacs, and all other manner of kids? Was it because many of those kids, like me, were athletic and geeky and academically ambitious all at the same time?

My senior year, the varsity basketball team had

an average GPA of 3.76. Out of the twelve guys on that team, eleven of us went on to get bachelor's degrees. The women's basketball team had that same level of academic accomplishment. This kind of scholarly achievement might be standard for an urban private school, but it seems improbable for a farm-town public high school of a hundred and fifty kids in a community of fifteen hundred people.

So perhaps I was the beneficiary of a white small town's honest meritocracy. I was good at everything that a Reardan kid was supposed to be good at—I could have simultaneously been portrayed as the nerd hero and compassionate jock in a 1980s teen movie—so maybe that made my indigenous and liberal identities of secondary importance to those white kids and their parents. But I wonder if my race would have been more of an issue if I'd been a nonathlete. If I'd been only an average student. If I'd been plain or overweight or socially awkward. Or if I hadn't been such a natural diplomat.

I was the best, or among the best, in the school at nearly every academic and extracurricular activity (though I never did repair that small engine in shop class and yes, yes, I twice set myself on fire while arc welding), so it was demonstrably impossible for anybody in Reardan to think of me as inferior to any of those white kids.

I think I overwhelmed most overt or latent racism with the sheer force and size of my abilities.

But was I also accepted because it's difficult to be actively racist, sexist, or homophobic on a one-to-one basis? It's hard to be anti-Indian when an Indian is sitting next to you in a classroom. Though I did learn it's pretty easy for a white conservative father and mother to be vocally anti-Indian when their daughter is dating a rez boy like me.

But, damn, after high school and college, and a decade into my very public and leftist artistic career, the town of Reardan asked me to be the grand marshal for their Community Day parade. I said yes, of course, and proudly rode on a mule-driven wagon through town while waving at so many of my old friends and teachers. How did that happen? How did all of those future Trump voters—all of those folks willing to validate and empower that rich man's bigotry—come to celebrate the poor brown boy who grew up in their white town?

I know the answer has a lot to do with basic human decency, and also with the seductive nature of fame, but I think the answer has most to do with compartmentalism. It's easy for a white racist to fall in love with and accept one member of a minority— one Indian—and their real and perceived talents and flaws. But it's much tougher for a racist to accept a dozen Indians. And impossible for a white racist to accept the entire race of Indians—or an entire race of any nonwhite people.

I would guess, perhaps too optimistically, that nearly every racist believes it is morally wrong to be racist. And since nearly every person thinks of themselves as being moral, then a racist must consciously and subconsciously employ tortured logic in order to explain away their racism—in order to believe themselves to be nonracist.

I have lost track of the number of times a white person, hilariously thinking they were being complimentary, has said to me, "But, Sherman, I don't think of you as an Indian."

Throughout my rural and urban life, among white conservatives and white liberals, I've heard many other variations on that same basic sentiment.

"Sherman, you're not like other Indians."

"Sherman, you're a credit to your race."

"Sherman, you barely seem Indian."

"Sherman, I don't think of you as being Indian. I think of you as being a person."

"Sherman, you're not just a Native writer. You're a writer."

"Sherman, I don't see color. I see the person inside."

All of these statements mean the same thing: "Sherman, in order to fit you and your indigenous identity into my worldview, I have to think of you as being like me—as being white like me."

I suspect that some of my white friends, if they are reading this, don't recognize themselves as a person who has said racist things directly to me—who cannot even recognize the racism present in such statements.

In being friends with white people, I've always had to live entirely inside their circle of experience—inside their white world. And my white friends have rarely, if ever, spent even a moment in my indigenous world. This inequality in my friendships has a lot to do with my own introverted nature; I am far more emotionally available when performing onstage and in the books I write than I am in person. But it happens mostly because "being American" means "being white," even for a brown boy like me.

So, at Reardan High School, I was successful and acceptable and loved because I was—and still am—great at negotiating with whiteness. But that means my white friends often mistakenly believe that my ability to successfully negotiate the white world means that I am white—or more white than Native. My white friends can mistakenly believe that my intellectual and artistic abilities are intrinsically white. And, yes, I am heavily influenced by Whitman, Dickinson, Springsteen, Hank Williams, and Dusty Springfield—and owe them and many other white and non-Native artists and intellectuals a huge debt—but I am also very much a product of my ancient tribal culture. I am the genetic, artistic, and political descendant of my mother and father, and grandmother, and thousands of years of salmon-fishing ancestors.

But here I must also indict the strange anti-Indian racism of many Native Americans who have, over my nearly-twenty-five-year literary career, sought to discount, discredit, and demolish me as a writer and as an indigenous person. These are the Natives who, like white racists, mistakenly attribute my success to my perceived whiteness. These are the Natives who cannot believe that a reservation-raised boy could ever become the man I am.

A few years into my career, and in the early, less universal age of the Internet, a rumor started that I wasn't a real Indian—that I was actually adopted and raised by a white family. Of course, that falsehood was primarily a grievous insult to those indigenous people, like one of my first cousins, who were taken from their birth families and given to white folks—an act of bureaucratic genocide so commonplace that the U.S. government needed to pass the Indian Child Welfare Act in order to stop the practice. But this mythology about white parentage was told about me, a Native man who grew up with two Native parents on his tribe's reservation in a government-built house located across the street from the tribal school. If my wholly indigenous identity can be viewed with suspicion—in the past, present, and future—then I sigh and grieve at the heinous shit that other Natives endure because they have a white parent or grew up in the city or fail to meet some other imaginary standard of Indianness.

And I laugh when I think about my wife, Diane, a Hidatsa/Ho-Chunk/Potawatomi, who called her sister after our first date and said, "He's way young and way rez."

And I think of the continent-sized leap I took in my early teens when I left the reservation school to attend Reardan.

I was a courageous explorer, scholarly adventurist, and terrified child. And none of you, Native or not, would have ever heard of me if I had not taken that first step onto the moon. I have been harshly judged by other Natives who were either too scared to take that step or who somehow think their first step was more pure—more Indian—than mine.

What does it feel like to experience such hypocritical anger from other Natives? Well, if dealing with white anti-Indian racists is like soft-shoeing through a minefield, then facing anti-Indian Indians is like dodging bullets from camouflaged snipers, sneaky and deadly.

But very few of even the most cruel Indians voted for Trump. So I must recall the ways in which my race, and my indigenous identity, did become problematic when I attended Reardan High School and spent five years in Trump Country.

I remember how my parliamentary-procedure-team coach and teammates sometimes called me Chief Gayfeather. And, yes, that's an obviously racist and homophobic insult, but it was also, impossibly enough, an affectionate acknowledgment and gentle mocking of my Native American identity and highly emotive personality. In high school, as now, I cried more easily than most people. I wrote poems and stories. I constantly expressed my love for people, places, and things. I was affectionate. So, when viewed through the hypermasculine lens of white small-town America, my emotional vulnerability was sometimes perceived as being stereotypically homosexual. One would think that an androgynous Indian boy would be tortured in a farm-town high school, but I was the androgynous and popular Indian boy who led that debate team to a state championship and made out with two of my female teammates, separately, while on road trips to debate meets. I would love to say I also made out with one of my male teammates, because it would make for a more dynamic story, but alas, I've always been approximately 84 percent straight.

Chief Gayfeather! I'm sure that shit would get students suspended and teachers fired in Reardan today. But it was acceptable in the 1980s. In some sad-ass spasm of self-denigration and self-preservation, I accepted that shit, too.

I also remember a basketball game we played against Freeman High School where I recognized one of the refs as we did warm-up drills. He had been, for years, notoriously and obviously biased against reservation-high-school teams. And though I was the only Native on my team and my parents were the only Native fans sitting in the bleachers, I knew that ref would still practice his official form of anti-Indian racism on me.

So I told my coach, a white man, of my suspicions about that racist ref.

I don't think my coach believed me. But that ref called a foul on me during the opening jump ball, then called two more fouls on me in the next two minutes, and then called the fourth and fifth fouls on me. The Freeman coach had understood what was happening and had ordered his players to purposely run into me and flop like soccer players.

I was sitting on the bench, disqualified by fouls, before the fourth quarter.

After the game, which my team won without me, my coach pulled me aside in the locker room and said he was sorry about what happened.

He didn't directly call it racism. But he tacitly acknowledged it.

I also remember a Future Farmers of America extemporaneous speech contest where three judges ruled that I'd either won first or second place while the fourth judge put me in sixth and last place. Her strange decision, and low score, meant I finished in third place and missed out on a trip to the state finals, because only the top two finishers moved on.

Afterward, we looked at her scorecard and saw that she'd deducted points for my "long hair" and "distracting foreign accent." Well, my hair was not quite as short as my competitors' crew cuts, but my singsong speaking voice could only be considered foreign if one thinks the Spokane Indian Reservation is an international destination.

I also remember when an adult community member in Reardan publicly objected to me being named basketball team captain. He said, in my presence, that only a "local boy" should be captain. I wish I'd been rowdy enough to point out that I'd been local for at least forty-five thousand years. This is the same guy who, after he read my novel about my first year in Reardan, wrote me to ask why I had to invent racist white characters.

And I also remember the pep rally where my great friend and fellow Spokane Indian and basketball star, Steve, and I were wildly cheered by our schoolmates. Steve had transferred to Reardan the year after I did and had become quite popular, too.

As Steve and I were being celebrated, one of our

white teammates leaned over and said, "You let two Indians in and they think they own the place."

Once again, I wish I'd been rowdy enough to tell my teammate to shut the fuck up because Spokane Indians had inhabited, if not officially owned, that very land for millennia.

Of course, I could tell you far more stories about the kindness of many Reardan folks than about the racism of a select few. And I could also tell you about the incongruent kindness of some racists. But I must point out that I was most often subjected to active and passive racism when I threatened the status quo—when I was the Native student who was smarter than the white kids or when I was a better basketball player or debater or actor or comedian or public speaker. Or, most revealingly, when a white girl fell in romantic like or love with me.

In Reardan, I was subjected to racism when certain white folks feared I was taking something away from them.

I was subjected to racism when certain white folks were afraid of me, the indigenous usurper.

So, in the context of the 2016 presidential election, does any of this sound familiar?

In 2016, white conservatives elected as president a serial liar who is likely the most fearful and paranoid and wildly insecure white man who has ever run for the office.

And those white folks elected him because they believe they are victims. Yes, I am a Spokane Indian—an indigenous American—who grew up with white folks who think this country is being stolen from them.

Hahahahahaahahahahaahahahaahahahaha.

I wonder if I could have changed a few votes if I'd campaigned for Hillary Clinton in Reardan and the rest of Lincoln County. I completely doubt it. I graduated high school over three decades ago and haven't stopped or spent any time in Reardan for over eleven years. The last I heard, my books are not taught in the school because they are "inappropriate" for the intended audience.

I wonder what my old Reardan friends think of me. I would guess they're proud of my success but chagrined and unsurprised by my continuing liberalism.

I wonder if any of them thought about me when they voted for Trump. I wonder if they remember how much they loved and were loved by me. I wonder if they know they've helped place me, a public-figure brown-skinned liberal, in danger. How much of that danger is real? I don't know. I am getting death threats. But I am more afraid of the quieter forms of right-wing anger and sociopathy that have found power with Donald Trump's election. I never directly feared for my life and career during a

Republican presidency until Trump won the office. I have never felt so scared for the peace and safety of the entire world.

And I fear that Reardan, the place where I was so loved and accepted and celebrated, is now just another little white town that I, in the name of personal and professional safety, might need to avoid.

Dear Reardan, I am afraid of you.

Does that make you sad? Or angry at me?

Dear Reardan, dear old friends, dear old lovers, do you realize that when you voted for Trump, you voted against me—against the memory of the person I used to be in your lives?

I was the indigenous immigrant, the first generation of my family to ever fully commit himself to the world outside of the reservation. I was the eccentric brown boy. I was the indigenous leftist. And for five years in the 1980s, I was a transformative figure. I made that little white town into a slightly more diverse and inclusive and accepting place.

Or maybe I didn't do any of that. Maybe I was just a cultural anomaly. And though many Natives—many Spokanes—have attended Reardan since I graduated and have maintained friendships and marriages with white people, I wonder if all of that is superficial. I wonder if my friendships in Reardan have always been superficial. Maybe I was loved only because of the ways in which I was not seen as typically and stereotypically Native. Maybe I was loved only in part. Maybe I was celebrated only in proportion to the positive press I brought to the town and school. And maybe, in this Trump era, I would now be ostracized and vilified in Reardan for being who I have always been.

In order to survive, I always knew I'd have to leave the tribe of my birth, leave the limited and limiting Spokane Indian Reservation, but I am only now realizing that, in order to keep surviving, I also had to flee from my other place of birth, from the equally limited and limiting Reardan, from all those white folks who became another tribe for me.

I have always been an escape artist.

Escaping is what I do.

So, old Reardan friends, if you don't hear from me for a while, then it means I am trying to escape you.

80.

I Am My Own Parasite

I dreamed that my spine was a spider
and my ribs were its legs.
It revolted and molted me, leaving me
husked in the dirt
While it put on my two best trousers
and two best shirts,
And scuttled onto the stage,
to claim that my rage,
And all of my stories and poems,
hatched from its eggs.

81.

Tribal Ties

Please remember
As you read my brutal poems

About rape and murder
And assault and dangerous

Loneliness ripped
From the earth

Like uranium—please
Remember as you read

These poems about
My dead mother

And my dead father
And all of my childhood

Pandemonium—
Please remember,

As I weep
Inside

My verse,
That nearly every Indian kid

I knew
Had it worse.

82.

Want List

I don't want to miss my mother. I don't
Want my *want* to be tangible. I don't want
My *tangible want* to be elemental. I don't want my
Mother to be a baptismal fire.

I don't need my mother to be clay and silt. I
    don't
Need my mother to be that basalt ridge. I don't
    need
My mother to be that evergreen. I don't need my
Mother like I need the enduring earth.

I don't love minor chords. I don't
Love every piano in the world. I don't love

My stereo's choir. I don't love my
Mother as much as I love song-drunk air.

I don't grieve everybody that I have lost. I don't
Grieve damned and dammed rivers. I don't
   grieve
My way like a salmon through the dark. I don't
   grieve my
Mother like I grieve the sacred waters.

I don't grieve my mother. I don't grieve
My mother. I don't grieve my mother.
I don't place my mother upon the pyre—
Yes, I do, yes, I do. I'm a goddamn liar.

83.

The Staging

In the weeks after my mother's death,
  I sleep
Four or five hours a night, often interrupted
By dreams, and take two or three naps a day.

It seems like enough. I can survive if I keep
This sleep schedule as it has been constructed
For me. But if it seems my reflexes are
  delayed,

Or if I sway when I walk, or weep or do not
  weep,
Please don't worry. I'm not under destruction.
My grief has cast me in a lethargic cabaret.

So pay the cover charge and take your
    seat.
This mourning has become a relentless
    production
And I've got seventy-eight roles to play.

84.

Assimilation

DRIVING IN THE Cascade foothills, I stop for the deer that had already stopped for me.

Growing up on the reservation, by choice and desperation, we ate almost every animal that walked, swam, or flew.

In my rez youth, I would have seen that roadside deer and thought, "Food."

In my urban adulthood, I saw that deer and *talked* to him. I rolled down my window and said, "You are way too tame, Mr. Four Point. Somebody is gonna shoot your ass."

85.

Litmus Test

AFTER READING MY stories and poems, people often ask me, "Why did your father drink so much?"

But some strangers, the ones who know the most about pain, hear my father's tragic story, and they ask, "Damn, why didn't he drink *more?*"

86.

Standardized Achievement

I wonder if my mother is at rest
Or if she's laughing at her bequest:
A rigorous seventy-eight-question test

That quantifies our devotion & grief.
This test will be proctored by a machine
That thinks "slight misdeed" & "fucking
   stampede

Of maternal rage-horses" are synonyms.
Or maybe everyone sits for this quiz
And writes long essays about phantom limbs

And how we children ache in that
  place—
Now sterilized & amputated—
Where our good and bad mothers
  graced.

87.

Everything You Need to Know About Being Indigenous in America

IN AUGUST 2015, as a huge forest fire burned on my reservation, as it burned within feet of the abandoned uranium mine, the United States government sent a representative to conduct a town hall to address the growing concerns and fears.

My sister texted me the play-by-play of the meeting.

"OMG!" she texted. "The government guy just said the USA doesn't believe the forest fire presents a serious danger to the Spokane Indian community, even if the fire burns right through the uranium mine."

88.

Fire

In AUGUST 2015, a forest fire burned nearly forty thousand acres on my reservation in eastern Washington State. Over three hundred miles away, in Seattle, I was able to log on to a U.S. Forest Service website and watch satellite images of that growing fire. Updated regularly, the images were snapshots of destruction. I was afraid for my siblings living only a few miles from the southern edge of the blaze.

"We've been ordered to prepare for evacuation," my sister texted me. "We've loaded up the two cars with the most important stuff."

"What stuff?" I texted back.

"All the photo albums," she texted. "And all the beaded stuff. And quilts. And the jewelry. And everybody's powwow regalia. And the Indian paintings."

"Good," I texted back. It had been only a few weeks since our mother died—since grief had started a flash fire in our bones—and now my brothers and sisters were facing another fire, which threatened to burn everything else.

"Can you see the fire?" I texted my sister.

"We can see huge smoke clouds on the horizon," she texted. "The sky and the smoke are glowing orange."

"Reflecting the fire probably," I texted.

"Yes," she texted. "It is scary and beautiful."

Grief is scary and beautiful, too, I thought, but did not text. I wondered if you can look at smoke clouds and see objects and animals like you can do with regular clouds floating in the sky. I wondered, if I had been standing beside my sister, if I would have seen our late mother's face in the smoke.

Yes, yes, yes, I would have forced myself to see her in the smoke. I would have invented her face. And thinking of my mother's face made me think of the paintings of Indian faces hanging on the walls of my childhood home.

"The paintings you put in the car?" I texted my sister. "You mean the ones Dad bought?"

"Yes," my sister texted.

I laughed. My father's paintings were cheap shopping-mall art that depicted wise Indians in eagle-feather headdresses floating majestically over golden desert landscapes. My sisters had packed those corny paintings in their cars along with family and tribal heirlooms that would fit beautifully in any Native American museum.

l laughed at the dichotomy between Indian art and Indian kitsch. And then I laughed at us, the Indians, who were equally in love with that same art and kitsch.

I laughed because I would have saved those silly paintings, too.

"Is the air okay?" I texted.

"It hurts a little to breathe," my sister texted back. "But we're okay."

Jesus, I thought, is there a better and more succinct definition of grief than *It hurts a little to breathe, but we're okay?*

"If you have to evacuate, where will you stay?" I texted.

"They have shelters in Reardan and Airway Heights," my sister texted back.

"No," I texted. "Just call me if they make you evacuate and I'll get you hotel rooms with kitchens."

"Okay," she texted. "Thank you."

Over the years, I'd often had to give money to my parents and siblings to save them from their own bad decisions. And I'd often been angry about my family's irresponsibility and would then feel guilty for harshly judging my loved ones. After all, wasn't

I the fucking progressive indigenous leftist who believed that every American should be guaranteed a minimum basic income? If I didn't happily help provide for at least some of my siblings' basic needs, then didn't that make me a bad liberal and worse Indian? But, hey, I felt no conflict in offering to shelter my siblings (and the good and bad Indian art) in a clean and decent hotel if they had to evacuate our reservation. Their lives were on fire! Hell, sometimes it feels like the whole country is on fire. Like a constant conflagration is burning too close to all poor people. Shouldn't rich-ass America be taking care of everybody?

"How many people are fighting the fire?" I texted my sister.

"About two hundred Spokane Indians," she texted. "And maybe one hundred Indians from other reservations."

"Is the government sending in their firefighters?"

"They said they're low on resources. Low on men and equipment. They don't know when they'll be able to send more help."

I briefly fantasized about driving to the rez to help fight the blaze. I would extinguish it all by myself. I'd blow out the flames with my epic and poetic breath like I was an Indian X-Man mutant. In reality, I knew I would throw out my bad back after scooping up maybe the sixth shovelful of dirt and ash.

Then some Indian or Indians would have to carry my sad-sack ass away from the fire line.

"Jerry, Tinker, and Steve are cutting firebreaks with their tractors," my sister texted. They were cousins, very good friends with my big brother but distant to me. I was proud to hear of their courage. They were blue-collar Indians. Their hands were callused from years of hard work. My hands are writer-smooth.

My late mother's hands were often rough from manual labor. She sold her quilts mostly to white people and sometimes to other Indians. During my childhood, for months at a time, my mother's quilt money was our minimum basic income.

"I'm scared of fire," I texted my sister.

"Me, too," she texted back.

My siblings and I have been afraid of flames ever since our big sister died in a trailer fire. I don't have to imagine her face when I stare into a fire. My dead sister's face screams at me from every fire—from the small embers of lit cigarettes to the massive fireworks shows in Seattle every Fourth of July and New Year's Eve. Looking at these satellite images of that forest fire on my reservation, I could see that it was burning closer and closer to the abandoned uranium mine.

Yes, that out-of-control forest fire was threatening to turn the abandoned uranium mine into Dante's rez-ferno.

That might be all you need to know about Native American history.

Or maybe you just need to know that my tribe survived that forest fire. And survived the much larger forest fire that burned a year later.

We Indians know how to survive every fire.

89.

Love Story

MY MATERNAL GRANDFATHER, James Cox, Spokane Indian and Scottish, died six years before I was born.

My paternal grandmother and grandfather, Susan and Adolph Alexie, Coeur d'Alene Indians, both died twenty years before I was born.

My maternal grandmother, Etta Adams, Spokane, died when I was fourteen.

So 75 percent of my direct connection to ancestral culture and history was gone before I was born. And 100 percent of that direct connection disappeared before I had a driver's license.

My mother and father taught me more about modern Indian powwows and Indian basketball than they did about ancient tribal practices and beliefs. Much more. Well, to be specific, my mother taught my sisters how to be powwow fanatics, and my father taught basketball to my brothers and me. My parents sometimes talked about their autobiographical histories. But, in telling their stories, my mother often aggressively lied and my father often passively omitted key details. I think they both sought to disguise and hide their trauma.

Until I began writing this book, and doing some fairly basic genealogical research, I didn't know that my father had uncles and aunts who died young. I had no inkling of any of this until I stood in Sacred Heart Mission Cemetery on the Coeur d'Alene Indian Reservation and saw the grave of a man named Edward Alexie.

"Who is Edward Alexie?" I texted my sister.

"Some relative, I guess," my sister texted back.

At Edward's graveside, I pulled out my iPad and did some quick research on him. Though I am half Coeur d'Alene through my father, I didn't grow up on that reservation. Culturally speaking, I am Spokane. So my knowledge of day-to-day Coeur d'Alene life is limited. I have family and friends on the CDA rez, but I see them only occasionally. And, after reading only a few documents, I called my sis. I needed to say more than texting would allow.

"Edward was Dad's uncle," I said. "He died the same year that Dad was born."

"What did he die of?" my sister asked.

"Smallpox, bubonic plague, Custer's ghost, I don't know," I said. "I'm an Indian on an iPad in an Indian cemetery with access to all the information on the Internet. But I can't find his cause of death."

"Why don't you call somebody with the Coeur d'Alene tribe? A historian or somebody? Or be really crazy and ask one of our cousins what they know."

"I can't," I said. "I'm too embarrassed to let them know how much I don't know."

"They're sure gonna find out how much you didn't know when you publish your book."

I laughed.

"This memoir," I said. "It's going to have a lot of blank spaces. I suppose I could really dig into the research and get stuff as accurate as possible. But I like the blank spaces. I like how they feel. I want my readers to feel how I feel. I want them to feel the loss. To feel our loss. I want them to know how guilty I feel for not knowing this stuff."

"It's not your fault," my sister said. "Dad never talked about bad things."

"And Mom lied so much," I said.

"Yes, she did," my sister said, and laughed. "Just like you."

I laughed.

"Okay," I said. "I gotta do more research."

I think nearly all of my father's uncles and aunts, and his mother and father, died young.

One aunt, named Mary Magdoline Alexie, was five years old when she died, on January 16, 1911. I don't know if her misspelled middle name was a typo on the official records or if it was misspelled on purpose by her parents. Two days after Mary Magdoline's death, Eugene Burton Ely landed his plane on the deck of the USS *Pennsylvania* in San Francisco Bay. That was the first time an airplane landed on a ship.

My father's other aunt, Mary Catherine Alexie, was only a year old when she died, on April 11, 1911. Six days after Mary Catherine's death, Southern Methodist University was chartered.

So, yes, while my great-aunts were dying young on the rez, some incredible things were happening in the outside world.

I can't find any evidence of where my great-aunts are buried. I don't know why they died. Were they buried in the old Coeur d'Alene way? Were they wrapped in blankets and placed in graves dug by their parents? I know those graves, unmarked and forgotten, must be located somewhere on my father's reservation. Probably close to the town, Desmet, Idaho, where they were born. But that town is surrounded by wheat fields now. So did my great-aunts long ago become part of a harvest? Did they help wheat to grow? Did my great-aunts become bread?

I don't know. I don't know.

There is another Mary Alexie. She was my father's great-aunt and lived until 1982. Early census reports have her listed as Mary Agatha Alexie, though her gravestone reads MARY AGATH ALEXIE, dropping the third *a* from Agatha. So which is mistaken, the early census reports or the gravestone? Has to be the gravestone that's correct, right?

But I don't know for certain. I don't know.

During my childhood, my father would often take me on long drives around his reservation. He'd mostly tell me stories about his athletic successes and failures. Sometimes, my father would park on the shoulder of a rez back road—a dirt-and-gravel one-lane history book—and then he'd stare out the window and remember things that he never shared with me. He'd gently ignore me. He wanted me to travel with him. He wanted my presence. But not my words. So I'd gently ignore him back and read my books and comic books.

On those road trips, my father would sometimes visit his great-aunt Mary Agath(a) Alexie, but I'd stay in the car. She looked so old that it was in-timidating. As a child, I didn't have the words to describe what Great-Aunt Mary evoked in me, but now I think it was something like *Holy shit, I am never, not once in my life, gonna be as Indian as that Indian is Indian.* I worried she might be a ghost. That was irrational, I know, but my father spent part of his childhood among Indians who were alive when Custer and Crazy Horse were battling each other. My father was alive on the reservation with a few old Coeur d'Alene Indians who had gone to war against George Wright and the Ninth U.S. Cavalry. My father toddled among indigenous warriors who had shot arrows at white soldiers.

There is a photo of my father with his mother, grandmother, and great-grandmother. In the absence of my father's stories—of his personal oral tradition—I only have photographs like this. I have studied it for hours. I love most the expression of my father's mother's face. Susan Alexie. The grandmother I never knew. So she's more like a stranger. No. That's not the right word. She's more like an idea. She's the Idea of a Grandmother. She is pregnant with my aunt Ellen, who would die of diabetes during my first year at Reardan. But, in that old photo, my grandmother appears to be looking at something or someone out of frame. Not her husband, since he was already serving in the U.S. Army. Whom is she looking at? And what is that expression on her face? Bemusement? Suspicion? Irritation? Shyness? She is the indigenous Mona Lisa.

Susan Alexie died of tuberculosis on August 30, 1945. I don't know why the exact date of her death is not on her gravestone. Perhaps it had been about money. Those extra letters and numbers might have been too expensive. I don't know. I don't know. I don't know. I could write "I don't know" one million times and publish that as my memoir. And, yes, it would be repetitive, experimental, and more metaphor than history, but it would also be emotionally accurate.

My father was only six years old when his mother and father died. I'd love to think that he didn't remember his parents—that time had erased his memory. But I can remember things that happened to me when I was only six. And it's not the good stuff that I recall. No. It's the most traumatic shit that plays in the 3D IMAX Theater of My Mind. So I know that my father remembered his dead parents. But he never said one word to me about them, not ever.

90.

Genocide

Grief is a sea
Creature, a predator
Newly discovered,
Or so you believe,

Until you remember,
Genetically,
That this same grief
Hunted your mother

And your father
And your grandparents
And all of the women
And men who created you.

Sherman Alexie

What happens to humans
Who live as prey?
We are furious, furious,
Furious, and afraid.

91.

Greek Chorus

THE UNITED STATES did not believe the forest fire burning through the uranium mine presented any danger to the Spokane Indian community.

92.

Roller Ball

I SAW YOUR MOM yesterday," Pernell said. "At church."

"So?" I asked.

Pernell was a nice Indian boy. He'd always been kind to me. We were reservation sixth-graders who'd never punched each other. That qualified as a close friendship. Some people called him Jack. I sometimes called him Jack, too. I have no idea how a kid ends up being named Jack and Pernell. And, no, Pernell wasn't his last name and I don't think his middle name was Jack or Pernell.

"Your mom sang a solo in the choir," Pernell said. "She sings really good."

My mother had a lovely singing voice. But I'd only heard her singing along with her favorite country songs or with Elvis. I'd rarely heard her sing any Christian spirituals because I'd never gone to church with her. She never asked or forced us kids to go to any of the various Christian churches she'd attended over the years. Inside our family, we children were allowed to practice the religion of our choice. I was vaguely Catholic for a time, then became an Assembly of God kid in order to romantically pursue a white girl from a little white town. She rejected me, so I quit going to that church. I quit all churches—white, Native, or anything else. Like most Indians nationwide, my sisters turned the powwow into their sole spiritual pursuit. My big brother has never made any declaration of faith, and my little brother became a fundamentalist Christian after marrying into a white Evangelical family. Our father was a childhood Catholic who spent his adulthood using vodka and fiery chili as his only Eucharist.

And now, as I write this, I realize that I'd rarely heard my mother sing any traditional Spokane songs—neither the formal religious hymns nor the casual stick-game gambling songs. She was always on the powwow trail, traveling from reservation to reservation to watch the dancers and drummers, but she didn't sing along. Or maybe she did sing along. I don't know. I rarely traveled to powwow with her. I was too busy playing basketball and reading books.

Spiritually speaking, my mother was as unknowable to me as any of her gods.

"And then after your mom was done singing in the choir," Pernell said, "I saw your mom rolling in the aisle and speaking in tongues."

"No way," I said. "She was probably just speaking Spokane."

My mother was one of the few tribal members who were still fluent in the old way of speaking Spokane.

"It wasn't Indian talk," Pernell said. "It was her Jesus voice."

There were quite a few Spokane Indians who fell in love with Pentecostal and Charismatic Christianity. I think it's rather easy for a universally damaged people like Native Americans to believe wholeheartedly in miracles, in the supernatural. But I'd never thought of my mother as a Spokane who'd go that far.

"I'm not lying," Pernell said.

"I believe you, Jack," I said, though I hoped he was mistaken.

When I got home from school, I immediately asked my mother if she'd been speaking in tongues.

"Yes," she said.

"Weird," I said, and walked downstairs to my room. I figured my mother was *pretending* to speak in tongues. She was just acting, I thought. It's like a one-woman show, I guessed. My mother had always been so dramatic. And what's more dramatic than an Indian woman rolling down the aisle of a little reservation church?

I tried to put it out of my mind, to allow my mother to freely practice her religion as much as she allowed me to fully practice my nonreligion. But, a few weeks later, I crawled out of my Sunday-morning slumber and walked the mile to her church.

And there she was, along with the white couple who led the church and a few dozen Spokane Indians, throwing books, magazines, and music albums onto a bonfire.

My mother and her fellow indigenous Charismatics were chanting something about the Devil— about the evil of the secular world—about all the sin-soaked novels and porn magazines and rock music.

I was grossed out.

On opposite sides of the bonfire, my mother and I made eye contact. But I think she was so deeply entranced—so hypnotized and self-hypnotized— that she didn't recognize me.

I hurried home to make sure my small personal library of books and records was intact and un-burned. And, yes, all was safe.

Later that night, at the dinner table, I told my

mother to leave my stuff alone or I'd burn down her church.

"You're a sinner," she said, and pointed her fork at me.

"And so are you," I said, and pointed my fork right back at her.

93.

Law & Order

Hey, shithead, if you're going to forgive
Your mother, then you better hurry—
But, hold on, maybe you can delay
Because you're the judge and one-man jury

And all of the lawyers and bailiffs.
Hell, you're the Bible and the ornate gavel.
Most of all, you're the journalist who opines
About justice kept whole or justice unraveled.

Hey, shithead, you've never worn a watch,
So I suspect this case will become eternal,
As you try and try and try your mother
For the crime of being unpredictably maternal.

94.

The Lillian Alexie
Review of Books

My late mother was once
Interviewed by the local news
About her son, me, the poet.

When asked if she knew
That I would become a writer,
She said, "I thought he was

Going to be a pediatrician.
There's still time for him
To become a doctor, I think."

She was also asked if it hurt
To read my most autobiographical
Stuff, the shit that detailed

How she used to drink and smoke
And punch old Indian women
In the face. She said, "I was ashamed,

And wished he used fake names,
But then I realized they made me
Think honestly about the past."

I don't know if she was telling
The truth. She mythologized herself
As much as I do. But I can testify

To this: Whenever I traveled near home
To read my poems, my mother
Would always sit in the third row

And gracefully withstand my utter lack
Of tact. Though, on the phone,
She once described me

As "13 percent book smart
And 87 percent dick jokes."
Ah, the things our mothers know...

95.

Painkiller

My sister reminds me
Of the time that I stepped
On a nail, screamed
In pain, and ran
With the nail and board
Still attached to my foot.

Also screaming, our mother
Chased me, wanting
To deliver first aid,
But I was probably
Trying to elude the pain
By running from everything

In the world. When
She finally caught me,

My mother pushed me down,
Pulled the nail and board
Off my foot, and then removed
My shoe. We all expected to
See blood. But, no, no, no,

The nail had miraculously
Passed between my toes
With barely a scratch.
That nail had been impaled
In my shoe and not
In my foot. We laughed

And Mom asked me why
I was screaming from
Pain when there was no pain.
I had no answer then.
But now I think
That I'd been anticipating

The pain, much like the rain
Dancer who is always successful
Because he doesn't stop
Dancing and praying
And dancing and praying
Until it rains and rains and
Rains and rains.

96.

Cultural Identity

FIFTEEN YEARS AGO, at a book reading in Philadelphia, a white man asked me what made my work so "particularly Indian." He said that my poems and stories didn't seem "all that Indian."

I said, "First of all, you're a white guy from Philadelphia. What do you know about Indians you didn't learn from some other white guy from Philadelphia? And secondly, would you ask a white guy what makes him so white? Well, let me tell you, pal, that question you just asked makes you the whitest asshole in Philadelphia right now."

Yes, before I went on bipolar medication, I would sometimes lose my temper in very public and aggressive and completely justified ways.

But as the years have gone by, I have often

pondered that white man's question. And I often think of the other white people and Indians who have questioned the "Indianness" of my identity. And I have experimented with various answers to their questions and challenges. I have considered the genetic, cultural, political, spiritual, and economic aspects of "Indianness." I have discussed the issue with other indigenous writers and scholars. I have read millions of words written by and about Indians.

So, if I could travel back in time to Philadelphia, I would answer that white man's question in a different way. I would have said, "The concept of 'Indianness' is amorphous and highly personal and eccentric. It's hard to say exactly what 'Indianness' is without reverting to generic notions of 'cultural construction' and 'postcolonialism.' But I will say that I have never been a dancer or singer. I have only intermittently believed in God. I used to be a math prodigy and now I'm a great storyteller. Does any of that make me more or less Indian? I don't think so. You know what makes me and my stories Indian? *All the goddamn funerals.*"

At that point, I'm sure that white man would have been trying to speak again, so I would have stepped forward and said, "You know what also makes me Indian? I could punch you in the face right now, do an improvised thirty-minute lecture on the sonnet poetry form, and then punch you again. And, hell, you might be a professional boxer who will kick my ass. But that doesn't matter to me as an Indian. *I will fight you even if I absolutely know I'm going to lose.* You could knock me out and I could wake up and still deliver that thirty-minute lecture on the sonnet *with a heavy-duty reservation accent.* I mean—dude, I come from an honor culture. Don't you know what that entails?"

And then, as a sort of concluding couplet, I would have said, "And also, in case you missed the subtext—in case you misheard—then let me say, 'Fuck off, fuck off, you colonial turd.'"

97.

Motherland

I TEND TO believe in government because it was
the U.S. government that paid for my brain surgery
when I was five months old and provided USDA
food so I wouldn't starve during my poverty-crushed
reservation childhood and built the HUD house that
kept us warm and gave me scholarship money for
the college education that freed me. Of course, the
government only gave me all of that good shit because they completely fucked over my great-grand-
parents and grandparents but, you know, at least
some official white folks keep some of their
promises.

98.

Glacial Pace

When I was thirteen, I coughed on some ice
   chips
And my mother quickly rose and belted
Me *hard* on the back one, two, three, four times.
Later, I said, "Mom, it was ice. It was gonna
   melt."

I was angry at her maybe because
I needed reasons to be pissed at her,
But she always turned life into a play.
She was a mother portrayed by an actor.

When I told my wife the Ice Chips Story,
She said, "Hey, *hey,* I'm on your mother's side

With this one. You can choke to death on ice.
Your mother was trying to save your life."

I scoffed but then did an Internet search
And learned that an ice cube can strangle you
If it's large enough and blocks the airway.
Then it becomes a race: Will that ice cube

Melt and slide free before you suffocate?
I told my wife what I'd learned. And she smiled
And said, "Now, you're racing against the ice.
Will you forgive your mother before you die?"

99.

Next Door to
Near-Death

I DON'T BELIEVE in God. I don't believe in Heaven. I think "afterlife" is only a pretty way of saying "death." But, in December 2015, when I was lying anesthetized on the surgery table in Seattle's Harborview Medical Center, with my skull cut open so the neurosurgeon could remove a small benign tumor, I dreamed myself in a wild grass field and saw my dead parents standing on the cliff above me. Depressed and angry most of their lives, my mother and father were magnetically joyous. They held hands. I don't recall seeing them ever holding hands in life.

I knew I was dreaming. I have endured monstrous nightmares most of my life, so I've learned many strategies for consciously escaping from subconscious dreams. But I didn't want to escape that dream of my late parents. In fact, as the sun rose behind them and above me, I felt the strong desire to climb that cliff and join them.

I would later learn, after my successful surgery, that my brain had bled so much that I'd needed four units of transfused blood and two units of platelets. I'd bled so much because the tumor had adhered to my dura mater, the tough membrane between the skull and brain. My dura mater had also adhered to my skull. And most serious, my tumor had grown into and adhered to the superior sagittal sinus, a rather large blood vessel running across the top of my brain. Despite multiple CAT and MRI scans of my skull, the doctors had not seen the extent of these adhesions. So when they'd cut into my head and removed the skull plate, usually the simplest part of any brain surgery, they were surprised to discover they'd also torn open the dura mater and sinus. It sounds terrifying, I know, but I was never in critical condition. It was relatively serious, but I was never near death. I'd only been next door to death. Or maybe even down the block and around the corner from death.

So I didn't have a near-death experience. Even though I was unconscious, I think I knew my brain was bleeding. I think I heard and felt the increased tension in the operating room. I think I was scared. And to comfort myself, I created the image of my late parents looking at me. Or rather, I'd created alternative parents, a mother and father who offered illuminating love and support instead of fear, doubt, and sadness. It worked. I enjoyed my dream. And I feel warm now as I write about the parents I'd imagined to replace my lost ones. So, yes, when it comes down to it, I comforted myself during surgery. I've always been good at comforting myself.

Of course, my neurosurgeon stopped the bleeding, removed the tumor, and repaired my brain. I have small titanium plates, screws, and mesh holding it all together. The doctor told me I wouldn't set off airport metal detectors. But I don't know why not. I don't know anything but the most general details about my surgery. I suppose I could do more research, but I prefer the mystery of medicine and healing. I prefer mystery in almost all things.

Near the end of my surgery, I dreamed of my parents again. This time, they were standing in that same grassy field with me. Still holding hands, they stood maybe fifty feet away. They weren't wearing white robes. They didn't have wings or halos. No, they were both dressed in the same clothes in which they'd been buried. My mother's favorite turquoise suit was simply tailored and beautiful, and my father's favorite sweatpants and Geronimo T-shirt looked comfortable and sloppy. They looked like the people I used to know. I waved hello. They smiled, waved good-bye, and walked away through the tall grass. I wasn't sad to see them go. I knew it was time to wake. And so I did.

100.

The Only Time

FOUR DAYS AFTER brain surgery, in a private room in Harborview Medical Center, I took a sip of ice-cold water and hiccupped.

I laughed. I often hiccupped after my first drink of any icy beverage. Just like my late father did. We shared that reflex.

Ice-cubed drink. One big hiccup. Laughter. Slight embarrassment if it was a public hiccup.

That was the routine.

But, after brain surgery, I hiccupped once, twice, three times in a minute. And then I hiccupped for eight straight hours.

Despite all the pain in my life—and the large number of tragedies—that was the only time I ever seriously considered suicide.

I was almost murdered by hiccups. How hilarious is that?

101.

Scanned

TWENTY-FOUR HOURS after my brain surgery, I met my ICU neurological nurse. Well, I'd met her the day before, but I didn't remember her because I'd been heavily medicated. I was still heavily medicated only a day after surgery, but I felt like I was mostly living in reality.

"Didn't you say something about being a fan of mine?" I asked her, needing as much external validation as possible. I had never felt more vulnerable in my adult life, and I was probably also feeling post-traumatic effects from the brain surgeries I had in my early childhood. Yeah, my current brain surgery was reminding me of my previous brain surgeries.

"I read your first book of poems my freshman year

of college," the nurse said. "And I have read everything since."

"That's cool," I said. "Thank you."

I felt happy. Safer. I figured that a person who loved my words would, by association, also love my brain, and would therefore pay special attention to me.

"I'll never tell anybody you are my patient," she said.

"Doesn't the law require you to protect my privacy?" I asked.

"Yes," she said. "HIPAA. The Health Insurance Portability and Accountability Act. But I won't even tell my husband you are my patient. I won't tell my dogs."

"HIPAA protects me," I said. "But I'm a writer. And I don't think there's anything that protects you from me. You're going to appear in my poems and stories. Well, the real you and the fictional version of you."

"Just make me awesome," she said.

"In some future book, I'm going to blend you with another fan," I said. "She loved my movie *Smoke Signals* and wouldn't date any guy who didn't love it as much as she did."

"I don't like that movie that much," she said. "It's so much tamer than your books. Too tame."

"See there," I said. "You're already becoming fictional."

"But based on real events," she said.

"Inspired by something resembling the truth," I said.

"Sounds like we're both protected," she said.

"Yes," I said. "But can I ask a favor?"

"What favor?"

"I'm going to be stoned on painkillers and other drugs for days and days, right?"

"Yes."

"And I have brain trauma from the surgery, right? No matter how well everything went?"

"Yes."

"So with all the pain and painkillers, and all the damage, I am going to forget things I say and do."

"Yes."

"So if I say something really good—something sad or funny or smart—then can you write it down—remember it—in case I can't?"

"Wow," she said. "I don't know if I can write it down."

"HIPAA rules?"

"Yes, HIPAA."

"But isn't monitoring my behavior part of your job?" I asked.

"Yes, it is," she said, and smiled.

"Why are you smiling?" I asked.

"Something funny happened right after surgery yesterday."

"What? What?" I asked. "Tell me. I need you to tell me the story so I can tell the story later."

"Okay, okay," she said. "Right after surgery, we took you into the MRI to check that everything looked good in your brain."

"Did it look okay?" I asked.

"Yes, everything was cool," she said. "And you were talking and—"

She hesitated.

"What? What?" I asked.

"You were being funny and smart right away," she said. "You were verbally coherent even though you were still so drugged up."

"What did I say?"

"You were flirting with everybody," she said. "Calling everybody beautiful and hot."

"Oh, no," I said. "I wasn't being a creep, was I?"

"No, no, you were very sweet. You were also talking about your beautiful wife. And you were flirting with the men and the women. I think you flirted with yourself and with the MRI machine, too."

"Oh, God, that's so embarrassing."

"There's more," she said. "There's more."

"I don't know if I want to hear anything else," I said. "No, I lied. I want to hear all of it."

"Okay, so when we lifted you from your gurney onto the MRI machine, your operating gown slipped off, and you were completely naked."

I laughed at the nude predicament that I could not remember being in.

"So you were naked," she said. "And you were apologizing. You kept saying sorry to all of us—"

"Wait, how many people were there?"

"Eight of us."

I laughed and laughed.

"So many people," I said. "It was like I was putting on a show."

"Yeah, you wouldn't stop apologizing and we're all trying to calm you down, saying it's okay, it's okay, we've seen it all before. And then you said, you said—"

"Oh, no, what, what, what?" I asked.

"You pointed at me," she said. "Then you told everybody I was a big fan of your books. And then you pointed at your...nudity...and said you didn't want to disappoint your loyal reader, me. You wanted to make sure we all knew you were a grower and not a show-er."

My nurse and I laughed together. I had worried about the size of my dick only an hour after brain surgery! Of course I did!

"Then you got all quiet," she said. "And put your hands over your privates and yelled, 'HIPAA! HIPAA! HIPAA!'"

My nurse and I laughed harder and harder, until I thought I might bust the stitchings in my skull.

"And that's when we started calling you the Unicorn," she said.

"Because of—"

"No, no, no, no, not because of your penis," she said. "Because you were talking so well after surgery. Because you recovered so fast. Because you and your brain were magical like a unicorn."

"So my dick isn't magical?" I asked.

"Oh, God, no," she said. "I'm a nurse, Sherman. There is nothing magical about anybody's dick."

My nurse and I laughed often during my three days in the ICU. I didn't know if I would ever see her again. Considering the state of my brain at the time, I didn't think I would recognize her again. But I thought she would read this book. I hoped she would read this book.

Dear Nurse, thank you for your honesty and humor. Thank you for taking care of me. Thank you for doing your job so gracefully. Thank you for remembering my stories when I could not.

102.

Brain Surgery
Ping-Pong

Three months after brain surgery, I played Ping-
  Pong
And found myself unable to adjust to the speed
Of the game. I could only follow the ball for one
  shot
At a time and couldn't anticipate my next move
Or where my opponent might hit it next. I
  wondered

What that might mean about my brain and its
  new
Normal. I had noticed those gaps in other ways,
  how

I forgot an interviewer's question five seconds after

I began to answer. How I stood onstage in front of 3,000 people

In Minneapolis and, for a brief terrifying moment, forgot

Why I was there. In the neurosurgery ICU, the nurse told me

They had to be extra diligent when assessing the brain health

Of imaginative people like me. She said, "You're the ones

Who can talk your way around your deficiencies." And I said,

"I've been talking my way around my deficiencies since I was born."

So, playing Ping-Pong, I tried to work around my sudden deficiencies

But I missed and lost and missed and lost. I didn't tell my friends

What I was feeling because I didn't want to ruin the fun

Or make excuses. My friends would have beaten me even if my brain

Were fully healthy. And I was in no danger. My neurologist said

It would take at least a year for my brain to fully
    heal.
So this is who I am now: a lesser Ping-Pong
    player.
That's hardly a tragedy. I played as well as I
    could.
And I sometimes hit good shots. And I was hav-
    ing fun,
Even as I recognized that I had lost a little

Of that connection between my eyes and hands.
But haven't I been losing shit all along? As we age,
Don't we all deteriorate? If I can't hit as many
    smashes
In table tennis or swish as many jump shots in
    basketball
Or write as many poems as I did before brain
    surgery,

Then so be it. I am alive! I am alive! I am alive!
And felt even more alive when my friends and I
    switched
From Ping-Pong singles to doubles. Playing with
    a teammate,
We alternated hits, and I was fucking overjoyed
    to realize
That I had enough time—another second or
    two—between shots

To recharge—to refresh, refresh, refresh—and
   put my paddle
On the ball with more accuracy and power. But
   I still didn't say
Anything about my Ping-Pong dilemma or my
   Ping-Pong epiphany
To my friends. I knew I would tell them later
   through a poem.
And this is their poem. Dear friends, I am often
   a lonely man,

Even in a room full of people who love me. Dear
   friends, my brain—
Unpredictable as it was—is even more unpre-
   dictable now.
But thank God for all of the ways in which we
   compensate
For our deficiencies. In order to play
   Ping-Pong—in order to make it
Through this crazy life—I needed somebody to
   step in and take

The next shot. So let's call this a Ping-Pong
   prayer. Let's call it
A Ping-Pong jubilation. I am not alone in this
   world. I am not
Alone in this world. I am not alone in this world.
   I am not alone

In this world. I will never be alone, my friends,
   and as long as I am
Alive to be your teammate, neither will any of
   you.

103.

Clarification

LET ME REPEAT.

Yes, I have repeated myself. Yes, I have been repetitious. That's what grief is.

Grief and repeat were sitting on the fence. Grief jumped off. Who was left?

Repeat.

Grief and repeat were sitting on the fence. Grief jumped off. Who was left?

Let me *repeat* the chorus.

Let me make things clear.

Five months after my mother died of cancerous tumors, I underwent surgery to remove a benign tumor from my brain.

The doctors tell me there's a 10 to 20 percent chance I will grow other benign brain tumors.

Depending on the location and size of these tumors, I could find myself in mortal danger.

Did you know that you can be killed by a benign tumor?

Imagine that news headline: *Native American poet killed by oxymoron.*

104.

Words

TEN MONTHS AFTER brain surgery, my neurological ICU nurse greeted me after my poetry reading in a tiny theater at Bumbershoot, a music and arts festival in Seattle.

I didn't recognize her until my wife said, "Sherman, this is _____. She was your ICU nurse after brain surgery."

I vaguely remembered her face. But I specifically remembered her kindness. I hugged her.

Then I stepped back. I felt so shy. She'd seen me at my most vulnerable. She'd seen me unarmored and afraid. She'd seen me in the worst pain of my life. She'd seen me weeping and tightly holding my skull because I thought it was burning and bleeding and breaking apart.

Standing in that tiny theater, I felt the urge to run away and hide. And then I realized I was still holding my nurse's hand. And that made me even more embarrassed. I dropped her hand and took another step back.

"Oh, God," I said. "It's so good to see you. I'm sorry I didn't remember your face. But I remember you. Does that make sense? I remember your spirit but not your face."

She laughed and said, "It's okay. You were on *so many* drugs."

I laughed and said, "I loved those drugs."

She said, "I remember how happy you were to be alive when you woke up. But you were even happier to have your stories intact. You just kept saying, 'I still have my words, I still have my words.'"

"I don't remember much about you," I said. "But I remember feeling safe. I felt so safe with you."

"That's the best thing a patient has ever said to me."

I hugged her again.

I remembered her scent better than I remembered her face. I closed my eyes and I remembered her standing in my dark hospital room. I remembered her asking me a series of questions to measure my cognition after brain surgery.

"You kept asking me questions," I said as I stepped away from her again.

"Yes," she said. "And you just kept telling stories

and jokes. So many jokes. You woke up from surgery and started talking and wouldn't stop. It was amazing. We'd never had a brain surgery patient come out so lucid. You were so funny. We couldn't believe how funny you were."

I remembered only bits and pieces of that time. I choked back tears.

"I must have been scared," I said. "I am funnier when I'm scared."

She hugged me this time.

And then I stepped away from her for the third or fourth or fifth time. Why was I so shy? I think it was because my nurse and I had shared a physical intimacy that went far beyond sex.

After brain surgery, it was her touch that brought me back into the world. Her touch gave me back my body. Her touch reintroduced me to the corporeal. Her touch began the healing process.

"Thank you," I said. "Thank you for taking care of me."

She smiled.

I wanted to thank her for being maternal—for being that compassionate woman at my bedside—for bringing me the magic and medicine. But I worried about how Oedipal and way Indian that would sound.

So I repeated myself, hoping the repetition itself would somehow let her know how important she was to me.

"Thank you," I said. "Thank you for your kindness. Thank you for your kindness. Thank you."

She said, "Please keep writing your stories. And I will keep reading them."

I said, "I will remember your face now. I will be able to place you more fully in my memories now. I won't feel so fragmented now."

I hugged her one more time, and then I had to say good-bye. I hurried away with my wife and friends.

Ten minutes later, walking to my car, my back spasmed so hard that I almost fell to the pavement. I cried out in pain and leaned against my wife and a friend to remain standing.

"Are you okay?" my wife asked.

"Yes," I said.

"I thought you were having a seizure," she said.

"No," I said. "The world is too fucking big. Sometimes, I can't even carry myself through all the love and fear."

With my wife holding my arm, I limped toward the car. I coached myself. I said, *Sherman, you can make it through this pain. You can always find your way through any pain.*

And, with my wife's help—always with my wife's strength—I made it into the car.

I was in great pain, but I took the time to write down these very words.

This is who I am. This is who I have always been.
I am in pain.
I am always in pain.
But I always find my way to the story. And I always find my way home.

105.

Therapy

1.

Today, for you, I will remember six of the worst things that have happened to me.

Give me a high five for my honesty.

Okay, I've decided to go with the four worst things.

Maybe three would be better.

I know it's only the two of us in this room. But I'm an Indian, so it always feels like my entire tribe is crushing into this—or any room—with me.

Maybe I should tell you one bad thing. And nothing too bad, either. I have to be careful. Other Indians are eavesdropping.

2.

In therapy, one hour equals fifty minutes.

An early memory: When I was two, I'd comfort myself by rubbing my face against my big sister's panty hose. No, she wasn't wearing the hose at the time. If that were true, it would bring up a whole different conversation. Okay, sometimes I rubbed my face against my sister's panty hose while she was wearing them. So, yes, I have, as they say, issues.

I don't want to talk about it. I don't want to talk about it. I don't want to talk about it.

I have four surviving siblings. My big sister died in a house fire. I often write about her death. Sometimes, I think I should stop. But why should I stop grieving in poems if I can't stop grieving in life?

Fire, fire, fire, fire, fire.

You know, something like 70 percent of the country is awake at 6 a.m. I get up at 6 a.m. and I'm ruined for the rest of the day. 6 a.m.! What is up with that?

3.

Okay, here are the six worst things that have happened to me:

1. Comic Book Swap
2. Butter Knives
3. St. Ignatius
4. _____
5. Lungs
6. Top Ten Toys

You'll notice that I listed only five things. I left one blank to account for the blank spots in my memory—for the sour relief of repression. You'll also notice that my list is vaguely metaphorical or metaphorically vague. You didn't really think I was going to give away everything, did you? This is a confessional poem, not a church confessional.

Hail Mary, full of grace. Hail Mary, full of grace. Hail Mary, full of grace. Hail Mary, full of grace.

When I was three, my big sister ran away and became a teenage mother. By the way, my big sister's name was Mary.

There's a photograph of Mary and me playing dueling grand pianos.

Ha ha ha ha ha ha ha ha ha ha! Did you really believe that a reservation Indian family would have even one grand piano? And if there is a reservation Indian family out there who does have a grand piano, then please mail me a photograph care of Shocked to Shit, Seattle, WA.

4.

Parked outside my therapist's office, I watched another therapist attempt to parallel park. When you grow up on a rural reservation, you only have to park parallel to the earth, so I was impressed as she parked skillfully in a very narrow space. But I guess it wasn't quite parallel enough, so she pulled out of the space and tried again. And again. I thought she parked well, but she thought otherwise. She parked, pulled out, parked, pulled out, parked, and pulled out for at least ten minutes. Finally, she parked in a way that pleased her. Or maybe she just abandoned the effort. But as she stepped out of her car and walked toward her office, I thought, "Damn, I want that one to be my therapist."

Two pills every day. The side effects are, well, interesting.

Three of the side effects: The urge to write prose poems; self-consciousness; night sweats.

I wake four times a night. Drenched in sweat. Sheets soaked. Pillow like a life preserver in Lake Sad-Ass.

Awake at 5 a.m., a full hour before most of the country, I pretend that I'm the only Indian who has survived genocide. It feels strangely familiar. I realize that every Indian often feels like he or she is the only Indian who has survived.

Today, as I walked around downtown Seattle, I studied strangers' faces and wondered what six most horrible things had happened to each of them.

5.

These are six worst things that have happened to people I know: Filmed while being gang-raped by a group of men wearing paper bags for masks; lost four sons in four separate car wrecks; lost mother to heart attack and then, during her funeral, lost father to heart attack; contracted AIDS while having sex for the first time; lost husband and three sons in the same plane wreck; lost mother to cancer and daughter to house fire in the same month.

Is there a cure for grief? Is there a cure for grief? Is there a cure for grief? Is there a cure for grief? Is there a cure for grief?

Be funny. Be funny. Be funny. Be funny.

Humor is a crutch. Humor is a crutch. Humor is a crutch.

Who are the two funniest human beings who have ever lived? Richard Pryor before he caught himself on fire while freebasing cocaine, and Richard Pryor after he caught himself on fire while freebasing cocaine.

One flame.

6.

One more flame.

People always said that Big Sister and I could have been twins. I'm lying. My sister and I looked nothing alike, and she was born thirteen years before me.

My other sisters, twins, are only one year younger than me. You could call us Irish triplets if we happened to be Irish. It's cute, but frankly, I prefer to be symbiotically connected with my dead sibling.

The fourth word of the Bible, King James Version, is "God." The fourth word of the Bible, New American Version, is "when."

When, God, when? When, God, when? When, God, when? When, God, when? When, God, when?

When I was six years old, I had an epileptic seizure while playing king of the hill on a woodpile, collapsed, rolled down the logs, and landed on the grass. I don't know what happened to my sister when she was six. I barely know anything about my sister's life, but I do know at least six things about her death.

106.

How Does My Highly Indigenous Family Relate to My Literary Fame?

HOME ON THE reservation, back from his colonoscopy in Spokane, my big brother texted me: "Dad used 2 say he knew you were famous when he found yr books at Goodwill. But I say yr famous when the ass nurse is asking me how I like havin a famous brother."

107.

Will the Big Seattle Earthquake Trigger a Tsunami the Size of God?

I have placed a big canoe on the roof.
Inside that boat: water, rope, airtight food,

First-aid kit, waterproof clothes, blankets,
Boots, fire starters, and my mother's ghost.

To access the roof from inside our home, tall
And narrow, there's a ladder in the hall

Closet near the bathroom on the third floor.
It's a collapsible ladder hung on the door.

To break the window glass, plaster, and joists,
I've got a hammer with steel points

And my mother's ghost. She'll protect my eyes
From every sharp and falling surprise.

I thought of purchasing a real gun,
Or a weapon that only gassed or stunned,

But didn't want that danger in my home,
No matter how useful. My mother's ghost,

Armed with over five centuries of grief,
Will repel post-disaster assholes and thieves.

Dear family and friends, dear blood, dear you,
I will paddle in the night to your rescue.

Look for me. I'll be in the endless boat
Illuminated by my mother's ghost.

108.

How Are You?

I'm honored by your concern. I would like
To gather all of the books that contain
The words "mother" and "grief," set them aflame,
And dance as they burn. I'm sleeping okay,

Five or six hours at night, then two naps
During the day. I want to sledgehammer
Every truck in a ten-block radius,
Push them into the lake, and build a reef

That will be named Mother-Grief on the map.
I'm overeating but I always eat
Too much, so I think I'm overeating
At my usual pace. Study my face.

I've always looked more like my father, but
This morning, I woke to see my mother
In the mirror. Grief is a plastic surgeon.
I'm not hiding from the world. I've seen

My psychiatrist three times in three weeks.
I remembered to put gas in my car.
There's an undiscovered animal perched
In that big tree in our backyard. It glows,

Has bluish claws and feathers, and sings old
Evangelical hymns. All my neighbors
Have tattooed my mother's name on their
   wrists.
I twisted my ankle while cooking brown rice

And chicken with habanero pepper.
But I think clumsiness is normal
At a time like this. My left eyelid twitches
But that's just stress. I bought a telescope

To distract myself by studying stars
And discovered a new constellation.
It's near Orion and it resembles
A Native mother cradling her son.

109.

Where the Creek Becomes River

I HAVE NOT worn a pair of moccasins in four decades.

Let me repeat that.

I have not worn a pair of moccasins in four decades.

Let those eleven words become a chorus.

I have not worn a pair of moccasins in four decades.

The last time I wore moccasins was in Arlee, Montana, on the Flathead Indian Reservation, during the Fourth of July Powwow in 1976.

Is there any greater oxymoron than *Bicentennial Powwow*?

A few days earlier, my father had run away from home on yet another multiday drinking binge. And my mother, as she often did in reaction to my father's escape act, had also impulsively run away from home. But she, as usual, took my little sisters and me along with her as she drove from our reservation across the Idaho and Montana borders into Arlee.

In the indigenous world, we assign sacred value to circles. But sometimes a circle just means you keep returning to the same shit again and again.

This book is a series of circles, sacred and profane.

As a teen, my mother had been married to man who lived in Arlee, but I didn't know about that marriage in 1976. Looking back, I suppose she took us to Arlee in some effort to reclaim her youth.

Or perhaps to reclaim a certain part of her youth—her sexuality.

Shortly after dropping my little sisters and me at the campsite of my aunt and cousins, my mother climbed into an RV with a man—a stranger to me— and drove away. I can't recall any physical details about the man. I don't know if he was Indian or white or something else. I only remember waving good-bye and crying as that man and my mother drove away on a dirt road. I remember all the dust kicked up by that RV's wheels. Even now, my throat constricts with that memory of dirt and tears—by the silt of abandonment.

My aunt, in an act of consolation, gave me a new pair of moccasins. She'd originally bought them to give to one of her sons as a gift, but she was desperate to stop my weeping. So she gave those moccasins to me instead. She knew I might cry for hours. She was probably scared I would rage and wail until my mother returned. And who knew when that would be?

My little sisters were sad, too, but they were powwow dancers. So they consoled themselves by wrapping shawls around their shoulders—like indigenous armor—and dancing in a collective circle with all of the other powwow dancers.

But I didn't dance. My childhood brain surgery and years of aftereffects and seizures and medications and hospital stays and subsequent illnesses had left me a physically and emotionally frail kid. I didn't have confidence in my body or soul. I didn't feel strong and graceful enough to dance. I didn't feel like I deserved to dance.

I didn't feel Indian enough to dance.

But, wow, looking at those new moccasins made me feel like a super Indian. They were deerskin with a thick sole. And lightly beaded. Just a few rows of beads—yellow, blue, and red—forming the outline of a five-pointed star. I still wasn't courageous enough to dance, but I pulled on those moccasins and ran through the powwow grounds. Soon enough, I saw a group of other Indian kids running and laughing. So I ran with them. That's what kids do.

In my memory, the Arlee powwow grounds were bordered on one side by a creek. Looking at Google maps, it appears that creek is farther away from the grounds than I remember. But I would swear that some Indian folks were camped almost next to that creek. I could easily fact check this geography by emailing my friends who live on that reservation. But, emotionally speaking, it feels more accurate to think of that creek as being a part of the powwow grounds rather than flowing a football field distance away.

I ran with those Indian kids to that creek, which was maybe two feet deep and flowing fast. The creek was perhaps five feet wide. And I remember running back and forth across a pedestrian bridge. A bridge across a creek? If my memory is true, then that creek must have been a popular destination. I remember those other Indian kids kicking off their sneakers and socks and splashing into the creek. It was only two feet deep. But I didn't know how to swim. And so I was afraid. But then, bravely and irrationally, I pulled off my new moccasins, set them on that little bridge, and stepped into the water.

The water was so cold that I gasped. And it was moving fast. Looking again at Google maps, it appears that creek flows into the Jocko River, so that might account for the speed of the current. The other Indian kids, stronger and more graceful than me, ran with and against the current. But I could only carefully and clumsily walk with the current. I remember the feel of the slippery rocks on the creek bottom. If my memory is correct, then that creek must have been flowing fast for many years in order to smooth those rocks. It was a very hot day, so the water felt good. And I splashed the cold water at the other kids as they splashed water at me. We laughed. It wasn't easy for me to make friends. But I thought these kids, who were nondancers like me, might become my friends for the rest of the pow-wow and help me forget my loneliness.

And then I heard a commotion behind me. A different kind of laughter. And I turned around to see an older Indian kid pick up my new moccasins from the bridge and drop them into the creek. I don't remember if I said anything. If I cursed or shouted. But I distinctly remember those moccasins floating and flowing down that fast creek toward me. More than that, I remember that eight or ten or twelve Indian kids stood still in the water and watched my moccasins pass by. And then it was just me, unsteady in the current, as I crouched like a soccer goalie and tried to intercept my moccasins. I reached for them and missed. And then I dove after them as they floated away. But I missed again. I was briefly submerged in the shallow creek, and when I got back to my feet, I watched my moccasins disappear around the bend and then presumably flow into the Jocko River.

I know this is a sad story. In the context of a different and better and calmer childhood, this sad story might not even be all that sad. It might be worth a sigh or two. But this sad story has mythic power for me. In fact, this story is so painful for me that I almost didn't include it in this book. Indeed, I added this chapter at the last possible moment before publication.

I vividly remember watching my new moccasins disappear. But I don't remember stepping out of that creek. I don't remember walking back to my aunt's campsite. I can only recall stepping into the tepee and telling my aunt that I had lost my moccasins.

And then she slapped me hard across the face.

I was stunned.

My father had never practiced any form of corporal punishment on me. And my mother had, at that point, only physically assaulted me once. And, yes, she'd used a thick twig to spank my butt. But she'd punished me that severely because I had forced my little sisters to smoke cigarettes until they vomited.

And while I'd been slapped, punched, and kicked by other kids, I had never been struck by an adult.

And then my aunt slapped me again.

I fell to the ground in a fetal ball as she continued to slap my head, arms, legs, and back. She slapped me at least a dozen times. I would have many bruises. She screamed at me for losing my moccasins. She reminded me again and again that she had bought them for her son, and not for me. She called me an idiot. She called me a loser.

And then I rolled away from her, ducked under the edge of the tepee, and made my escape.

I didn't return to my aunt's campsite that night. I walked the powwow, barefoot and alone, for hours. Until the sun went down. Until the last powwow song ended. Until the food stands closed. Until even the last drunk had passed out. I was nine years old. I was angry and afraid. But I wasn't going back to my aunt's campsite. I refused to surrender, to concede, to seek her shelter.

I don't remember if I slept that night. I do remember that an old Indian woman gave me a piece of fry bread the next morning. She took pity on me, I guess. I give thanks to her.

And then I walked around the powwow all that next day and again into the night until I heard my mother call out to me. She had returned to the powwow.

I remember she was carrying my shoes.

I remember that I fell asleep in the backseat of our car as she drove us back to our reservation.

I don't remember arriving back home on our reservation.

When my father returned home from that

particular drinking binge, he had shaved his hair into a mohawk.

I was embarrassed for him. Embarrassed for me. Embarrassed for every Indian in the world.

"I look like a warrior now," he said to me.

"No, you don't," I said.

As I finished the first draft of this chapter, I smelled ozone, a common olfactory hallucination that happens to epileptics. I also tasted mud and tears. Silt. I thought of my mother carrying my shoes. I thought of my father removing his cowboy hat to reveal that mohawk hair.

A few years after I lost my new moccasins, my sister died in St. Ignatius, Montana, less than twenty miles away from the bridge across the creek.

Ozone.

Ozone.

Ozone.

I didn't have a seizure while writing this chapter. But I smelled ozone. I smelled the dank water of that creek flowing away from me.

And I tasted blood in my mouth.

Over the last four decades, I have visited my friends and family on the Flathead Indian Reservation, but I have never again stepped foot on the Arlee powwow grounds.

And I have not worn a pair of moccasins in four decades.

110.

Kind

AFTER BEING PSYCHOLOGICALLY and physically tortured by our missionary teachers—by all of those cruel white women and men—and after finding little solace at home from our Native parents and grandparents, who'd been tortured in the same way, we Indian kids are hungry for any tenderness from anybody.

We fall in love too easily.

We get pregnant too young.

We run away with strangers.

Then we run away with other strangers.

Or we fall in love with the same boy or girl who was tortured alongside us. We spend our lives with the person who has the same scars in the same places. We make love with the person whose open wounds snap into ours like LEGO pieces. And then, of course, we rage at our neediness.

We might turn racist and sexist and homophobic—turning against those people as powerless as or more powerless than us.

We hate power.

We hate weakness.

We hate all white people.

Or we fall in love with all white people.

Or we fall in love with the white liberals who want to heal us.

Or we fall in love with the white conservatives who want to hurt us again.

We reenact the racist torture and salvation in our beds.

We cry in the arms of white people.

We cry in the arms of other Indians.

We boast and brag.

We insist our damage is greater than all of the damage suffered by all of the other damaged people. We are the gold medalists in the Genocide Olympics. Or maybe just the silver medalists. Or maybe we just win the bronze because Custer was only 25 percent as bad as Hitler.

In response to our generational pain, we Indian kids become addicted to torture—to the memory of torture. Or, wait, no, maybe we are addicted to gentleness—to gentle white people.

Hello, my name is Sherman and I am addicted to white people.

Or maybe, after centuries of being tortured by white civilization, I am addicted to those white folks who will reward me for being Indian. I am addicted to those white folks who will not torture me.

Does any of this sound like love?

111.

Tribalism

A NON-NATIVE friend said, "Native Americans were the victims of genocide. So why isn't there a Museum of the Native American Genocide?"

And I said, "Because we Indians would spend years arguing about whose tribe suffered the worst massacre."

I have visited museums of genocide in other countries. Though I realize "visited" is the wrong verb. "Endured" is too self-serving. Perhaps the best sentence is "I have experienced museums of genocide in other countries."

And what do I remember?

I remember that I kept having to close my eyes

against the pain. I often had to look away from the pain. I often had to sit on benches and stare at the blank floors.

And what do I make of the genocide museum in our own country? What do I make of the United States Holocaust Memorial Museum?

It is a vital place. It is a grievous reminder. A warning. It is as necessary as any museum ever built.

But it also proves to me how the United States closes its eyes against the pain it has caused. The United States often looks away from the pain it has caused. The United States often sits on benches and stares at the blank floors.

So, if ever built, what will the United States Native American Genocide Memorial Museum contain? What will it exhibit?

It will be one room, a fifty-foot square with the same large photo filling the walls, ceiling, and floor.

There will only be one visitor allowed at any one time.

There will be no furniture.

That one visitor will have to stand or sit on the floor.

Or lie on the floor if they feel the need.

That visitor must remain in that room for one hour.

There will be no music.

The only soundtrack will be random gunshots from rifles used throughout American history.

Reverberation.

What will that one photo be?

It will be an Indian baby, shredded by a Gatling gun, lying dead and bloody in the snow.

It is a photo taken by a U.S. Cavalry soldier in the nineteenth century.

Very few people have seen that photo.

I have not seen that photo.

But I know it exists.

The Smithsonian keeps such photos locked away from us.

The United States wants all of us to forget the crimes it committed against the indigenous.

The United States wants us to forget.

The United States wants us to forget.

The United States wants us to forget.

* * *

A non-Native friend said, "Native Americans were the victims of genocide. So why isn't there a Museum of the Native American Genocide?"

And I said, "Because we Indians would spend years arguing about whose tribe suffered the worst massacre."

112.

Security Clearance

AFTER I'D AGREED to teach a writing workshop in a women's prison, I received an application in the mail that asked me to "list the names of any relatives or close associates who have served or are currently serving time in correctional facilities anywhere in the world."

I thought of my father and brother and uncles and reservation friends and cousins who'd been inmates. Then I called an official number. I was transferred, put on hold, ignored, interrogated, dismissed, and finally I was helped.

"So I'm supposed to list all of the people I know, or are related to, who have been in jail or prison?" I asked the friendly clerk.

"Yes," he said.

"Even the ones I haven't seen in years? Or decades?"

"Well, it's safer to answer as completely as possible."

"What if they're dead?"

"Put them down and write 'Deceased' by their names."

"Okay, okay," I said. "You're sure I need to put all of them?"

"That's what I advise," he said. "And what kind of crimes are we talking about here?"

"Murder and attempted murder," I said. "Rape, child rape. Assault. Robbery. Drug possession and drug dealing. Domestic violence. Forgery. Failure to appear in court. Failure to pay criminal fines. Contempt of court. Theft. Public intoxication. Driving while intoxicated."

"Wow," the clerk said. "Have you ever been convicted of a crime?"

"Two speeding tickets," I said. "One in nineteen eighty-nine, and one in two thousand eight."

"That's it?"

"Yeah, I'm the rebel of the family."

I again looked down at the small space where I was supposed to supply the required information about my convict family.

"You know," I said. "There's not enough room on the application to list everybody."

"You can put them on a separate sheet," he said. "And attach it to the application."

"Are you sure it's okay to do that?" I asked.

"You wouldn't be the first," he said. "Some people have attached two additional pages."

"Wow," I said, and laughed.

Then I said my good-byes and, as a long-distance and complete nonparticipant in a one-page indigenous criminal clan, I listed all of those felons who share at least some of my genetics.

It took me approximately an hour.

113.

Ode to Gray

Has anybody written an ode to gray?
Well, if not, then let me be the first. Let me
  praise
The charcoal pit, tweed suit, and cloudy X-ray

That reveals, to your amateur dismay,
Nothing you understand. Who has been amazed
Enough to write a breathy love song to gray and
  gray's

Nearly imperceptible interplay
With other grays? Oh, how beautiful the haze
Of charcoal pits, tweed suits, and cloudy X-rays

Of airport luggage. I love the dog day,
The long delay, the existential malaise.
Has anybody written an ode to gray?

If not, then let me proceed without delay.
Oh, let me construct an army made of clay.
Marching, marching, they will be my ode to
  gray,
To charcoal pit, tweed suit, and cloudy X-ray.

114.

Tyrannosaurus Rez

Yes, I've survived
All of the genocidal shit that killed
So many in my tribe,

And it is absurd
That I've made a great career
Out of nouns and verbs,

But, look,
It's a miracle when any writer
Sells even one damn book.

So listen to me: I was conceived
With twenty thousand years
Of my ancestors' stories

Locked in my gray matter
And flooding my marrow.
So don't think I'm flattered

With your homily
About how I must be
Some kind of anomaly.

I am my mother's son.
I am my father's child.
And they left me a trust fund

Of words, words, and words
That exist in me
Like dinosaurs live in birds.

115.

Objectify

"Desire is the inconvenience of its object.
Lourdes isn't Lourdes if you live in Lourdes."
> —Don Paterson, *Best Thought,*
> *Worst Thought*

How often have I walked through my front door
And forgotten to exult? Why won't I roar
For all of the objects that I adore?
When did I stop praising the books I hoard
And the bookcases, lovingly restored?

Why do I ignore the baskets and gourds?
O Lord, let my love for things be reborn.

Let me sanctify my hand drums, adorned
With feather, paint, and bead. Let me drum for
The star quilts piled on the beds and floors.
I own so much yet want for so much more.
Why do I greet the sacred with my scorn?
From this day forward, let us be forewarned:
Lourdes isn't Lourdes if you live in Lourdes.

116.

My Mother as Wolf

Reintroduced into the wilderness, my mother
Struggles to remember what
Her wolf ancestors knew in their DNA—

and here, just as this poem begins, I have to tell
you that when that first stanza originally popped
into my head, I dropped into a fugue state that had
me flying through the universe while dodging plan-
ets and suns. This flying-through-the-universe thing
had previously happened only when I tried to meditate. Whether guided by teachers or during some
half-assed attempts of my own, I'd never been able
to calm myself and empty my mind. Instead, moments into any attempts to meditate, I'd fly with

light speed through the endless dark. I'd be awed by the beauty of the universe and terrified by the isolation. Some friends tell me that I might have been in a meditative state anyway. I don't believe it because I'd fly for only a minute or two before I'd fall asleep. So I think I might have been disassociating instead of meditating. Maybe I'm too terrified to let go of this terrifying world. Maybe I'm just sleep-deprived. I often get sleepy during moments of stress. I could fall asleep during a gunfight. Sounds like disassociating, right? And it seems to me that disassociating is the opposite of meditating—

Reintroduced into the wilderness, my mother
Struggles to remember what
Her wolf ancestors knew in their DNA—

When this first stanza arrived in my head, I was sitting next to my wife, watching a married couple reenacting an argument. Onstage, the woman recounted how she, as an eight-year-old, contracted polio from a bad sugar-cube immunization. She speculated that she was one of only three people in the United States who caught polio from inoculate because her immune system was already burned out from the case of mumps that her physician father didn't care to notice. "My father was a great healer," she said. "For everybody except his own children."

At that very moment, I thought of my late mother as a wolf, and of her immense and intimidating and feral power, and then I disassociated and launched into my flight across the universe—

> My mother, pack-hungry, lopes
> Through the tall wild grass
> In search of other wolves
> And other mothers—

So, yes, I did end up writing a second stanza about my mother as a wolf, even after that first stanza disassociated me. But here's the crazy thing: After the woman onstage talked about her polio— and after I'd disassociated, fallen asleep for a few minutes sitting in my chair, and was awakened by audience applause—I turned to my wife and smiled. I was going to joke about falling asleep, but my wife said, "Why'd you leave?" I was confused. "I've been sitting here the whole time," I said. "But you got up and left," my wife said. "You bumped my shoulder and then you were gone. And I didn't even realize you'd come back until you smiled at me." I laughed and told her about my flight through the universe and quick nap, and she said, "Childhood trauma can give you superpowers, right?"

My mother stalks a small pack of sheep.
She knows these animals are protected
By humans with rifles—with metal and fire.
My mother doesn't have a word for "rifle,"

But she knows one hundred ways
To say "hungry" and "blood" and "tooth."
And, yes, she taught me those words.
So watch me now as I rend, gnash, and chew.

117.

All My Relations

I AM RELATED, by blood and marriage, to men who hit women, and to men and women who hit children, and to men and women in jail and in prison and on parole for stealing and robbing and raping and shooting and stabbing and punching and kicking and forging and abetting and neglecting and manslaughtering and murdering and dealing and buying and muling and abandoning and vandalizing and breaking and entering and jacking and driving without insurance and driving under the influence and driving without a license and vehicular homiciding and shoplifting and deserting and violating and failing to pay on time and failing to pay at all and failing to yield and failing to stop and failing and failing and failing and failing.

So many felonies and misdemeanors.

Therefore, I have been at parties, weddings, births, barbecues, tailgaters, games, proms, funerals, baptisms, and graduations with convicts and ex-convicts whom I love and whom I hate and whom I have met only once and hope to never see again.

I have been victimized by some of these criminals. I have been the subject and object of their misdemeanors and felonies.

Scholars talk about the endless cycle of poverty and racism and classism and crime. But I don't see it as a cycle, as a circle. I see it as a locked room filled with the people who share my DNA. This room has recently been set afire and there's only one escape hatch, ten feet off the ground. And I know I have to build a ladder out of the bones of my fallen family in order to climb to safety.

118.

How to Argue with a Colonialist

SHERMAN," SAYS Mr. Blanc. "I am sorry that you Interior Salish Indians lost your wild salmon to the Grand Coulee Dam. But, honestly, can't you do your religious ceremonies and cultural stuff with wild salmon from elsewhere? Or with salmon you farm yourself?"

"Yes," I say to Mr. Blanc. "Many of us Interior Salish Indians do order wild salmon at restaurants. We definitely eat and enjoy wild salmon caught in rivers not our own. And, yes, we also farm our own salmon as well. But, honestly, Mr. Blanc, comparing outsider and farmed salmon to our own wild salmon is like comparing bobblehead Jesus to the real Jesus. One is plastic and the other one is blood."

119.

Dear Native Critics, Dear Native Detractors

I WRITE ABOUT this shit because this shit happened to me.

Did shit like this happen to you? Did this shit happen to some Indian you love? Some Indian you know? Some Indian you knew?

This shit happened to me. This shit happened to Indians I love. This shit happened to Indians I hate.

This shit happened. This shit happened. This shit happened. This shit happened. This shit happened. This shit happened. This shit happened. This shit happened. This shit happened. This shit happened. This shit happened. This shit happened. This shit happened.

Now, let's pick up a hand drum and sing it together.

This shit happened. Way ya hi ya. This shit happened. Way ya hi ya. This shit happened. Way ya hi ya. This shit happened. Way ya hi ya. This shit happened to me. Way ya hi ya. This shit happened to you. Way ya hi ya. This shit happened to Indians I love and hate. Way ya way ya way ya way ya ho.

This shit happened.

This shit happens.

This shit is happening now.

But if this shit didn't happen to you, dear Indian, if this shit never happened to you, then I am happy for you, I am happy for you, way ya hi ya, I am happy for you, if this shit didn't happen to you, then I feel joy for you, I feel joy for you.

I feel joy for you, way ya hi ya, so much joy for you.

But, dear Indian, if this shit didn't happen to you, then why do you need to judge the shit that happened to other Indians?

Why do you, like a schoolteacher, hand out grades to the shit that happened to us?

Why do you shame us?

Why do you shame us?

Why do you shame us?

Why do you shame us for the shit that was done to us?

Why do you shame us, the already shamed, who sing our poems and tell our stories because we want to be unashamed?

I am the Indian trying to be unashamed.

Way ya hi ya.

I want to be unashamed.

Way ya hi ya.

I am a Child of the Sun.

Way ya hi ya.

And there is nothing that can clean you like the sun.

Way ya hi ya.

I expose my shame to the sun.

Way ya hi ya.

I illuminate my shame.

Way ya hi ya.

I want my shame to burn, to burn, way ya hi ya, to burn, way ya hi ya, to burn away, burn away, burn away.

And maybe, maybe, as I sing, maybe, maybe, I can teach other Indians, the Clan of the Ashamed, to leave that clan and start anew.

Let us leave the Clan of the Ashamed and start anew.

Let us leave the Clan of the Ashamed and start anew.

Let us leave the Clan of the Ashamed and start anew.

Let us leave the Clan of the Ashamed and start anew.

Dear Native Critic, dear Native Detractor, do you judge me because I want to be new? Do you judge me because I am not the same kind of Indian as you?

120.

Slight

In Seattle, a street magician fucks up.
He's publicly performing a year too early.
A little girl shouts, "I can see your fake thumb!"
I hurry away from his embarrassment,

As I recall when I've gone public too early
With intimations and declarations of love.
Who hasn't been crushed by embarrassment?
I gave an awkward eulogy at my mother's
    funeral;

It certainly wasn't a declaration of love.
I delivered half-jokes, half-truths, and half-
    apologies.
My eulogy for my mother needed its own eulogy.
But my self-deprecation is just another form

Of narcissism, right? What kind of ass apologizes

For his eulogy? I'm a magician fucking up his act.

And now I've gone public with my embarrassment

As my dead mother shouts, "I can see your fake thumb."

121.

Psalm of Myself

At my mother's funeral, a stranger said,
"It hurts more to lose your mother than your fa-
   ther."
At first, I scoffed, "Oh, you never had the honor
Of meeting my mom. She was army-ant intense."

And yet, weeks after her funeral, I'm still swarmed
By her memory's teeth. I mean—it was easy
To love my father. He always sought to appease.
He was addicted to surrendering. He harmed

Nobody. I don't think he had one enemy.
But my mom? She waged war on everything
   that moved.

She indicted and convicted before she accused.
She mocked oxygen and scolded gravity.

And, yes, I'm aware of how much I resemble her.
I'm the child with all of her vanity and rage.
I'm the actor who needs and needs to take the
stage
And, with tender spite, seek to reassemble her.

But have I created her in my image? Am I playing God?
She belonged to herself and not to me. She
birthed me,
Not the other way around. She is my mortal
deity.
To emulate her, I'll be arrogant, angry, beautiful,
and odd.

122.

Hunger Games

I crave grief for breakfast, lunch, and dinner.
Sweet grief, salted grief, I want so much
To swallow you whole. I'm a damn sinner

Who can only be saved by your fingers.
Hurry, place the sacred grief on my tongue
And consecrate breakfast, lunch, and dinner—

Or maybe not. I wish I were slimmer
And more disciplined—a secular monk.
But I lust, lust, and lust. I'm a sinner

Who seeds, threshes, harvests, feasts, and shivers.
Forgive me. Condemn me. I need flesh and
    blood
And grief at each breakfast, lunch, and dinner.

I want to want too much. I know what hinders
and troubles you. But join me in this flood.
Look at me. I'm your beloved sinner.

Sit with me, please. Let's talk. Please. Linger.
Let's touch and eat everything that we touch.
Let us stay through breakfast, lunch, and dinner.
Let's become each other's favorite sinner.

123.

Communal

THIRTEEN MONTHS AFTER my mother died, my sister texted me that her refrigerator had finally given up.

"It's leaking everywhere," she texted. "We unplugged it. And all the food is in plastic coolers with ice."

That dead refrigerator was in the kitchen of my childhood home on the reservation. Our family home. Then our mother's home after our father died. And now, my sister and niece's home.

I remembered that I bought the refrigerator maybe ten or twelve years earlier, not long after my father had died.

My sisters live on low-paying jobs and disability checks. They long ago destroyed their credit ratings, so they can't buy a refrigerator all at once or in monthly payments.

"Send me the dimensions of the old fridge," I texted back to my sister. "And I will order you a new one from Sears."

A few moments later, my sister texted, "64 inches high, 29 inches wide, 31 inches deep."

I scanned the Sears website for good deals on fridges, for one that would fit the space and had an ice maker. I was goofily happy to think of an ice-making refrigerator in my childhood home. It felt like an earned extravagance.

But ice-making fridges cost over $1,000. I could have afforded that, but I didn't want to spend that much money. I've often had to financially rescue my siblings and parents over the years. I resent it sometimes—being the family hero—but I deal with my resentment by setting limits.

So I bought an Amana that cost only $600. And I texted my sister and suggested she get some cousin to pick it up from Sears in Spokane. Otherwise, it would cost me another $200 to have it delivered to the reservation.

"Okay," my sister texted. "Can you send me gas money for whoever picks it up?"

"Okay," I texted, and transferred cash to her bank account. "There's money for all of you. Split it evenly. And pay somebody to get the fridge."

A week later, my sister texted me a photo of the new refrigerator, looking rather Darth Vaderesque, wedged into the space where the old fridge had been.

"Thank you," my sister texted. "Everything cold is cold. And everything frozen is frozen."

I realized the new fridge resembled a new coffin or a large black tombstone. I realized that I'd never have to send emergency cash to my dead mother ever again. I'd never have to rescue her from her poor financial decisions—from the poverty she'd created for herself and for the poverty forced upon her.

But I know I will be rescuing my siblings until all of them are dead—or until I'm dead.

"My doctor ordered me to only eat food that grows or walks," my sister texted me a few days later. "Healthy food is so expensive."

"I'll send you some green to buy greens," I texted her. "Some lettuce to buy lettuce. So you can become a skinny rez rabbit."

Except I typed "rabbi" instead of "rabbit." A funny mistake.

"Can a woman be a rabbi?" my sister texted me back with a smiling emoji.

"Yes," I texted back. "That's one of the cooler things about Jewish cultures. Women can be spiritual leaders. A woman was president of Israel."

"I think Mom was like a rabbi," my sister texted.

"Ha," I texted back. "But remember she lost by twenty votes when she ran for Tribal Council."

It was a close election. I thought of Hillary Clinton and her close loss to Donald Trump. Our tribe survived the man who defeated our mother. I don't know if our country will survive Trump.

"I looked up 'rabbi' online," my sister said. "It means 'teacher.'"

Was our mother a teacher? Was she holy?

I think so. I'm not sure. Maybe.

So I texted her old cell phone. I didn't know if her number had already been assigned in the months since her death. I didn't know who might receive my text. So, in not knowing its destination, it felt like a prayer.

"How sacred were you?" I texted my mother's ghost.

I am still waiting for a response.

124.

Your Theology or Mine?

THREE HUNDRED AND seventy-one days after my mother's death—after enduring what can only be described as the worst year of my adult life—after maternal loss and forest fires and uranium radiation and brain surgery and seizures and more forest fires—and after a fevered and flawed and grief-driven study of family and tribal history, I realize that I am equally a child of Jesuit and Salish cultures.

I might be an atheist—driven more by my reaction to the politics of religion than its practical theology—but I am also the progeny of the mystical Jesus and the mystical salmon. I would argue that Jesus is made of salmon and each salmon is made of many parts of Jesus. And, yes, I know these are contradictory thoughts for an atheist to express.

So what?

If you believers want to corner me—if you force me to choose the Word—then I am going to choose only one word. And that one word is going to be a verb. And that one verb will be "return," for I am always compelled to return, return, return to my place of birth, to my reservation, to my unfinished childhood home, and ultimately to my mother, my ultimate salmon.

I return to her, my mother, who, in these pages, dies and dies and dies and is continually reborn.

125.

Review, Reprise, Revision

AT SOME POINT in my childhood—in my early teens—my mother, Lillian, told me the most painful secret of her life. I have repeated this conversation in my head many times over the years. I repeat it in this book. I can't help but repeat it. I repeat the same words, sentences, and paragraphs. That's what happens. Great pain is repetitive. Grief is repetitive. And, maybe, this repetition can become a chant inside a healing ceremony.

"Junior," she said. "I am the daughter of a rape."

"What?" I asked, unsure that I'd heard her correctly.

"A man raped my mother. And she got pregnant with me because of it."

"Who was the rapist?"

My mother, Lillian, said his name. He was a man who'd died years earlier. I'd never known him, but I knew his children and went to the tribal school with his grandchildren. They were among the tallest kids on the reservation. Unlike my siblings and parents, I was tall, too. I'd always wondered why I was so much taller than the rest of my family. Why I was darker. I'd sometimes worried that perhaps I wasn't my father's biological child. But I have the same widow's-peak cowlick—a rebellious lock of black hair that defies styling—as my father. My biological older brother and my younger twin sisters have that cowlick, too. Plus, as I've aged from a skinny dark kid into a chubby paler man (having lived in sunless Seattle for twenty-three years), I have come to strongly resemble my father and my siblings.

But not in height.

"The man who raped your mother," I said. "Your father..."

"He's not my father," my mother said. She was angry. "My father is James Cox, the man who raised me."

I was always afraid of her anger. Everybody was afraid of Lillian's anger. We were always trying to mollify her.

"I'm sorry," I said. "The rapist. Was he tall?"

My mother immediately understood what I was asking.

"Yes," she said. "That's where you get your height."

I didn't ask my mother anything else. I didn't have the emotional vocabulary. And I'm not sure she had the emotional vocabulary, either.

Rape was common on my reservation. But it was rarely discussed. And never prosecuted. Why not? I would guess it has something to do with the strict social rules of a tribe. White folks love to think that Native American culture is liberal. But it is actually repressive. Indians are quick to socially judge one another. And even quicker to publicly condemn and ostracize. I wouldn't realize it until I read more widely in college, but living on an Indian reservation was like living inside an Edith Wharton novel. Disruption was not tolerated. And I think I know the source of intolerance. For thousands of years, we Spokane had endured and enjoyed subsistence lives. We'd lived communally. Every member of the tribe had a job. And each job was vital. So, inside a subsistence culture, a socially disruptive tribal member would have been mortally dangerous to everybody else.

But there is a logical problem with that, isn't there? First of all, we were living in the twentieth century and not the fourteenth or fifteenth.

And if that were still true—if socially disruptive tribal members were traditionally punished no matter the century—then wouldn't it make more sense for the tribe to ostracize and even expel rapists? Well, not if the rapist was a culturally significant figure. Not if the rapist, however economically poor, was socially rich and powerful. Not if the rapist could put on an eagle-feather headdress and make a beautiful and powerful entrance into the powwow arena.

And what would happen inside a small tribe if every minor or major crime, if every small or large transgression, was made public? What if we Natives practiced the same kind of justice inside our own communities as the justice that we demand from white society? Of course, centuries of genocidal acts by white Americans have certainly helped teach us Natives how to commit genocidal acts against one another. But at what point do we Native American victims start demanding more justice and freedom from our Native American oppressors?

And what happens if those indigenous oppressors happen to be our parents?

For over three decades, I believed that one of my biological grandfathers was a rapist.

I thought I was the grandson of rape.

But in July 2016, just over a year after my mother died, I had a telephone conversation with my sister Arlene. We were discussing our half sister, Mary, and her convoluted parentage. I wanted to get the details correct for this memoir.

"Mary was the child of a rape," my sister said.

"Wait," I said. "You mean Mom was the child of a rape."

"No," she said. "Mom was the child of an affair."

"No," I said. "Mom told me she was the child of a rape."

"She never told me that. Who did she say she was raped by?"

I gave her the name of the accused rapist.

"No," my sister said. "Mom's mom was having an affair with him and they got pregnant."

I laughed. I didn't mean to laugh. It wasn't funny. But its awful seriousness is what made it hilarious. Jesus, I'd believed yet another one of my mother's fabrications. Or wait, maybe my sister had been fooled again by our mother. Or maybe she'd told us two different lies. Would our mother lie about rape?

"And you know what's really messed up?" my sister said.

"What?" I asked, wondering what could possibly be worse than lying about rape.

"You want to know what our cheating grandma and her cheating boyfriend did?"

"What?"

"Well," my sister said. "Do you know the name of the cheater's wife?"

I said her last name.

"Yeah, that's it," my sister said. "But do you know what her first name was?"

"No," I said.

"Guess."

"Tell me."

"No, guess."

"I have no idea."

"Okay," my sister said. "Just think about it. What's the worst thing a husband and his affair snag could name their adultery kid?"

I thought about it. And then I suddenly understood.

"Oh, shit," I said. "They named Mom after the wife."

"Yep, Mom is Lillian. That poor wife was also Lillian."

I threw my cell phone on the couch. And walked away. I paced. Was this completely fucked-up story just another one of my mother's grandiose falsehoods?

But, wait, wait, wait, I kept thinking. What if my mother was telling the truth about some of it. What if it was the partial truth? She'd always been such a damaged person. And that damage had to have been inflicted by somebody. So what if my mother lied about the specific details of her pain but was always emotionally honest about the volume of her suffering?

If it's fiction, then it better be true.

And then I remembered the original topic of my

conversation with my sister. So I picked my phone back up and laughed and cursed while my sister laughed and cursed.

"So who raped Mom?" I asked. "Who raped Lillian the Second and got her pregnant with our sister?"

My sister then told me an even more awful story.

When my mother was rapidly becoming a rebellious teen, her parents sent her to Sacramento to live with her older sister and her husband, who'd been relocated to Northern California as part of the Indian Relocation Act of 1956. Relocation was meant to educate Indians, give them new life and job skills, and help them assimilate into mainstream culture. And it accomplished all of that while also damaging and destroying cultural bonds among thousands of Indians and their ancestral homelands and cultures.

"Jesus," I said. "Mom told me she was relocated. But she always said she traveled alone to Sacramento, got off the bus downtown, had a bowl of soup, and caught the next bus back home to Spokane."

"Nope," my sister said. "She lived there for a few months with her big sister and big sister's first husband."

I wanted to hang up the phone.

"So the husband raped Mom," I said.

"Yes," my sister said.

"So, Mary is the child of a rape."

"Yes."

"So Mary is our mother's daughter and her niece?"

"I hadn't thought about that," my sister said. "But you're right."

"And Mary is our half sister and our half first cousin, too."

"Something like that," my sister said.

"How come I've never heard any of this before?"

"Come on, Junior," my sister said. "You haven't lived on the rez in thirty-six years. So many stories and secrets get told. Time goes by. Time goes by."

My sister was telling the truth. I am disconnected from my tribe. By my choice. And, yes, I am disconnected from my immediate family, too. By my choice. I have traveled the world. My sister has lived in the same house for forty-four years.

"Man," I said. "Mom was so full of shit. What are we supposed to believe? Where did all that bullshit come from? What are we supposed to do with all this bullshit?"

"Well," my sister said. "You got famous on that bullshit."

And we laughed.

126.

The Widow's Son's Lament

My mother and I'd held each other hostage
For thirty-six years. But then my dad died,
And Mom and I were too damn exhausted
To be jailers anymore. We untied

Old knots and unlocked cell doors in tandem
And walked free in separate directions.
Neither of us demanded a ransom.
She remained on the reservation

And I took refuge in the city. We still
Phone-gossiped about friends and family.
I sent her money to pay past-due bills
From power and satellite companies.

We met in person a few times a year.
We laughed too loudly in public places.
We never mentioned the old pain and fear.
We somehow achieved homeostasis.

We didn't speak of forgiveness.
We didn't play that ruse.
No, we were mother and son
And we'd declared a truce.

127.

Physics

I want to reverse this earth
And give birth to my mother
Because I do not believe
That she was ever adored.

I want to mother the mother
Who often did not mother me.
I was mothered and adored
By mothers not my own,

And learned how to be adoring
By being adored. So if I adore
my mother after giving birth
to this new version of her,

Will she change history
And become one
Who openly and freely adores
Her daughters and sons?

I don't know. I don't know
If it's possible in any potential world.
But build me a time machine
And I'll give this shit a whirl.

128.

Spring Cleaning

If attics are the eggs, then steamer trunks are the
  yolks.

Thirteen years after my father died,
And thirteen months after my mother's death,

I open my father's steamer trunk—his chest-
  egg—and find
Toy guns, basketball cards, and cigar smoke.

Evoke! Evoke!

My father designed this strange collection with
  my sons in mind

(My glorious boys are part egg and part yolk),
But I think that he meant it as a joke—
Affectionate and unkind—

Because he knew that I love basketball, but hate
 guns and smoke.
Suddenly choked,
Blind,

And broken open like an egg and spilled like a
 yolk,

I mourn my mother. I mourn my father. I some-
 times wear his coat,
An outdated big-collar consign
That, I realize, also smells of toy guns, basketball
 cards,
And cigar smoke.

I want my grief to be baroque,
But damn it, it's as simply designed
As an egg and its yolk,
And as unrefined

As a chest heavy with guns (and mothers) and
 hoops and smoke.

129

Discourse

MY FRIEND JOHN SIROIS is a Colville Indian singer, drummer, and Dartmouth graduate currently working to protect the upper Columbia and Spokane rivers. An Ivy League Indian and a powwow Indian and a wild salmon restoration champion can easily be the same person.

Yes, a Native can be highly educated, live in the city, and be the guy you call when you need a beautiful prayer and hand-drum honor song.

I often get asked, "Sherman, how do the indigenous live in two worlds? How is it possible?"

And I'm all "Shiiiiiiiiiiit, I code-switch eighteen times before I drink my first cup of coffee."

Don't you white folks understand that Indians turn everything we do into something Indian?

That's how we reverse colonialism. By taking back most of the good things that were stolen from us and grabbing some of your good things, too.

And when like-minded Indians get together? Oh, man, you get some classical drama. I love my friend John Sirois like Pythias loved Damon. Yeah, that's right, I just claimed two mythical Greek dudes as my own. I compared their love to my love for another Indian man. You call that assimilation? I say maybe John and I will write a powwow song about Pythias and Damon:

Philia, Philia
Way ya hi yo
Philia, Philia
Way ya hi yo
This Indian is my brother
He's my brother
And I love him so
I love him so
Aho!

John is also a very handsome dude. When he met my late mother-in-law for the first time, she turned to her daughter, Diane—my wife!—and asked, "How come you didn't marry John?"

I met John at the same academic camp for Indian kids where I met Diane. John was mentoring high school kids from his reservation. Diane was running the whole thing. And I was a judge for the essay competition. Yes, John, Diane, and I were born into the Clan of Indigenous Brainiacs. Whatchu gotta say about that?

John was one of the Indian guys, along with a few high school kids, who gave me the courage to ask Diane for a first date.

John also knew my mother.

"I was thinking about the times we'd be at your readings," John texted, "and your mom was always asking me to keep you from cussing."

"Ha Ha Ha!" I texted back.

I am profane but nearly always for specific reasons. My profanity has an aesthetic. And Indians, in general, have dirty mouths. But those same privately filthy Indians will turn into Warriors of Decorum in public venues, especially when white folks are in the audience. I think many Indians consciously and subconsciously seek the approval of white folks. As a colonized people, we tend to perform our Indianness as a way of asserting our identities. These performances can be full of sovereign pride and co-dependent groveling *at the same time from the same person.* I want to get the attention of white folks, too, but I enjoy positive and negative reactions. I am the author of one of the most banned and challenged books in American history, and that makes me giddy with joy. But, all in all, I am most gleeful about inciting the wrath of other Indians.

"You were bullied as a kid by your own tribe," my therapist once said. "So it's not surprising you'd strongly react to bullying, or what you think feels like bullying. It's not surprising you fight back. That you *enjoy* fighting back, especially against other Indians."

"Being bullied can turn you into a bully," I said to my therapist.

"Yes," she said. "The stuff that you hate in others is often the stuff you hate in yourself. But perhaps you can learn something about yourself when this happens. When you are angry at somebody, what does that say about who *you* are?"

Maybe John Sirois and I should write an honor song for my therapist. And ninety-nine more honor songs for my mother.

"Your mom was so serious," John texted. "Please say something to Junior about his cussing when he gets onstage, she'd say. He will listen to you, she'd say. And I was, like, uh, sure, I'll talk to him. LOL!"

"But I don't listen to anybody!" I texted.

"I know. But I didn't have the heart to tell her otherwise. You know you just got to listen to and respect mothers! She felt better knowing I would talk to you."

"Wait, I'm older than you!" I texted. "Why was my mom telling you to be my elder?"

"What would I have said to you?" John texted. "Without laughing?"

"I would have started my talk by repeating what Mom had just asked you to say to me."

"I know! LOL! Maybe that's why I never said anything to you!"

"You know me!"

"Your mom knew you better than everybody else!"

Later, as I reread my conversation with John, I thought about the ways in which my mother tried to play good mother/bad mother against me. I thought how she often tried to make me obey the Edith Whartonian social rules of the reservation: Respect your elders even if they're dumb or lazy or ass-wipes; you can bring crying babies to any and all events and nobody will mind all that much; don't talk about the felonies, but you can endlessly gossip about the misdemeanors; make sure you clap for all the powwow dancers and not just your favorite category; even though you know your tribe is the best, that doesn't mean you're the best of your tribe; you can tell the truth about Indians in private, but don't tell the truth if white people are listening.

My mother often disobeyed those rules and many others.

I miss her constant rebellion.

I miss her inconsistent mothering.

I miss her stern and hypocritical judgment.

I miss the courtroom inside her heart.

I miss Lillian Alexie, my most beloved and failed censor.

130.

Self-Exam

Dear audience, please stand if you were raised
By a terrible mother. Okay, okay,

Approximately half of you. So I'd say
That terrible mothers are commonplace.

Just like terrible fathers. So let's mourn
For the children who never knew childhood.

Our grief is justified. Our anger is good.
I won't blame children for childish scorn.

But there comes a day when a broken child
Becomes an adult. On that day, you'll need

To choose between the domestic and wild.
You'll need to escalate war or declare peace.

I tell you this because I'm the kid, mother-stung,
Who became a terrible adult son.

And I'm to blame for that. I made that mess.
Because I am the Amateur of Forgiveness.

131.

The No

So we must forgive all those
Who trespass against us?

Fuck that shit.
I'm not some charitable trust.

There are people I will hate
Even after I'm ashes and dust.

132.

Jungian

Even as I deny the idea of God,
The idea of God interrogates me.

Even as I pretend that my love
For my mother is conflicted,

It's my mother who, in my dreams,
Emerges from a door marked "adore"

An image so overtly self-subversive
That it drops me—laughing

And praying—to the floor.

133.

Side Effects

TEN MONTHS AFTER brain surgery, I realized that my unilateral hearing loss had worsened. While I could still hear normally out of my left ear, my impaired right ear seemed to be slightly more damaged. That made it difficult for me to understand speech in crowded and noisy environments. Even when my wife and sons and I talked during a relatively quiet dinner at home, I often missed or misheard words and phrases. A simple sentence like "Pass the potatoes" could turn into a mysterious and inexplicable stew of disconnected words.

But I also noticed that my brain, rather than accept the blank spots and lines of nonsense, would reach deep into its memory files and pull out a familiar word or phrase as a replacement. My brain was always working hard to make sense out of nonsense.

So, one day in a crowded restaurant, when a waiter recited the daily specials to me, I heard him say, "American woman, get away from me," instead of whatever he said about the salad du jour.

Yes, in crowded rooms, my confused and hard-working brain works like a jukebox. Or maybe more like the shuffle on an iPod. My brain translates mis-heard language into song lyrics I know by heart. And like every pop culture addict, I can sing along with hundreds—perhaps thousands—of top-forty rock hits. I know my brain contains a vast data bank of lyrics, so I laugh at the possibilities. Which song-writer's poetry will I hear the next time a stranger or friend or family member speaks to me in a crowded room?

I hope to hear Prince's sexy lyrics more often than Air Supply's sappy shit. But I won't be in control of that process.

After neurosurgery, I have learned that my brain is a boardinghouse where my waking consciousness rents one room with a hot plate and a black-and-white TV while the rest of the rooms are occupied by a random assortment of banshees, ghosts, mimes wearing eagle feathers, and approximately twelve thousand strangers who look exactly like me.

And, oh, there's an auditorium in my mind where Hank Williams is always singing. So, if I ever meet you in a crowded airport or bookstore, and you say something like "I love [or hate] your books, I've been reading [or ignoring] them for years," I might think you said something like "I'm so lonesome I could cry."

This auditory phenomenon is somewhat scary. But it also feels like a piece of magic.

And what's the magic word? It is *compensation*.

134.

Hydrotherapy

I don't know how to swim.
I can't think of a much worse
Place to be than immersed
In water. But I live in a city
Surrounded by lakes
And canals and bays.
What can I say? You must bless
Your enemies lest they continually
Defeat you. My mother

Was terrified of the water
And never learned to swim either,
So did I inherit,
By nature and/or nurture,

My hydrophobia from her?
My sisters and brothers can swim
From one side
Of the river to the other.
So what happened to me? Well,
I was born hydrocephalic
And had brain surgery as an infant.
So, for years, my damaged head throbbed
And quaked
From any atmospheric pressure
Like driving into the mountains
Or into the valleys. So imagine how
Much it hurt to be underwater.
Imagine how much it hurt

To watch my siblings learn to swim
And then to swim freely
In the dozens of rivers, streams,
Lakes, and ponds
On our reservation or at some city pool.
My father swam, too,
With a stroke as lazy as he was.
But, on the shore, always removed
From the water,
My mother and I sat
And watched our family swimming
Away from us.
"Why are you afraid

To swim?" I asked her once
And she said something vague about
Drowning when she was a kid.
"You mean you almost drowned," I said.
"No," she said. "I drowned.
And then I came back."
And, listen, my mother was a liar

So I don't know how much of this is true.
But she never fully entered a body
Of water
And would only sometimes
Sit on a dock or shore or poolside
And soak her feet.
So I wonder: Will a person who has drowned,
Or almost drowned, always feel
Like they're drowning,
Even after they've been saved?
Did my mother's continual rages originate,
In some large or small way, from
Her drowning
Or near-drowning?
I don't know. But I remain terrified
That I'll die in a plane crash, but not

From striking the earth. No,
I'm afraid that my plane
Will plummet into water.

I'm terrified that I will drown
Inside an airplane.
And, as I say this fear aloud, I laugh
And laugh and laugh at death. Hell,
When death comes, I'll laugh
And say, "Hey, Mr. Death,
It's nice to meet you.
That sickle makes you look fat."
Because you must mock your enemies
Lest they defeat you.
Because you must bless your enemies
Even if they don't bless you.
So I bless the water, my provider
And my nemesis. And I bless
My mother, who gave birth to me
In water, by water, near water,
And in honor and fear of water.

135.

My Food Channel

My mother frying baloney. It curls
At the edges and rises
Off the cast-iron pan.
This is not acceptable. We are poor
But we do not deserve
Fried baloney that is crispy hot
In the middle of its circle
But cool and fleshy around its diameter.

Fried means fried.
Partially fried means it ain't fried at all.
So my mother slices the meat
Incompletely,
Four cuts from rim halfway to midpoint,

Just enough to make the baloney go flat
In the pan and cook evenly.
This culinary display doesn't take very long.
We children, hungry enough
To eat everybody's sins, listen
To the sizzle, sizzle and realize, realize
It's one of my mother's love songs.

136.

Triangle of Needs

Too poor in most winters
To afford cold-weather clothes,
I fought snowball battles
Using old socks for gloves.
Doesn't sound so bad, I know,
But my jacket was thin cotton
And I also wore Kmart tennis shoes
That we called rez boots.
My cousins had uranium money
So they had warm stuff
To wear. I pretended to be
Okay when we fought

For hours in the freeze.
I suppose I could have stayed
Inside. But I was a kid,
And like all other kids,
I needed to play.
And I would keep playing
In the midwinter ice
Until I started to shake
Uncontrollably. I wonder
How often I was close
To hypothermia.
I wonder how near
I fell to dangerously
Low body temperatures.
In December 1974
Or 1975, I stumbled
Through two miles
Of slush and freezing rain
And arrived home
Only to discover
That we'd lost electricity.
We had no heat.
My mother, wrapped
In an old and thin quilt,
Was constructing
A new and thicker quilt.
"What happened
To the lights?" I asked.

"We had no money
To pay the bill,"
She said. "So I need
To finish this quilt
And sell it to this
White woman in Spokane
So I can pay the bill
And maybe get some
Tomato soup and Pepsi, too."
Shivering, I cried
And said, "But I'm cold now."
So my mother told me
To take off my wet clothes.
And then, wearing only
Underwear, I crawled beneath
The old and new quilts, next
To my mother's legs
And eventually got warm.
And, yes, my mother finished
And sold that quilt

For less than it was worth,
But she paid the bill—
She moved the goddamn earth—
And got our electricity back.

137.

Artist Statement

ON OUR FIRST date, my future wife said she'd once broken up with a boyfriend because his favorite song was the Eagles' "Desperado."

Well, I remembered that my wife had revealed that goofy bit of information to me. But she always insisted that she'd never said it and that it wasn't true. She'd never dated a man like that. And I insisted just as strongly that she had told me about her Eagles-loving former beau and was just retroactively embarrassed by that particular romantic partner.

We argued about it for years.

Then, one evening, my wife and I watched a *Seinfeld* rerun.

"Hey, Elaine," Jerry said. "What happened to that guy?"

"Ah," Elaine said. "I dumped him."

"Why?"

"Because his favorite song is 'Desperado.'"

I kept staring at the television as my wife stared at me. I had confused my real life with an episode of a classic situation comedy. So, yeah, I think you know by now that I am definitely going to conflate shit.

138.

Sonnet, with Fabric
Softener

1. This is a poem about an epiphany. 2. This is also a poem about folding laundry. 3. It may have been Mark Twain who said, "The coldest winter I ever spent was a summer in San Francisco." 4. I live in Seattle, whose weather is much like San Francisco's. 5. I believe it was Tom Robbins who said, in describing Seattle, "It wasn't really raining, but everything was wet." 6. I say, "Our laundry room, even in summer, used to be the fucking coldest place south of Alaska." 7. I'm one of those husbands and fathers who love to do laundry but don't fold the clean clothes with any regularity. This greatly irritates my wife. "You already did the laundry," she often says. "Why can't you go the extra step and fold it?" I never have an answer to that particular

question. 8. Marriage is filled with, among many other things, laundry and unanswered questions. 9. For sixteen years, my wife and I cleaned and folded (or did not fold) laundry, and froze while doing so. 10. And yes, it was a minor annoyance—we weren't risking hypothermia—but why shouldn't one be comfortable in one's home? 11. On a bright note, the cold room truly made us love wrapping ourselves in sheets hot from the dryer. 12. For sixteen years, I often thought of wrapping my fresh-out-of-the-shower wife in sheets hot from the dryer, but it was too damn cold to be naked anywhere near the laundry room. 13. Then, one day, I bought insulated curtains at Target and hung them in all the doorways of the basement, where our laundry room is located. This immediately made the laundry room at least fifteen degrees warmer. "That's all it took?" my wife asked. "Yes," I said. Technically speaking, this is called an epiphany. 14. Dear wife, I'm sorry that I am mysteriously incapable of folding clean laundry, but I iron, oh, I iron. Sweetheart, I'll make your white shirt so crisp and sharp that it will split atoms as you walk.

139.

Complications

IN 2016, WHILE traveling to a Journey concert with my wife and older son, my brain crafted a mixtape of ballads.

Sad songs about unrequited love.

Minor chords.

One piano key.

The silence between notes. The silence between songs on the mixtape. The hiss of absence.

"You know," I said to my wife as she drove us along. "I just realized that every Indian boy on my rez who ever punched me is dead."

"They were all your age?" my wife asked.

"My age or older. A couple of them were eight or ten years older."

"Are you sure they're all dead?"

"Yeah, pretty sure," I said. "None of them made it to fifty. Most of them didn't make it to forty. A few didn't make thirty."

What is a person supposed to feel when they realize all of their physically violent childhood bullies are dead? And dead so young?

I felt like I didn't have the right to mourn my tormentors' deaths. I didn't love them. They didn't love me.

"Why am I so sad about them dying?" I asked.

"Maybe you believe in redemption," my wife said. "Maybe you were always hoping for some reconciliation."

"Maybe it's survivor's guilt," I said.

"Maybe," she said.

I remembered the day when one of my worst bullies caught me alone on the outdoor basketball court behind the school. He wrestled me to the pavement, sat on my chest, and spat in my face.

I closed my eyes and pressed my lips together.

But then he held my nostrils closed.

I tried to hold my breath.

I tried to hold my breath.

I tried to hold my breath.

But then I gasped for air.

And my bully spat in my mouth.

This happened almost forty years ago. I don't think about it often. Maybe once or twice a year.

Only once or twice a year. Only once or twice. Once or twice.

A friend asked me if I would trade some of my childhood trauma for some of my stories and poems.

"Straight-up trade," my friend said. "God takes away one pain in exchange for one poem. Would you do it?"

"No way," I said. But I think the real answer is "Yes, yes, of course I would, of course. Let me make a list. Let me trade away the worst three things— that Unholy Trinity—but I want to keep all the rest."

140.

Photograph

ONE EVENING, NEAR midnight, I called my little sister and told her that I was going to reveal, in this memoir, that our mother was the child of a rape. It was a family secret that I would not have publicly disclosed while my mother was alive. In order to write honestly about my mother—about her cruelty toward me—I knew I needed to reveal that she was conceived by a cruel act. There are reasons, justifiable or not, that my mother was so often vindictive toward me and the rest of the world. But she was also generous and kind to many people. She was generous and kind to me. She was contradictory. She was an unpredictable person—a random mother. And she was angry, yes, but she *angrily* provided for her children. She kept us mostly warm and mostly safe and mostly fed. And that was no small accomplishment for a woman who'd been hurt so much—who was the child of the greatest hurt. And I know you have read this story in this book a few times. But I must tell it again and again.

"But Mom wasn't made by rape," my sister said. "She was raped. And that's where Mary came from."

Mary was our half sister. Our big sister.

"But Mom told me she was conceived during a rape," I said to my sister. "I was, like, twelve or thirteen, and she sat me down and told me her mother was raped. She told me who raped her mother. And that she is the daughter of that rape."

"No," my sister said. "Mom was raped when she lived in California when she was a teenager. In Sacramento. By the husband of the woman she was living with."

"Mom told me she only spent a day in Sacramento," I said. "She said she got off the bus, had a bowl of soup in the bus station, then got on the next bus heading back to Spokane."

"I don't know anything about that," my sister said. "But Mom was sent to California because she was being so difficult on the rez, I guess. Then she was raped in Cali. But nobody believed her. They blamed her. Then she came back to the rez pregnant. Then, later, after she gave birth to Mary, she moved to Montana and married a Flathead Indian."

"Yeah, but I thought that guy was Mary's father," I said.

"He raised her as a daughter," my sister said. "But he was not her birth father."

I remembered that my big sister, as an adult, had moved to Montana to be closer to her father and other half siblings. But I now realized that Mary had moved closer to the man, not biologically related, who'd raised her as his own blood. He'd chosen to love her as a daughter; my big sister had chosen him as a father. They'd chosen each other. I was overwhelmed by the enormity of love. I had to get off the phone. I said good-bye to my sister and paced around my office.

My mother was a liar. A bold liar. But she was not an accomplished liar. Her falsehoods were often so obvious that we could immediately discount them. But had she successfully lied to my sister and me about rape—about two rapes? And why had she told me about the rape when I was only a young boy—when I was beginning my separation from her? Was it a way to keep me close? Was it a way to include me in some personal conspiracy? Did she worry that I might become a rapist? Was that story a warning? A call to self-examination? Did that rape story serve as my mother's highly dysfunctional version of the Sex Talk? Was she trying to help me? Or hurt me? I paced and paced and paced. I thought about my mother. I thought about her various deceptions.

Then I called my sister again.

"Why did Mom divorce that Montana Indian?" I asked.

"She missed our rez," my sister said. "She loved our rez."

"And he loved his rez too much to leave his," I said, anticipating the narrative.

"Yep," my sister said. "Mom gave him an ultimatum. Move to the Spokane rez or get divorced."

I laughed. That seemed utterly logical. That is exactly how much an Indian can love their own reservation.

"So, it's like Mom was having an affair with the Spokane rez," I said.

"And that Montana guy was sleeping around with his rez," my sister said, filling in the narrative.

We laughed.

I said good-bye again.

And then I wept, not for long. I cried so often while writing this book. It became a ceremony, equal parts healing and wounding. I often get asked if my writing is "therapeutic," and I always say, "Well, I think it can be therapeutic for other people. But for me? Well..."

I thought more about my mother. About her lifetime of myths, lies, and exaggerations. And then I realized something new: I don't think my mother ever told a lie about something as tragic and epic as rape. She was a fabulist but not criminally so. She manipulated us with her lies. She hurt our feelings. She exhausted us. But she never put us in physical danger with a lie. Can a liar have a code of ethics? No matter how cruel my mother could be, I cannot imagine her being cruel enough to invent two rapes.

So I believe that my mother told my sister the truth about being raped and giving birth to Mary, the daughter of that rape.

I also believe that my mother told the truth when she said that she was, like her daughter, conceived by rape.

But why did my mother apportion the truth? Why did she tell me one version of history and tell another to my sister? I imagine my mother's pain and shame were so huge that she could only approach them piece by piece. I also think my mother was afraid to burden any of her children with the entire truth. My mother needed us to know. She needed to tell her story. But each of her children only got one piece—one chapter—of the book. I imagine my other siblings—and perhaps nieces, nephews, and cousins—were also given parts of my mother's most painful and truthful stories.

And, in this way, I recognize the way in which I have protected myself through the careful apportioning of secrets, of personal details, of emotions. I know how I reveal certain parts of myself only to certain groups of people.

"Sherman," a friend once said to me. "How come you're so much funnier around strangers than you are around me?"

That line made me laugh and wince with self-recognition.

"I think the realest version of me isn't funny," I said to him. "If I'm being funny, it usually means I'm uncomfortable. It usually means I'm angry. Maybe being unfunny around you is me trying to be your real friend. And not just your funny friend. Maybe being unfunny is my way of showing you love. I mean—I don't want to perform for you."

"Okay," he said. "That makes sense. But could you maybe try to be funnier sometimes? Because that version of you is so entertaining."

My friend and I laughed again. And I winced again. That friend knows I am a secretive person. And he will someday read this book and he will have more questions. And I might tell him things—good and bad stuff—that are not contained within these pages.

But I will also still keep my secrets. I don't want him to know the worst stuff, not all of it, or maybe not any of it.

You want to talk tribal sovereignty? Well, let me

tell you about my personal sovereignty. Let me tell you about my one-man reservation. Let me tell you about My Clan of Me.

Let me tell you that, yes, I am my mother's son. And I am so much like her. We lived in separate, but related, villages forever across the river from each other. We belonged to the Ever-Nomadic Tribe of Obfuscation.

But I still have questions I want to ask her. There are questions I want to ask of the whole world. As a man, I don't feel I have the right to formulate answers to these questions. I don't want to pretend that I am wise about anything, let alone a subject as complicated and horrific as the meaning of rape. But, as the son and brother of rape victims, as a man who feels the primal need to understand and protect his loved ones, I have questions. I have questions. I have questions.

What were my grandmother and mother thinking and feeling as they gave birth to daughters of rape? As they raised those daughters? Did they often think about how their daughter was conceived? Did they willfully forget? Did they love that child less than their other children? Or did they love those daughters most? Is my big sister's early death somehow psychologically connected to her conception? Was my big sister's difficult life an inevitable result of the horrific way she was created? How does the child of a rape develop self-esteem? How does it feel to look into a mirror and see your rapist father's face? How does it feel to look into your child's face and see your rapist's features? How much forgiveness does it take to survive all of that?

I asked my wife these questions, because she's the woman I know best, because she's Native American, and because I needed her counsel, and she said, "Think of the history of war. Think of the aftermath of war. Think of what men have always done after victory. Think of the rich and poor. Think of the way entire groups of people—of women—were treated by invading armies. It happened in ancient times. In every age. It happened very recently. It's happening now. It's happening to most Native women right now. There have been millions of children who've been conceived by rape. And millions of mothers who love those children."

I didn't have any response to my wife's history lesson. I knew she was telling the truth. I knew she was right.

"Rape culture" might be a recently created descriptive phrase, but that phrase retroactively and accurately describes the collected history of human beings.

And it also describes the culture on my reservation. If some evil scientist had wanted to create a place where rape would become a primary element of a culture, then he would have built something very much like an Indian reservation. That scientist would have put sociopathic and capitalistic politicians, priests, and soldiers in absolute control of a dispossessed people—of a people stripped of their language, art, religion, history, land, and economy. And then, after decades of horrific physical, emotional, spiritual, and sexual torture, that scientist would have removed those torturing politicians, priests, and soldiers, and watched as an epically wounded people tried to rebuild their dignity. And, finally, that scientist would have taken notes as some of those wounded people turned their rage on other wounded people.

My family did not escape that mad scientist's experiment. In my most blasphemous moments, I think of that evil scientist as God.

So look again at the photo on the book's jacket.

Look anew.

Perhaps you assumed this is a photo of my mother and me. Other people have made that assumption. I'm the author of this book, so it makes aesthetic sense that my face, along with my mother's, would be on the jacket.

But that baby on the jacket is Mary, my big sister. She looks pissed about being a part of the photograph. And that woman on the cover is my mother at seventeen. She looks happy and not bothered by her daughter's anger.

That's a mother and daughter on the jacket of this book. Those are two women who, with strength and grace, loved each other. They led incredibly painful lives. One died tragically young. One endured catastrophic losses.

Look at that mother and daughter.

Look at those two Native American women.

Think of their grief.

Think of their grace.

Think of their pain.

Think of their power.

Sing them an honor song.

141.

Dear Mother

I'm going to sleep now.
Since you died, I've only dreamed

Of ordinary errands:
Groceries, driving the boys

To baseball and saxophone,
Folding laundry at noon.

But, in these dreams, you
Are always there, mute,

Five or six feet away,
And younger than I am now.

I do my best to ignore you
(As I did in life)
But your persistent
Presence is maddening.

These aren't nightmares
And, yet, I tell myself

To remain calm,
To remain calm.

Eventually, in these dreams,
I lose my shit

And scream, "What
Do you want?"

And you nod
And smile

As beautifully as ever
And turn away.

Mother, what a trickster
You have become.

After seventy-eight years
Of words, words, words,

And words, you are now
Mocking me

With your silence,
So complete, so absurd.

142

The Urban Indian Boy
Dreams of the Hunt

On the reservation,
My big brother kills an elk
And cuts open its belly—
Intending to eat its heart
And praise the animal's sacrifice—
But instead finds the six hearts
Of his six best friends who
Have died in drunken car wrecks
Over the last twenty years.
Kneeling beside the elk,
My brother pauses—
Even a reservation Indian can be
Surprised by the bloody magic of things—

Then feasts on his friends' hearts
And thanks God for the brief
Moments when we are loved well
And for those stretched-taut days
When we are barely loved at all.

143.

Dialogue

Is my mother still dead? *Yes, she is still*
Dead. Are you sure that my mother is dead?
We are positive that your mother is
Dead because we are looking at her grave.

It's been a year since her death. *Yes, we know*
Because we can no longer sense her breath
Or body heat. Is that why you have come
To my home? *We're not dumb. We need fresh blood.*

I've built homemade traps. *We've seen the lights*
Floating in the shallow bowls of soapy
Water. We can't resist the lure. I've drowned
Over one hundred of you. *There are more*

Of us alive than dead: adults, pupae,
Larvae, and eggs. The four stages of fleas?
We're not unlike the Five Stages of Grief.
We can be temporarily submerged

But we always return. I have summoned
An exterminator. She reminds me
Of Darth Vader. *Eh, as she poisons us,*
She will also be poisoning your ass.

I'm desperate. I'll do what I must to end
Your invasion. I'll burn my fucking house.
Hey, pal, you're practicing some evasion.
It's not us you hate. You hate your own blood.

But don't worry. We love the salt in you.
Be still. Our bites don't pinch. They only itch.
I want my mother back. *You're lying.*
You might ache now but she caused you far more

Pain when she was alive. Your grief might itch
But it stings less and less with each new day.
So shut up and bare your legs, bare your arms.
Damn, you're not fooled by my false pleas or
    charm,

Are you? Oh, come on, dude, it's not us fleas
You need to flatter. You don't require

495

Our approval. Okay, maybe you're right.
Maybe life is better since my mom died,

But what about my sisters and brothers?
What about their pain? *Do you aspire*
To be like us now? Do you want to feast
On their blood? I want to honor their grief.

Fuck you. You're a writer. You're a damned thief.
No, no, no, no, I love my siblings.
They're more important than my scribbling,
Than these sad-sack rhymes. *Okay, if that's true*

Then tell them, say it aloud, testify.
Okay, I will, I will. *Let's hear it now.*
Dear sisters, dear brothers, I am sorry
For being a ghost, for not loving you

And our mother as much as all of you
Have loved me. I'm sorry for being so
Incomplete. *Okay, pal, we'll grade that a C.*
Maybe a C-minus. But now you need

To tell us how you're going to atone.
I don't know. *What?* I don't know. I don't know.
Should I kneel and thrash my back with thorns?
Listen, pilgrim, we're not Catholic. We're fleas.

We just want you to bleed and bleed and bleed
And bleed and bleed, but not to death.
No, we need you alive. We need your pain
To be close to the surface and bite-sized.

You are not my God. You don't control me.
You can't escape us. You are beyond help.
Fuck this, fuck death, fuck grief. Nice try, Junior,
But cursing fleas is like cursing yourself.

144.

Tantrums

First Set

What should I do with my rage against death?
I grab the exercise ball, lift it above
My head at full extension and throw it
Down against the floor with all of my strength.
This is called a tantrum and I'm supposed

To throw the fucking ball through the fucking
Floor. Of course, nobody is strong enough
To actually break the floor. But we must want
To break the floor. We must attempt to break
The floor. We must *need* to break the floor.

So a few days after my mother's death,
I tantrum that fucking ball fifteen times.
I need to throw it through the floor. I need
To throw it through the wall. I need to break
Down my muscles and rebuild them again.

Second Set

And then I rest and marvel at how hard
This simple exercise works my shoulders
And back and arms and legs. I'm out of breath
As I think of my mother's funeral
And how fucking childish I felt

As I looked at all of the mourners—
My fellow Spokane Indians—and realized
How desperately I'd always wanted
To be beloved by them. And how unloved
I'd always felt. Yeah, my mom was dead

But I was more worried about my life.
Angry at my narcissism, I grab
That exercise ball and tantrum the thing
Fifteen more times. I want to throw
That ball through the walls I'd created...

Third Set

Between me and my tribe. I didn't belong
Because maybe I never wanted

To belong. When everybody else danced and
   sang,
I silently sat in my room with books,
Books, and books. I used books for self-defense

And as stealth bombers: I am better than you
Because I have read more books than you; I am
Beloved by these books; I am beloved by words.
Ah, bullshit, bullshit, bullshit. I tantrum
That ball fifteen more times. Can I break

The earth itself and throw this fucking ball
Through the crust, mantle, and core? No, no,
No, no. I grow weaker with each throw. I stop.
I stagger. I surrender to the invincible floor,
This Indian boy can't tantrum anymore.

145

The End of a Half-Assed Basketball Career

As a teenager, I was a basketball star, I suppose,
But only on a dozen or so Indian reservations
And in twenty or thirty white farm towns.
I was good enough to be the ninth man

On an average community college team, if I'd
    chosen
That route, but I took the academic scholarships
To a Jesuit college instead, played intramural
    hoops,
And dominated fellow students who could've
    been

The tenth and eleventh men on a CC squad,
If they'd chosen that route instead of the books.
Then I drank myself away from the Catholics
To the public land grant university,

Where I learned how to write free verse poems.
I sobered up but never stopped playing ball.
And was probably better at age twenty-eight
Than I'd ever been. I helped my teams win

City league championships in Spokane
And Seattle. And once scored 55 in an all-Indian
    game
Where my team lost by 100 points. I played
    street ball
Against pro and college players and was
    humiliated

By my superiors only four or five hundred times.
I once blocked John Stockton's fast break lay-in,
An impetuous play that enraged and energized
    him.
He guarded me so closely and scored on me so
    easily

For the next ten minutes that I had to surrender
    and walk
Off the court. I was always slow and unorthodox

And only scored because I learned how to take and make
Shots from ridiculous angles. I played an old man's game

When I was twelve so I thought I would play forever.
But I hurt my back in 2002 and hurt it again and again and
Again for the next fourteen years. And then I broke my mouth
Playing hoops. And then I broke my hand. And then,

In December 2015, I had brain surgery to remove a benign tumor.
And then, in August 2016, I again collapsed to the floor
With a back spasm and wept with pain. When that spasm ended,
I stood and knew I would never play hoops again.

Chronic bad backs have ended the basketball careers
Of infinitely greater athletes than me (Tracy McGrady, for one),
So I didn't feel bad about my body's decline. Instead,

I shrugged and wondered what smaller sport I
    would learn

How to play. How strange to be fifty years old
    and still be
In search of a new game. A few months after my
    quiet
Retirement, I don't miss playing much, if at all.
    Instead,
I realize that my basketball obsession had lim-
    ited me

In certain ways. I see that certain friends were
    only
My friends because of basketball. So I've ended
Those friendships because they aren't nurturing
Off the court. I want to say that I'll have more

Free time for other friends and family but, in
    truth,
It means I will spend more time in solitude.
I played basketball like others practiced religion.
I was a single-minded monk. And now, I am

A basketball agnostic. I still love to watch
    LeBron
And Curry and Durant, but I don't daydream
About when I will play next. I don't need to pray

That I won't get hurt. I don't need to pray

That I will hit a few pretty shots, make a few
    prettier
Assists, grab a few rebounds, and maybe make
    one
Great defensive play. Better yet, I don't have
    to lie
Awake in the night and rewind the three hours

Of shitty basketball I just played. I don't carry
    around
The shame about my hoops decrepitude. I no
    longer
Have to uselessly flail against the younger
    friends who are
So much better than me. I no longer have to sit
    and sit

And sit and sit because the losers always sit.
I still shoot hoops by myself. I know, one day,
I'll be the old man who surprises
His grandkids by hitting ten long set shots in a
    row.

And, hey, this is a poem less about basketball
And more about mortality. I will soon have to
    give up

Other things, like walking steep stairs, like driving
A car, like sex. And, yes, yes, yes, yes, yes, yes,

I will eventually look at a blank piece of paper
Or blank computer screen and realize that I've run out
Of words. I will smile, shed a tear, walk outside,
Sit on my porch, and misidentify the local birds.

146.

When I Die

Bury me in my city. Bury me
Near the hospitals where my sons were born.
Bury me near the parks, pools, and playgrounds
Where they learned to crawl, walk, run, swim,
  and climb.

Bury me near the rooms
Where my sons admired
And doubted me. Entomb

My body near the libraries and bookstores
Where folks listened to my stories and poems—
Where my words were mostly celebrated
And sometimes ignored. Bury me upright

Near a taxi stand, train stop, and bus line.
Bury me near one thousand restaurants,
Good and bad. Bury me close to my friends,
Alive, dying, and dead. Bury me where

I'll get visited at least once a week—
Okay, once a month or bimonthly,
At least. Bury me facing north, east,

South, or west, I don't have a preference,
Religious or otherwise. Bury me
Next to my wife. Oh, damn, it hurts and hurts

To say this, but if I'm the first to go
Then bury me within walking distance
Of my home, so that my wife, my widow,
Can stroll over and keep me company.

Maybe she'll marry again. Maybe she won't.
But whatever happens, bury me near her.
Please, please, let me be her favorite ghost.

147.

Filtered Ways

ON A WEDNESDAY in August 2016, Shelly Boyd texted me to ask if I might be part of a special tribute to her late husband, Jim Boyd, to be held at the Native American Music Awards in Buffalo, New York, that September.

Jim had died, at age sixty, of natural causes—of complications from preexisting health conditions—on June 21, 2016, two weeks short of a year after the death of my mother.

I called Shelly and said, "I want to do the tribute. I want to do this for Jim, but I have to take care of my brain. Let me talk to Diane."

"Oh, Sherman," Shelly said. "Your wife has veto power over everything, right? Especially when it comes to your health, right?"

Jim had ignored many warning signs in the days before his death. He'd run out of his high-blood-pressure medication and had delayed in getting it refilled. He was serving as the chairman of the Colville Tribal Business Council and was rushing from place to place, working too hard and not getting enough rest. He hadn't played much music either after entering tribal politics. He'd often promised Shelly that he'd get to the doctor. That he would get more sleep. That he would play more music.

"Yes," I said to Shelly on the phone. "I will talk to Diane. I will listen to her. I promise."

Like many men—indigenous and not—I don't always take good care of myself.

In December 2015, I'd had brain surgery to remove a benign tumor that had grown dangerously large and was intruding on vital areas of my brain. I'd first learned about the tumor in 2007 when I underwent an MRI scan while filming a documentary about my childhood hydrocephalus.

"It's small," my neurologist had said about the meningioma. "The size of a pea. Come back in a year and we'll look at it again."

And then I ignored that tumor for eight years. And would likely have continued to ignore it if not for the death, by brain cancer, of a good friend in November 2015. Shortly after his funeral, I went in for another MRI and learned that my tumor was significantly larger—about ten times larger.

Three days later, I underwent successful brain surgery. But after five months of steady recovery, and the resumption of my hectic literary job, I started to suffer simple partial brain seizures. My neurologist put me on antiseizure meds and told me to make my life simpler. So I canceled all of my business travel for the next eight months. I vowed to gift myself more silence and solitude. And to spend more time with my closest friends and family. During my twenty-four-year literary career, I'd earned nearly two million frequent-flyer miles and had performed at more than three hundred colleges. I needed to stop. I needed to heal. I needed to step away from the applause, applause, applause. At least, one step away, maybe two.

"I want to do the tribute to Jim," I said again to Shelly on the phone. "I will call you tomorrow and let you know after I've talked to Diane."

Shelly and Jim and I became friends in 1992 when I met them at the Columbia Folk Festival, being held at a rustic outdoor performance space north of Spokane that was, I think, also a pumpkin patch, Christmas-tree farm, and kitschy country art vendor. My first book had been published only a few months earlier, so I was new to the spectacular randomness and oddness of live performance.

Jim was a Colville Indian musician who'd played for years in local cover bands and a few nationally famous Native American rock bands, including XIT and WinterHawk. But he'd recently gone solo and was playing a personal blend of folk, country, and blues mixed with traditional Native vocables, drums, and cedar flute. Of course, the white organizers put Jim and me, the Indians, back to back on the bill. Jim played first, and I was amazed by his music, especially a song called "Filtered Ways," which turned an Interior Salish stick-game song into a nostalgic rock ballad about lost youth. Then I stood and shouted my angry and nostalgic poems about my lost youth.

Afterward, I sat at a picnic table, feeling that post-performance emotional letdown (that I would later, thanks to Brene Brown, be able to more accurately describe as a "vulnerability hangover"), and smiled when Jim sat across from me.

"Your poems are cool," Jim said.

"Your music is awesome," I said.

Jim smiled. He was so instantly kind and shy. He was certainly one of the kindest and shyest people I have ever known. And, aside from my late father, Jim was probably the most gentle and shy Indian man in my life. In fact, as I type this, I think I was so immediately drawn to Jim because he reminded me of my father.

As Indian strangers will do upon meeting for the first time, Jim and I tried to figure out which Indians—cousins and friends—we had in common. Jim had traveled the world as an air force brat, but he'd also spent many years living in Inchelium, Washington, on the Colville Indian Reservation, a much larger rez, which sat across the Columbia River from my reservation. Jim was an urban Indian who'd gone rez, and I was a rez boy who'd gone urban. Different directions but still the same journey. We knew a lot of the same people, including my mother and big brother.

Then Jim and I talked about music and poetry.

That was the first time I'd ever had a long and detailed discussion about art—and the creation of art—with another Indian man.

Jim and I were also alcoholics who'd recently made the decision to get and stay sober.

So, yes, pretty quickly, I realized that I had a new brother.

"Did you ever think about putting your poems to music?" Jim asked.

"I used to write lyrics in high school," I said. "But they were like REO Speedwagon love songs."

"You should write some lyrics," he said. "Indian lyrics like in your poems. And I'll put them to music."

That night, I went back to my cheap apartment in Spokane and wrote these lyrics:

Sometimes, Father, you and I,
are like a three-legged horse
who can't get across the finish line
no matter how hard he tries and tries and tries.

Sometimes, Father, you and I
are like a warrior
who can only paint half of his face
while the other half cries and cries and cries and
   cries.

Now, can I ask you, Father,
if you know how much farther we need to go?
Now, can I ask you, Father,
if you know how much farther we have to go?

Father and farther,
Father and farther,
'til we know?
Father and farther,
Father and farther,
'til we know?

Sometimes, Father, you and I
are like two old drunks
who spend their whole lives in the bars
swallowing down all those lies and lies and lies.

Sometimes, Father, you and I
are like dirty ghosts
who wear the same sheets every day
as one more piece of us just dies and dies and
  dies.

Now, can I ask you, Father,
if you know how much farther we need to go?
Now, can I ask you, Father,
If you know how much farther we have to go?

Father and farther,
Father and farther,
'til we know?
Father and farther,
Father and farther,
'til we know?
Father and farther,
Father and farther,
'til we know?
Father and farther,
yeah, how much farther
'til we know?

Sometimes, Father, you and I
are like a three-legged horse
who can't get across the finish line
no matter how hard he tries and tries and tries...

That was two years before I owned a computer and three years before I had logged on to the Internet, so I wrote the first few rough drafts of those lyrics by hand, then typed a few more drafts on my Brother word processor, printed the final draft, folded it into an envelope, drove over to Jim and Shelly's house on the other side of Spokane, and dropped it in their mailbox.

A week later, Jim called me.

"I finished the song," he said. "Come over to my work. And we'll listen."

Jim was working as a counselor at a residential addiction treatment center for Native teenagers. At the front door, he handed me a cassette tape.

"There's the song," he said. "Listen to it and let me know what you think."

I walked back to my car and slid the tape into the stereo and heard the first chords of "Father and Farther." And, as I listened, I noticed that Jim was outside playing basketball with a few of the at-risk youth. Jim was a good athlete. He was funny. He and those boys laughed and laughed as they shot hoops. And I heard that sad and beautiful song for the first time.

Jim and I had created art together. It was the first time I had collaborated with another artist. It was the beginning of a personal and creative friendship that would lead Jim and me, along with Jerry

Stensgar, bass player, and Alfonso Kolb, drummer, to share the stage with the Indigo Girls, Jackson Browne, Bonnie Raitt, and Dar Williams. We played dozens of shows at music venues in Spokane, Seattle, Chicago, San Francisco, Los Angeles, New York, and Boston, and at numerous colleges in big and small towns.

Jim, Jerry, and Alfonso would play the songs that Jim and I had written together. And they'd play Jim's songs. And they would play music as I read my poems. And we'd perform songs where Jim sang as I read poetry.

When I first performed with Jim, I did it in character, as a Spokane Indian man named Lester FallsApart, a drunk and homeless Indian who wasn't afraid to be profane and brutally honest. As Lester FallsApart, I was able to break through my inhibitions and improvise stories. I learned how to be funny onstage.

"I don't know how you do it," Jim once said to me. "You get onstage and you're not afraid of anything. I get onstage and I'm afraid of everything."

"It's because of you," I said. "You and your music are like armor for me."

Over the years, I dropped the Lester FallsApart character and performed only as myself.

Jim and I wrote songs together that appeared on the soundtracks of the two movies I wrote, *Smoke Signals* and *The Business of Fancydancing*.

Jim and I self-released an album, *Reservation Blues,* to accompany my novel of the same name about an all-Indian Catholic rock 'n' roll band.

At my wedding to Diane, my powerful Hidatsa wife, Jim played a cover of Peter Gabriel's "In Your Eyes," and Shelly was our official photographer.

The years and events blend together. I cannot give you the exact chronology. Jim and I are artists. We are reservation-raised Indians. We are indigenous poets. Time works differently for us than it does for most other people.

But I do know that, somewhere during our separate and paired journeys, Jim and I lost the creative spark we had together. We stayed friends, but our artistic careers went in separate directions. He released many other albums, traveled the world with his music, and was inducted into the Native American Music Hall of Fame. I published many books, traveled the world, and was inducted into the American Academy of Arts and Letters.

Jerry Stensgar, the bass player, died.

Alfonso Kolb, the drummer, moved back to his reservation in California and serves on their Tribal Council.

Jim and Shelly lost a son to a sudden suicide.

My father died of alcoholism, a slow suicide.

At my father's funeral, Jim played "Father and Farther," and I wept harder than I ever have in my life.

After that, Jim and I would talk on the phone once or twice a year. I'd often bump into him when I was visiting Spokane.

We always promised to write a new song together.

To do another show.

To share the stage.

He and Shelly came to my mother's funeral. And I was positive that he played a song in honor of my mother, but now I'm not sure if he did. My memory, often distorted by my storyteller's impulse, is now also distorted by the aftereffects of my brain surgery and seizures.

Then, eleven months after my mother's death, I received a text in the night from John Sirois, another Colville Indian and one of my best friends.

Jim was dead.

A week after Jim's funeral, at the Bing Theater in Spokane, John Sirois sang one last honor song for Jim, and I improvised a eulogy.

I said, "Jim was so beautiful. He was so damn Indian-looking, too. He was like the Before Columbus Indian, and I am the After Columbus Indian."

I said, "At my wedding, Jim was walking in the hotel in front of me in the lobby. And some little white kid, a stranger, looked at Jim and said, 'Mom, that's a real Indian.' His embarrassed mother tried to shush her kid. But I said, 'It's okay, I'm an Indian, too,' and that little shit white kid pointed at Jim and said, 'But not Indian like him.'"

I said, "Jim was the first Indian man to ever tell me how much he liked my poems."

I said, "I always figured Jim and I would get back onstage someday. Like we'd do an Honoring the Ancient Elders concert where we'd honor the ancient elders we'd become."

I said, "Jim was a musician you could always trust onstage. And he was a person you could always trust offstage."

I said, "I don't have any regrets about my life with Jim. We didn't get to share the stage one last time. But he and I made art together. And we had so many adventures on the road. We laughed so much."

I said, "He and I were flying in a little plane together. Before nine-eleven. When you could see the pilots in the cockpit. When you could walk right up to them if you wanted. We were flying and hit some turbulence. And it felt like the plane almost flipped upside down. The plane was bumping up and down. It was scary. Jim and I were sitting across the aisle from each other. We looked at each other. Then we looked at the pilots. Those pilots looked at each other and laughed about the turbulence. So Jim and I looked at each other and laughed about the turbulence, too. And I guess that's what I will always remember most about him. That will be my most lasting memory. My brother, Jim Boyd, laughing about turbulence."

"Shelly Boyd called me," I said to my wife. "She asked if I would perform at the tribute to Jim in Buffalo."

"When?" my wife asked.

"In a month," I said. "At the Native American Music Awards."

My wife looked into my eyes. We've been in love for twenty-five years. We know the what of the what about each other.

"I can't do it," I said. "My brain. I will get too tired. I don't want to get all exhausted and start having seizures again. I have to stay home. And I don't want to fall over if Shelly is there. I'm not going to die, but think how much that would traumatize her."

"I know," she said. "You have to tell her you can't go."

But I didn't want to hurt Shelly's feelings, so I performed a highly sacred indigenous trick: I avoided making a final decision by avoiding the person who needed me to make my final decision. This didn't work when Indian tribes tried to avoid signing treaties with the U.S. government, and it didn't work when I tried to avoid Shelly.

A few days after she'd asked me to consider performing at the tribute, Shelly texted me: "If you and/or Diane have time, I'm in town till Wednesday morning if you want to meet for lunch or dinner. I'm visiting the Burke."

Located on the University of Washington campus, the Burke Museum has a cool collection of Native American art and artifacts. I'm not always a big fan of Native American museums or the Native collections of larger museums. I feel like museums too often lock us Natives in the past, but the Burke does a good job of honoring contemporary Native Americans while honoring our past. Plus, they have an Egyptian mummy in private storage, and drawers filled with bird wings.

After I read Shelly's message about the Burke, I called her.

"Hey, it's Sherman," I said. "You better watch out. You're so Indian and beautiful, the Burke might catch you and put you in an exhibit."

"I'll be all right as long as they put me in a canoe," Shelly said. "And feed me lots of salmon."

"It'll be good salmon, too," I said. "Remember, they still have wild salmon on this side of the mountains."

"That sounds better than how my life is going now," she said. "I might do it."

I could hear the grief in her voice. I didn't want to disappoint her about the tribute. But I had to tell her the truth.

"Shelly," I said. "I'm sorry. But I can't do the show in Buffalo. I think it would cause me problems. I get so tired now. I would be too exhausted."

"Oh, Sherman, I understand. But I'm sad. We were thinking we'd get some of Jim's musician friends to learn one of the songs you and Jim did together. And then you'd perform it with his friends and that would be the tribute."

"Oh, God," I said, and cried into the phone, fully understanding for the first time that Jim and I would never again perform together. I felt the full force of my grief.

"Oh, Shelly," I said, barely getting out the words. "I don't think I could even make it through the first few bars of the song. I don't think I'd be able to talk."

"Oh, I know, I know," Shelly said. "Sometimes I can barely talk about Jim."

"The sadness snuck up on me there," I said. "It hit me hard like a storm."

I realized at that moment that I'd have to stop listening to Jim's music for a while. In my family, we cut our hair to grieve death. In 2003, I'd scissored off my ponytail after my father died. And I never grew it back. I became a short-haired Indian. For my mother's death, I had no hair to cut. But I am writing this book about her. For Jim's death, I would have to put away the music he and I wrote together. I didn't know when I would be able to listen to it again.

"I miss Jim," I said to Shelly. "I am always going to miss him."

"I am going to miss him forever, too," she said. "You and I are alike. Because I am going to miss your mom forever, too."

I knew that Shelly and my mother had grown closer over the years. But I hadn't realized how close. I also knew that Shelly had, for personal and spiritual reasons, decided to learn how to speak her tribal language. My mother was one of the last fluent speakers of our tribal language, a dialect related to Shelly's language. Some words are the same or similar. Most are not.

"Your mom was so supportive of us learning our language," Shelly said. "She encouraged us so much. I always wished she lived in Inchelium so we could hear her talk all the time. It's a different language, I know, but we wanted to hear your mother speak it. We wanted to hear her fluency. We learn the language now, and we know phrases and we can talk to each other. But not like your mom. I told her she should come talk to us in her language. I told her she could talk about cutting her toenails and it would be beautiful to us."

"She never taught us how to speak the language," I said.

And Shelly said, "She didn't teach you because she loved you."

That made me weep again. I couldn't talk for ten or fifteen seconds. And then I said, "Oh, Shelly, I have never heard it that clear."

"Sometimes," she said, "you don't know something is true until you hear it for the first time."

And I understood that Shelly, in learning to speak her tribal language, had tapped into something ancient and powerful. In reclaiming her language, Shelly now understood something beautiful and painful about the loss of language. And she had just taught me what she had learned. She had said it in English, but it spoke to my soul in the old way.

I realized that my mother had not taught us the tribal language because she knew her children would not be strong enough to carry the responsibility of being the last fluent speakers. She protected us from that spiritual burden. She protected us from that loneliness.

During my teen years, my mother sometimes said to me, "Junior, English will be your best weapon." I had always understood that as a motivational sentence, but I now realize it was also about love. And how psychic was my mother about my relationship with English? At the very least, she perfectly predicted my eventual job description.

"Before your mom got really sick," Shelly said, "she was supposed to come to Inchelium and talk in Spokane to us. She was going to tell us stories. And then a big snowstorm hit. And closed us off from the east, west, and south. But the north was open. Isn't that funny? A big snowstorm but the north was open."

I cried as I listened to Shelly speak.

"Your mom called me and cried," Shelly continued. "She couldn't get through the snow. She was so sad. You know, Sherman, I get so mad at some of the people in your tribe. Your mom knew all the words, and those people wouldn't use your mother's knowledge. They wouldn't let her teach anywhere."

I thought of how difficult my mother had been over the years. About how many enemies she made within our tribe. And then I thought about how my mother and I had stopped fighting but had never truly reconciled. I thought about my poor, poor mother trying to reconcile with our tribe—with her enemies—and being turned away.

"Shelly," I said. "Mom and I struggled with each other over the years."

"I know, I know," she said. "I know."

I sobbed again.

"Is this who you're going to be now?" I asked. "Are you going to call up Indian men and make them cry?"

"That might be good," Shelly said. "It might be fun to become an old Indian heartbreaker."

We laughed.

"Your mother knew things that no other Spokane Indian knew," Shelly said. "Words. Ideas. Stories. Songs. History. It's all gone now. Buried with your mother."

I suddenly understood that Shelly had become my teacher. And, maybe, by loving my mother so much and being so loved by my mother in return, Shelly was also my mother's messenger.

"Oh, shit," I said. "You are saying amazing things."

"Oh, I'm just talking," Shelly said. "Just talking."

I felt blessed by her words.

"You know," she said. "Our languages are amazing. Our languages do things that English just can't do. There's a word we use in Inchelium. And a word used in Wellpinit, too."

Shelly said a word in Salish that I did not recognize, but I didn't ask her to repeat it because I wanted her to keep telling the stories I did understand.

"That word means 'earth-dream.' And, depending on how you use it, it means we, the people, are dreaming the earth into being. And it also means the earth is dreaming us, the people, into being. We are dreaming each other. And making each other real. And it means other things, too, that I don't understand. That I might never understand. But I am going to keep learning."

Shelly and I said our good-byes and made plans to

see each other in person. I told her that I would need to talk to her because of Jim and because of Lillian. I realized that Shelly would become my mother's voice, at least my mother's Salish voice. And I realized that my mother, Lillian, had dreamed me into being. And that I had dreamed her, my mother, into being. And that she and I would keep dreaming each other into being.

I don't know the Spokane word or words that mean "The son dreams the mother as the mother dreams the son." But I know how to say it in English. I know how to spell it. I know how to put it in a book. And that will make it magic enough for me.

148.

Epigraphs for
My Tombstone

1.

You shouldn't worry
If you haven't lately heard me
Tell a joke about death.
I'm just catching my breath.

2.

I'm buried
Two hundred and seventy-nine miles
From the graves
Of my mother and father.
That seems perfect.
No closer.
No farther.

3.

If I died
As an elderly man
In his unarmored sleep,
Then count
My quiet departure
As an indigenous victory.

4.

Oh, shit!
Crank the pulleys
And lift me into the endless span.
I hope to be remembered
As the kind and generous man
Who always fought the bullies.

5.

I'm sorry
If I sneeze myself dumb.
But I'm allergic
To 78 percent of the dust,
Ashes, pollen, and plants
That I've become.

149.

After Brain Surgery

I forget what I was trying to say.
One word or another gets in the way
Of the word I meant to use. Nothing stays.
I forget what I was trying to say,
So I say something else. I compensate.
Like a broken horse, I've learned a new gait.
But wait! Are these the words I meant to say?
I think these rhymes help me to map the way.

I think these rhymes help me to map the way.
But wait! Are these the words I meant to say?
Am I a broken horse? Is this my new gait?
Damn! I've lost the path, so I'll compensate

By repeating the words I meant to say.
But these words migrate. They refuse to stay
In place. This is my new life. My new way.
I forget what I was trying to say.

150.

Fluent

MY FRIEND SHELLY BOYD, a Colville Indian and dear friend of my late mother's, made an observation during a dinner that keeps echoing in my head.

She pointed out that my siblings and I might be the youngest people who were raised in a household with two fluent Salish speakers—with a mother and father who were raised in households where they were fluent in Salish before they were fluent in English.

Shelly said, "Both of your parents thought in Salish. They dreamed in Salish."

But, as I told Shelly, I don't even think of my late father as being a fluent speaker because he so rarely spoke the language. In my lifetime, I heard him say Salish words maybe ten times.

Sometimes, when she was very angry, my mother yelled at my father in Salish, in the Spokane dialect, and my father listened and listened and listened. And then, maybe two or three times in all those years, he snapped a word or two back at her in Salish, something so powerful and shocking in the Spokane or Coeur d'Alene dialects that it would cause my mother to turn and immediately leave the room.

And yet my siblings and I are not fluent. My brothers and sisters, having lived on the reservation their entire lives, know far more words than me now. Growing up together, we shared the same limited vocabulary. But now, twenty-six years after I last lived on my rez, I can barely count to ten in Spokane.

Our parents did not teach us our tribal language. And that was mostly because of shame. The white government, white military, and white church worked together to shame indigenous people for being indigenous—for speaking the language.

But I also think our parents and grandparents hoarded the language. In a real sense, the original Salish language, in all of its dialects, was the most valuable treasure that any dispossessed Indian could hide—could keep for themselves.

Being fluent is perhaps the last and best defense against American colonialism.

So I think it was a combination of shame and possessiveness that prevented our parents from teaching us to be fluent.

But Shelly also made this observation: "Sherman, I have known you for almost thirty years and you have always been mysterious to me. I don't understand how your brain works—how you see the world as you do. But I was thinking about you the other day, about being raised by two people with Salish brains. Who always thought first in Salish. Who, since birth and until their death, watched the world with Salish eyes. And so I think that, even though you and your brothers and sisters don't speak Spokane fluently, maybe all of you have these Salish/English brains that nobody else has. Sherman, I think maybe your English has Salish hidden inside of it."

I don't know if that's true. I have serious doubts that it's true. But my siblings and I do have a unique relationship with the Salish language, and with its tragic history of destruction, self-destruction, near-disappearance, and recent resurgence.

But the new Salish language is not the same as the old Salish language.

"When a fluent elder dies," Shelly said, "it's like a river has disappeared. And inside the disappeared river are Salish words—Salish concepts—that have also disappeared."

My siblings and I could have been taught that old language. We could have learned how to navigate all of those ancient rivers of words and concepts.

My siblings and I could have become the last guardians of the old Spokane language.

But we are not.

My siblings are everyday citizens of our reservation. They speak only English. And I, crazily enough, have turned English into my only vocation and greatest avocation.

I speak and dream in English. I am a gifted writer and speaker of English. And that fact, in the small world of the Salish language and of the Spokane Indians, is cause for unequal amounts of celebration and grief.

151.

Thursday Is a Good Day to Find an Empty Church Where You Can Be Alone

I want to believe
That my father and mother
Have found each other
In the afterlife
And become a new kind
Of husband and wife.
I hope they've built
A home by water
And have guest rooms
For all of us sons
And daughters.

But I don't want to be
The atheist who prays
Only for himself,
So let me just say
That my mother and father
Would certainly prefer
To be alive and alive.
Maybe they can return
As birds. Listen.
I know this magic
Will never happen.
And maybe my faith,
Or lack of faith,
Is odd. But I don't need
Answers. I just want
To be heard by somebody—
By the real and/or imaginary God.

152.

Pine

And now I need
To do something
Excessively Indian

So I will name
All of the pine trees
On the reservation.

That one is Mother
And that one over
There is Mother

And so is that third
Pine in the valley
And that tall one

On the ridge is Mother.
Okay, I'm either lazy
Or I have an arboreal strain

Of Oedipus complex.
So let me take this down
A few degrees.

That pine, the closest one
To my mother's grave—
I imagine its roots

Will eventually feed
On what my mother
Will become

After many years
In the earth.
So let my mother

Be that tree
And let that one tree
Be my mother.

And let my Mother Tree
Turn every toxin
Into oxygen

So that my siblings
And I can finally
And simply breathe.

153.

Ancestry

My late mother is
The grandmother
Of this poem.
It is her
Descendant,
Disrespectful
Enough to reveal
That my late mother
Was conceived
By rape,
That most vicious
Of amendments.
Unlike me, this poem
Will question

My late mother
About her conception
And self-conception:
I'm sorry
To interrogate you.
I know you're the victim
And should be treated
With respect.
But there are things
I'd like to know.
When did you first learn
You were the child
Of rape? Who
Told you? Why
Did they tell you?
Should I even
Call him
Your father?
Nobody wants
To be known
As a rapist's daughter,
Do they?
I should tell
Everybody
You were raised
By a good man
Named James,
And not

By your biological
Father, yes?
Are you angry
With me
Because I've revealed
What you chose
To conceal?
I'm sorry
For this
Intrusion.
But I need
To know if you saw
The rapist's face
When you looked
Into the mirror?
Did your mother see him
When she looked
At you?
Is it possible
That your mother
Loved you less
Than your siblings
Because of how
You were created?
Did you ever learn
How to be
Anything other
Than devastated?

Okay, stop, stop,
I want to stop
This poem
And drop
The facade.
I, Sherman Alexie,
Am the child
Of Lillian Alexie,
who was the child
Of rape.
I, Sherman Alexie,
Am the grandchild
Of rape.
My children are
The great-grandchildren
Of rape.
All of these descendants
Exist
Because of rape.
Rape is
Our ancestor.
Rape is
Our creator.
Rape is
Our Book
Of Genesis.
Rape is
Our Adam & Eve.

And yet.
And yet.
We never
Forget
That my mother chose
My father
Because of love.
I chose my wife
Because of love.
Our children
And grandchildren
Will choose
Their spouses
Because of love.
We continue
Lovingly
Despite
The crimes
Committed
Against any
And all
Of us.
How miraculous
Is that?
Dear Mother,
Dear Lillian,
Thank you
For choosing me.

Thank you
For your gifts,
Borrowed
And renewed.
Thank you
For my birth.
And for all
The plentitude
Of this
Half-vicious
And half-forgiving
Earth.

154

Things I Never Said to My Mother

1.

I have two sons—your grandchildren—
One dark-skinned and one light.

That means they'll have to fight
Slightly different enemies.

My dark son will have to be wary
Of angry white men with guns.

My light son will have to verbally battle
Angry Indians with sharp tongues.

2.

My sons ride city buses
To and from school.

They walk among thousands
Of strangers arranging

And rearranging themselves.
There are so many new

Skyscrapers
Being built

In our city of rain,
I wonder if

Everybody's spirit animal
Is now the construction crane.

3.

Dear Mother, I live and work
In a black neighborhood. Well,

In a black neighborhood being
Gentrified. It's good. I love it here.

Late one night, at my office
One mile from home, I stared

Out my window in an insomniac haze.
Remember how crazed I used to be?

Turns out eight hours of sleep
Is the only vision quest I need.

Anyhow, as I stared out that window,
I saw a transformer sizzle

And spark down the block.
Accidental and gorgeous fireworks.

Then that transformer boomed
And turned the neighborhood

Into one large and powerless room.
In five minutes, the closed supermarket

Parking lot below me was crowded
With dozens of black teens and young
    adults.

A sudden party! And the bass that shook
Their car windows shook my office
    window!

Then, three minutes after the party started,
Six police cars pulled into the parking lot.

Oh, shit! Oh, shit! I wondered if somebody
Was going to get shot! But the cops stayed

In their cars, content to just be reminders
Of more dangerous possibilities,
While the black teens behaved like teens.
Twenty minutes later, the power came back.

I was surprised that it had been fixed
So quickly. Soon enough, the black kids

Vacated the lot. And the cops did, too.
It was one of those city nights where

Bad things could have happened.
But it was good things that shook the air.

The music and car engines and laughter
Only singing about love, not disaster.

4.

I ask my older son to define "abundant,"
And he shrugs and says, "That's when

You have too much stuff. Like us."
My younger son wants to maybe become a
   rapper,

But he doesn't want to exploit black culture.
He wants to tell his urban Indian truth,

But he doesn't want to be a colonial asshole.
He says, "Dad, I know I've got money and
   power,

Even though I'm just a kid. But I want to talk
About all the evil shit in the world." I say, "Son,
You just gotta be honest when you're trying
To be a socially conscious artist in your village."

And he says, "I'm gonna be honest from the
   start
Because my rap name will be Lil' Privilege."

5.

Dear Mother, at your funeral,
Your grandson said, "I didn't know her

Very well. And I think I missed out
On good things, didn't I?"

I said to him, "Kid, you didn't learn
About some magic. That's true.

But we have also kept you
Two hundred and ninety-two miles

Removed from the tragic.
I mean—you have never seen

Another Indian even take a sip of booze.
That's the best kind of indigenous news."

A few weeks later, back in Seattle,
My son imitated me at the supermarket.

He hunched over the cart, puffed out
His belly, and said in his best rez accent,
"Ah, shit, I hate that tofu disguised as meat.
It's phony. Now go find me some turkey
    baloney."

Ah, I love that my sons trust me enough
To mock me to my face.

That's the best kind
Of familial grace.

6.

I once saw the moon fully
Reflected in a mirrored skyscraper

Then fracture into one hundred moons
As I drove under and beyond.

There are a million freeway exits
And I've taken maybe 99 of them.

There's a dude who sells hot dogs
Half price if you prove you're half in love.

Everything, everything, everything
Can be installation art.

7.

Mother, I know
I was a sad little fucker.
I cried all the time.
It wasn't pretty.

But I wasn't always
Crying because of you.

I was crying because
I was born to live in the city.

And now I do.
Thank God, I do.

155.

Tattoo

WHEN THEY WERE very young and dating, my mother and father, Lillian and Sherman, got tattoos of each other's names on their left wrists.

It was my mother's first and only tattoo. My father would eventually get forty-two tattoos, but most of them were of the ink-pen-and-lighter variety. He received none of them while sober. And he got at least a dozen of them while in jail.

But my parents were sober and inexperienced when they got those first tattoos. They couldn't take the pain.

So my father stopped his tattoo at "Lil," short for Lillian, though nobody ever called my mother Lil.

And my mother stopped her tattoo at "Sh."

156.

Scrabble

In the last hours of writing the last draft of this book, I realized that *memoir* is a partial anagram for *mom noir*.

157.

Public Art

At an open mike, I heard a poet proclaim
That her sadness was a beached whale on the
    shore,

And I complimented her on that metaphor.
But the poem that she had performed was not
    the same

As the poem that I'd heard. That poet seemed
    peeved
By my misinterpretation and turned away.

But I remain positive that her poem contained
Whales and sadness. And I happen to believe

That my sadness does beach me like a confused
   whale,
While my mania turns me into the love child

Of a rescued whale and hummingbird, too wild
To remain in the sea and too overscaled
For flight. But, wait, sometimes, my mania lets me
Become the great blue whale hovering over

A single orchid. Sometimes, being bipolar
Lets me ignore physics. Ha! Who needs gravity?

Look at me! Look at me! I am antimatter!
I am mammal and the opposite of mammal.

My wings are carved from glass. My flukes are
   enamel.
Watch me fly. Watch me fall. Applaud when I
   shatter.

158.

What I Have Learned

THE SPOKANE INDIAN word for salmon is pronounced *shim-schleets.*

The Spokane Indian word for a male's mother is pronounced *skoo-ee.*

These are approximate pronunciations. This is phonetics. I can't say the words very well. I have not learned how to *hear* the words, either. But I am practicing.

I will never be fluent in my tribal language, but I believe these are the two most important words for me to know.

My mother.

Skoo-ee.

My salmon.

Shim-schleets.

My wild salmon.
My wild mother.
Skoo-ee.
Shim-schleets.
Skoo-ee.
My mother as salmon.
My mother as salmon.
Skoo-ee.
Shim-schleets.

159.

Like a Bird

ON A SATURDAY morning in a hotel room in Bellingham—in an Oxford Suites that had three-dimensional art in the bathroom that spelled WASH in huge wooden capital letters—I confessed to my wife of twenty-four years that I had always been deeply ashamed of my acne-scarred back.

"Yes," she said.

During the course of our long relationship, I'd admitted to a certain percentage of my various shames, like our marriage was a recipe and I needed to add a small, precise amount of vulnerability—but not a teaspoon more—in order for everything to turn out well.

"I have never told you the full extent of my embarrassment," I said. "I need to tell you now. So, okay, I have always moved and dodged and hid my back under sheets and pillows. I have used angles of light and shadows to avoid you being able to fully see my back. Even when we bathed or showered together. Even during sex. I've operated like an escape artist for two decades."

She didn't say anything. I couldn't tell what she was thinking. I tend to fall in love with the unnamable. Then she spoke.

"I've seen your back," she said.

"I want you to see it better," I said.

"Okay," she said. She looked amused, irritated, slightly baffled. She knew that she was again part of two narratives, one that was happening in real time and another that I was revising and editing even as the first was taking place.

That two-simultaneous-narratives shit must be equally aggravating and attractive to the nonwriter lovers of ever-distracted writers.

"This freaks me out," I said. "But I am going to get naked and lie facedown on the bed. And I want you to look at my back. I want you to study my back. I want you to study my scars. I want you to tell me what they look like. I want you to touch the scars. I want you to trace their outlines with your fingertips. I want to feel you feeling my scars."

I felt an odd combination of fear, pride, and idiocy, like I was about to jump out of a plane into deep woods where I would hunt a brown bear with a pocketknife. And so I allowed my wife—who'd seen me naked and touched me thousands of times—to finally touch me in those places where I had hoarded so much of my pain and shame.

Before I met my wife, a Hidatsa/Ho-Chunk/ Potawatomi Indian, I had never, as an adult, been romantically loved by any other Native woman. But don't feel too bad for me. Growing up on the rez, as a preteen, I kissed four girls.

In kindergarten, I grew so dizzy while sitting on a spinning merry-go-round that I laid my head back on the metal and closed my eyes. A few moments later, I opened my eyes and was startled to see a girl staring down at me. Then I was even more startled when she kissed me, jumped off the merry-go-round, and never kissed me again.

That merry-go-round kisser was a white girl, the daughter of white parents who worked for the Bureau of Indian Affairs. I kissed a girl for the second time in fourth grade when I leaned through her open basement-bedroom window and smashed my mouth into hers. She was a white girl, and she fell laughing back onto her bed next to her best friend, an Indian girl, who asked, "What was it like?"

"He tastes like salt," the white girl said.

They laughed together. I ran away, fearing

something was wrong with my mouth. Only much later in life, after I had kissed other girls, did I realize that the taste of salt can make a kiss pretty damn spectacular.

In fifth grade, I kissed a white girl who was a little bit Indian. Or maybe she was an Indian girl who was mostly white. In any case, on the rez, she was treated and mistreated like she was a white girl, no matter how Indian she was or was not.

I think she was the first girl I loved.

One day, at recess, she gave me a necklace. A silver cross. Then she kissed me. I realized that I had always wanted her to kiss me. That's a powerful feeling at any point in one's life, but it's a naked Las Vegas Cirque du Soleil of the soul the first time you feel it.

I lived across the road from the tribal school, so I immediately ran home and asked my mother if she had a necklace I could give to my first love.

And my mother smiled, said yes, and gave me a silver necklace with a pendant-coin that featured an embossed buffalo on one side and an Indian head on the other.

That piece of jewelry was not exactly romantic, but I didn't know any better. I guess my mother didn't know any better either. And, despite my mother's other major and minor crimes against me, I absolutely refuse to believe that she deliberately sabotaged her young son's courtship effort.

Proudly swinging that half-Indian/half-buffalo necklace, I ran back to school and presented it to that mostly white girl. She accepted the gift but with a look of such obvious disdain that I turned and ran. And, as I ran, I heard her laughing with other girls, the mostly and fully Indian girls who had often laughed at me, at my thick government-provided eyeglasses, at my large hydrocephalic skull, at my epically crooked teeth, at my stutter and lisp.

I was a special-needs kid before needs were considered special. I was a kid Somewhere on the Spectrum when the spectrum was only "normal" or "not normal." I was the Official Tribal Fool living one hundred years after fools were last thought to be holy. I was a mess, a mysterious casserole slowly going bad in a half-assed freezer. I was social carrion. I was nearsighted in one eye and farsighted in the other. I was uncorrected and uncorrectable. I was the Boy Who Cannot Contain His Emotions. I was the kid who could not run fast or jump high. I was the kid scared of heights on a reservation that is essentially an endless pine forest. I was the Indian who didn't know how to swim on a reservation bordered on two sides by one great river and one damn good river. I was the Runt of the Rez.

I stole my fourth and last reservation kiss from another white girl. I was in sixth grade. She was an older woman. An eighth-grader. She was the white daughter of white teachers. And I saw her sitting on a big rock on the playground. Her eyes were closed. Her face was turned toward the October sun. I quietly climbed the rock, leaned toward her, and kissed her. She slowly opened her eyes, not surprised at all, as if she'd expected to be kissed by somebody, and said, "Never do that again."

She was absolutely justified in judging and rebuffing me that way.

Later that same school year, I was sitting on a second flight of interior school stairs while two Indian girls sat talking on the first flight of stairs. I could hear every word they said, but they didn't know I was listening.

They talked about their friends—all the girls they thought were the coolest and the ones who were the least cool—and then they talked about the boys they liked and the boys they loved.

I wanted to hear them talk about me, but I also wanted them *not* to talk about me.

"You know who you should like?" the first Indian girl asked the other Indian girl.

"Who?" she asked.

"Junior," said the first Indian girl. She said my name. Oh, shit, she said my name.

"Junior is nice," said the second Indian girl. "And he's supersmart. But he is so ugly."

I know that every person reading this has

experienced that kind of romantic devastation and personal destruction. But it doesn't make me feel any better to know that it's a universal experience. And I hope only a few people have experienced what happened to me after that moment on the stairs.

The next day, some other Indian girls began to call me ugly. They said it to my face, in public, at school, at sporting events, at ceremonies, everywhere. When they walked by my house, they'd yell "Ugly" loud enough for me to hear it in my basement bedroom. Insulting me suddenly became a wildly popular thing to do. I'd been randomly bullied and insulted for years, but I quickly became the target of an organized harassment campaign.

So many insults, so many names.

They invented a disparagement for me that I'm embarrassed to repeat so many years later.

"Junior High Honky," they chanted at me. "Junior High Honky. Junior High Honky."

That's a stupid insult, right? Inane. It hardly seems like it would be damaging. But, like water falling drop by drop onto your face for hours and days and weeks, that tiny insult slowly came to have enormous power over me.

So how did those mean girls invent that particular appellation? What is its etymology?

Junior High Honky. Junior High Honky.

Such a silly damn insult. I was an Indian being

racially insulted by other Indians. I was being called white by Indians who had a white mother or father. I was being called white by Indian kids who'd known me since our births. Many of us had played together as babies in cribs. So they were racially insulting me for the whiteness they knew I didn't possess. Well, my maternal grandfather was partly descended from a Scottish traveler, but he died years before I was born. Some of my uncles, aunts, and cousins had married white folks and had biracial kids, but every one of my living blood relatives was an official member of one tribe or another. A few of my cousins were distant urban Indians. That didn't make them any less Indian. It just meant they weren't reservation Indians. But I was the child of two reservation Indians who were the children of reservation Indians who were the children of reservation Indians. It was ridiculous and maddening to be called white by Indians who were less Indian than me.

As an adult, I can now intellectually understand why they called me white. In the Indian world, "white" is our enemy. "White" is the conqueror. "White" is the liar, killer, and rapist. So, if one Indian wants to inflict a grievous emotional wound on another Indian, then "white" is the Big Fucking Gun of insults. The bullies wanted to hurt me as much as possible. So, despite the fact that I was culturally, economically, politically, racially, and geographically a full member of the tribe—as much a Spokane In-dian as any other Spokane—I was called white, not because I was white, but because I was the frail kid. I was the easiest target. In the Land of Others, I was the Otherest. These days, you can go online and read other indigenous people's scholarly and less-than-scholarly reviews of my books, and you'll discover that some of those assholes overtly and subtly ac-cuse me of whiteness. And, sure, it hurts my feelings. It definitely gives me PTSD flashbacks to childhood shame. But it also makes me shrug, sigh, and laugh. I used to be bullied because I was the Indian with the least social power. Now, I'm sometimes bullied because I'm one of the Indians with the most so-cial power. So, yeah, when another Indian, especially one of the smart ones chasing that *completely* nonas-similative prize known as academic tenure, accuses me of whiteness, I think, "Different bully; same bul-lying." And, sometimes, when I'm being the best version of myself, I will remember that bullies are created—that bullies seek to torture because they've been tortured. When other Indians—friends, ac-quaintances, or strangers—talk shit about me, I try to remember they are acting out of their own weak-ness, their own crisis of self-identity, their own pain and fear and paranoia. I try to instantly forgive them.

I try. I try. I try.

But my adult understanding of this indigenous

cultural cruelty does nothing to help the bullied rez kid I was. My intellectualism, empathy, and self-empathy cannot time-travel.

"Junior High Honky, Junior High Honky, Junior High Honky," my bullies chanted at me.

They chanted, "You're so ugly. Ugly. Ugly. Oh, uh-ha! Oh, uh-ha! You're ugly!"

Not all of the Spokane Indian girls called me names. I distinctly remember the kindness of many girls. Those kind girls have grown into kind women. But there were three girls in particular who incessantly bullied me. And they happened to be beautiful and overwhelmingly popular. Shit, one of them owned her own snowmobile and a full-body snow-suit she could have worn to climb Mount Everest.

A snowmobile! A fucking snowmobile on the rez! I didn't even have my own radio. I didn't have a bicycle. I had to wear my only pair of shoes—tennis shoes bought in Kmart—during winter.

"But, Sherman," my critics like to say. "Not all Indians are poor on the reservation."

So, yes, yes, yes, I agree, there were a few rich Indians, relatively speaking, who lived on my reservation. There were also a few middle-class Indians living on my rez. And nearly all of those rich and middle-class Indians were dickheads. There was income inequality on my rez. There was a 99 percent and a 1 percent. There was social and political separation based on economic and cultural class. I can't imagine how those class differences play out now within tribes that have serious casino money. Or maybe I can imagine it. There are plenty of tribes disenrolling their members—legally destroying their tribal identities—exiling them. I think of those wildly successful casino tribes, and I wonder if their reservations have come to resemble and mimic the inequities of the United States itself. Doesn't an Indian tribe finally surrender to colonization by becoming as capitalistic as our conquerors? Isn't indigenous economic sovereignty one of the sneakiest damn oxymorons of all time?

I was a poor rez boy, and from the spring of 1978 through the fall of 1979, I was intensely belittled by three Indians who had some family money—whose parents had and kept jobs. My father died at age sixty-four without ever having had a checking account in his name. So, yes, I was a poor kid and those three rich Indian girls bullied and brainwashed me. They called me ugly with such cruel and constant precision that I came to fully believe that I was ugly. I looked in the mirror and said, "You're ugly, ugly, ugly." I often look in the mirror now and say, "You're ugly, ugly, ugly."

That same fall, during the first few days of seventh grade, I opened my math book and saw my mother's maiden name written on the inside cover.

I cursed at the obvious injustice. They had handed me that ancient math book because I was an Indian kid and because I was a reservation kid and because I was a small-town kid and because I was poor and because I was a poor reservation Indian from a small town in a small state in a region of the country where almost every kid, no matter their race, is treated like shit by the rich and powerful. I was enraged at the racism and classism. I felt doomed. I felt like all my classmates, my fellow tribal members, were also doomed. In real life, I stood and threw that thirty-year-old math book across the room and impaled it three inches deep into the wall. In the fictional version of that incident, as detailed in my novel *The Absolutely True Diary of a Part-Time Indian*, my autobiographical avatar throws that math book across the room and breaks the teacher's nose. The fictional version is much more satisfying.

My childhood dream had been to become a pediatrician, like all of the doctors who had treated me so well during my sickly childhood, but the reservation school was so shitty at that point—so devoid of advanced math and science curricula—that I might as well have been dreaming of becoming bulletproof, invisible, and ten feet tall.

When I got home from school that day, after being suspended for three days for throwing that old math book into the wall, I asked my mother and father if I could leave the reservation school and go somewhere different, somewhere better.

My father had gone, *on purpose,* to Immaculate Heart of Mary Academy, a Catholic school in Coeur d'Alene, where he and his sister were the only Indians. So I don't think it was a shocking idea to him that I might want to see more of the world. He'd been in the army. He'd traveled on all-Indian basketball teams through Canada, Montana, the Dakotas, Idaho, Oregon, and Northern California. When he was drunk, he often bragged that he used to have a Japanese girlfriend who lived in San Francisco. He'd written the first thirty pages of an "autobiographical" novel about his love affair with her. I doubt she was real, but he'd *wanted* her to be real. My father's lifelong dream had been to live in Phoenix, Arizona.

He said, "I want to live in a place where it never gets cold."

So, by action and ambition, my father had always been a traveler.

But my mother, except for a brief period where she became a teen mother in Sacramento and another where she became a teen bride in Arlee, Montana, had never lived off the reservation. And difficult and terrible things had happened to her when she had traveled away from the rez.

So, considering their respective histories with

adventure, it is not surprising that my father supported my escape. But I remain stunned that my mother gave her consent. I know I was brave to leave the reservation school, but I think my parents were far more courageous in letting me go. I was so young. I was a fucked-up Indian boy. And, despite being descended from thousands of years of traditional Native people and their conservative lives, my parents said yes when I asked to be a total radical and leave my tribal school.

My mother, despite all the pain she caused me, saved my life twice. The first time, in 1973, she saved my siblings and me when she stopped drinking and made our home a safe—a relatively safe—place to live. And then she saved my life again when she let me walk away from the Spokane Indian Reservation in 1979, never to fully return.

This is a familiar story for those readers who already know my work. But I have never fully told the truth about all of my reasons for leaving the reservation school for the white high school twenty-two miles away. So, for the first time in print, here's my most honest account for my actions: I left the reservation in the desperate pursuit of a higher and better education—in search of a more epic life. But, with an equal amount of desperation, I also fled the reservation because I believed that no Spokane Indian woman would ever marry me. Because I was too ugly to be loved by any of them. I set sail on an academic adventure, but I was also on a mission to find love. So, after a year-long effort in building courage, I transferred to the farm-town junior high in Reardan, where I became Jason, and my ambitions became the Argonauts.

I allowed my wife—who'd seen me naked and touched me thousands of times—to finally touch me in those places where I had hoarded so much of my pain and shame.

While I was working on the early drafts of this chapter, I said to my wife, "You know, I have been thinking about the rez. And what would have happened to me if I hadn't left. I have been trying to figure out which Spokane Indian woman I would have married if I'd stayed. And, you know, I don't think any of them would have married me. I really don't. And not any women from other tribes living on our rez either."

My wife was reluctant to follow that particular line of conversation with me. What person wants to debate the merits, the possibilities, of their real spouse's imaginary husbands or wives? At the time, I was miffed that she was unwilling to hear me think out loud about potential lovers and spouses. But, shit, I was obsessed with this book and its ideas. Like every other writer, I'd set aside my real-world manners in order to rudely pursue an idea.

So I continued to ponder the question by myself: If I'd stayed on the reservation, then who would I have loved, and who would have loved me? *Nobody, nobody, nobody.*

And then I remembered Angie, the white daughter of a white traveling salesman. Sounds like the beginnings of a dirty joke, right? I met Angie during my tribe's Memorial Day Powwow in 1979. I was almost thirteen and she was fourteen. Angie's father owned and operated a mobile arts-and-crafts and toy shop. That description is way too polite. So let me try again. Angie and her family lived in a rugged RV that also served as the warehouse and storefront for glass jewelry and polyester T-shirts and stuffed animals that resembled no living creature and thin plastic toys that broke within hours and candies that were clumsy-ass rip-offs of famous brands. So, yeah, maybe Hershey's chocolate bars were your favorite candy, but that's only because you never had a bag of Horshey's Choco-Dust.

Angie and her family lived in Seattle or Tacoma, I think. But they spent their summers and school-year weekends traveling from powwow to state fair to rodeo to car shows to wherever they could park their RV and sell their cheap goods.

In 1979, twenty or thirty of those traveling

vendors had set up shop at our powwow grounds. And we Indian kids—the ones who didn't dance powwow—would "walk the circle" of those vendors like we were cruising in cars. Around and around we'd go, examining and reexamining the cheap merchandise, eating fry bread and cotton candy and sno-cones, and staring at all the Indians we knew and all of those Indians who were strangers. And we'd also stare at the white tourists and vendors.

It was past 10 p.m. as I walked by Angie and her family's booth for the first time. I stopped and stared. She was a very skinny and pale girl with brown hair. Rather plain, I guess, but a confident and loud salesperson.

"What are you staring at?" she asked me.

"Your shirt," I said.

She looked down as if she'd forgotten what she was wearing. On the front of her shirt, on her flattish chest, was the image of an old radio with two anatomical-looking dials. Below that radio was the printed command DON'T TOUCH THESE KNOBS! THEY'RE WELL ADJUSTED!

Angie laughed at her sexually suggestive shirt, then turned around. On the back of her shirt was the message FROM BEHIND, IT'S ALL THE SAME.

At that time, I was too young and damaged to understand the explicit pedophilia of that shirt. I was only twelve. But there were hundreds of adults who must have seen the young girl wearing that shirt. What did they think when they saw it?

"T-shirts are five dollars each," Angie said. "Or three for ten bucks."

"I don't have any money," I said.

"Then why are you here?" she asked.

I didn't have an answer.

"Do you like me?" she asked.

I think I took a step back because she took two steps toward me.

"Come back in an hour," she said. "I have my bathroom break. We can walk. In the dark."

She was only fourteen, but she was as brash as her shirt. I was terrified and intrigued.

"Okay," I said.

I didn't have any clue what to do for that next hour. So I reverted to habit and kept walking the circle and walked by Angie eight or ten times. I would smile at her: she'd smile at me. I didn't know a thing about romance, so I didn't realize that my aimless circles had become courtship.

Finally, after an hour, Angie ran to me, grabbed my hand, and pulled me away into the dark parking lot near the darker and unused rodeo arena. She sat on a truck bumper, and I leaned against a light pole.

"What's your name?" she asked.

"Junior," I said.

"I'm Angie. Some people call me Annie or AJ. My dad says I shouldn't be chasing after Indian boys."

She leaned toward me and whispered, *"My dad hates Indians."*

I wasn't surprised by the racism. I've rarely been surprised to encounter racism.

"Do you like Indians?" I asked.

"I like you," she said. "Do you want to kiss me?"

I couldn't talk. But I could move. So I sat on the bumper next to her. I leaned in for the kiss, but she leaned away. I leaned toward her again, and she leaned away again. To and fro. To and fro. Almost a kiss. Not a kiss. Almost a kiss. Not a kiss. I worried that Angie was making fun of me, but then I realized she was having fun. She was enjoying me. I was having fun, too, but I was confused, and obviously not as experienced as she was. And it troubles me now to think about why she was expertly flirtatious.

Then I heard a mocking voice.

"Hey, Junior, who's your girlfriend?"

It was one of my regular bullies, a muscular Spokane Indian boy who would die young.

"Junior," he said again. "Who's your girlfriend?"

My bully was drunk. His two friends, also drunk, laughed. I sensed real danger.

"Run!" I yelled.

So Angie ran. She was the fastest sprinter I had ever seen. She *disappeared* into the dark before I could take a few steps. I have always been slow. And slow is not a good thing to be when you're a reservation prey animal.

My three drunk bullies quickly caught me. But they didn't hurt me too badly. They slapped me in the balls a few times, made fun of my speech impediments, and let me go.

I thought about looking for Angie, but I was scared my bullies would hunt me down again. So I ran the two miles home, crawled into my bed, and did not return to the powwow that year. I skipped the 1980 powwow entirely because I was publicly preparing to leave the rez school for the white high school.

I allowed my wife—who'd seen me naked and touched me thousands of times—to finally touch me in those places where I had hoarded so much of my pain and shame.

While working on this chapter, I texted my sister, "If I stayed on the rez, who do you think I would have married?"

"Ah, you would have met some girl at an all-Indian basketball tourney," my sister texted back. "Probably some urban Indian from Portland or Seattle. You would have married some Coastal Salish college girl and moved to the city. You woulda got a tattoo of a killer whale."

"But do you think anybody from our rez would have married me?"

"Doesn't matter," my sister texted. "You were always going to leave. You were always going to end up urban."

★　★　★

In 1981, after my first year among the white folks of Reardan, I returned to our tribe's Memorial Day powwow. I thought I might get bullied, but I'd grown physically and emotionally stronger in a short time. I was no longer an easy mark. I'd become a popular and admired kid in Reardan, as a scholar and basketball player and, yes, as a potential boyfriend. The girls in Reardan paid attention to me. They asked me questions. I asked them questions. We listened to each other's answers. I had kissed one girl on a school bus and another in a hayloft.

So, at that powwow, my new and overt self-esteem must have shone like knight's armor.

One Spokane boy looked at me and said, "Damn, you're growing like a weed."

And his friend, another Spokane, said, "His skull is growing even bigger now. It's a fucking planet."

I was ready to throw punches, but they kept laughing and walked past.

Both of those Indian boys died before they turned forty. I don't remember them with anger. Well, I still feel residual anger. But, mostly, I think about how lonely and desperate they must have felt in their short and tragic lives. How much pain had they suffered? How many dark secrets did they have to keep? Why had they always felt the need to pick on me?

That was the last time I felt physically threatened by a bully on my reservation. After that, my reservation enemies and detractors would only gossip about me. And rarely in my presence.

Alone, I walked the powwow circle of vendors. And then stopped when I saw Angie again. Of course, I remembered the white girl I had almost kissed at the powwow two years earlier. I was now almost fifteen. She was sixteen. And she was obviously pregnant and ready to give birth at any moment.

She was working at an ice cream truck, scooping out freezer-burned chocolate and vanilla ("Two flavors is better than one!") for rez kids. Her big belly—the T-shirt stretched taut over her belly—was smeared with ice cream.

I was stunned by her pregnancy. I remember thinking, "Shit, if things had happened differently two years earlier, maybe I would have gotten her pregnant. Maybe I would be a teen father."

Then I felt irrationally jealous and possessive, as if Angie and I had been seriously involved, as if we had real-world ties to each other. But, damn, we'd only held hands. Our brief powwow date had lasted maybe fifteen minutes. I didn't know her last name or where she lived. She lived somewhere that wasn't the reservation. That was her full address: Pregnant Angie, Not the Reservation, USA.

I was also scared for her. Even then, I knew that, by getting pregnant so young, she had made her life infinitely more difficult. And I kept imagining that other difficult world where I was the father of her child. And then I had to talk to her. I needed to talk to her. So I stood in line and made my slow way toward her.

"What flavor you want?" she asked me when it was finally my turn. She didn't recognize me. She barely looked at me.

"Chocolate in a plain cone," I said.

She must have recognized my voice—my lispy, stammering tenor—because she studied my face.

"I know you," she said.

I didn't know what to say. I felt suddenly embarrassed and shy.

"*I know you,*" she said again.

I can't explain why I felt so much shame at that moment. It almost felt like I was the father of her child and I had abandoned her. And I suspect there's something patriarchal and narcissistic about feeling that way, but I can't exactly explain that either. I think perhaps I had never been so clearly reminded of the nonfatal ways in which I could have trapped myself on the rez.

"Your name is Junior," Angie said. She didn't smile. She didn't look upset. She had remembered my name, which should have been flattering, I suppose.

"You're Junior, right?" Angie asked.

At that moment, I thought about who I had become in the two years since I had last seen her.

"My name isn't Junior," I said. "I'm Sherman."

She knew I was lying. But she didn't challenge me. She didn't say anything as I turned and walked away.

I allowed my wife—who'd seen me naked and touched me thousands of times—to finally touch me in those places where I had hoarded so much of my pain and shame.

A few years ago, I wrote a poem based on my extremely brief relationship with Angie, but I wrote it as if our relationship had been far more substantial, as if she and I had been older and more desperate, as if the worst things I feared about her life and my life had come true:

White Girl Powwow Love

She was skinny and buttermilk-pale.
She wore her hair with a rattail.
And I knew I'd two-step to jail

For her love, which was the no-fail
Pickup line that year. "I'm in jail,"
I said. "And only you got the bail

To rescue me." She smelled like stale
Everything, and though I was frail,
I talked her into chucking the bale

And disobeying her dad, a whale
Who thought everything was for sale,
Especially the sacred. So we sailed,
Her and me, on the powwow trail,
Until my dirty joke splat-failed—
The porno punch line was "Snails."

White Girl Angry, she dug her nails
Into my skin and said, "Why you males
Have to heave and hove and dog wail

Such awful shit?" She was a gale—
A storm through a trailer park vale—
An F5 on the tornado scale—

And I wanted to push aside her veil
And touch and memorize her pale
Skin like a blind man touches
    Braille,

And so I did. Virgin-clumsy, I flailed
At her buttons, and that tough rail
Of a girl went all weakness and quail.

I thought I was all rez-prevail,
But then she put on her chain-mail
Armor and golf-ball-sized-hailed

Me with this confessional tale:
"My daddy is a goddamn Whale
Killer," she said. "Ain't no scale

To weigh his evil. His devil pail
Is filled to the brim." She wailed
Tears like anvils and then bailed

On me. She ran back down the trail,
And I ran after her, but I failed
To catch her. Her pain felt like nails.

And though I never saw her pale
Self again, I pray, without fail,
When I think of her stuck in jail,

Or maybe still walking powwow trail—
A white girl, skinny, hard, and frail—
And likely wed to a killer of whales.

After reading an early draft of this chapter, my friend, a white woman, asked me, "Why didn't those Spokane Indian girls like you?"

"Most of them liked me," I said. "But only as a goofy geek. I didn't possess any of those qualities deemed sexually attractive to the women of my reservation. I still don't have any of those qualities."

"And what were those qualities?" my friend asked.

"I didn't dance or sing powwow," I said. "I didn't stick-game. I wasn't a church kid. I didn't become a good basketball player until I left the rez. I had speech impediments. I was bookish and shy. I cried all the time. I hardly ever left my basement bedroom. I was ugly."

"You weren't ugly," my friend said. "I have known you for thirty years. And I have seen the photos of you when you were a kid. You were always cute. And you wore purple striped shirts."

"Nobody thought I was cute until I left the rez."

"The Indian Ugly Duckling syndrome."

"That sounds so corny," I said. "But I don't think it's inaccurate. There might be some truth to it."

"You're trying to write the truth, aren't you?" my friend asked.

"My highly flawed version of the truth," I said.

"Then why don't you call up those Indian women

you grew up with? Why don't you ask them why they never fell in love with you?"

I laughed and laughed.

"Oh, God," I said. "That feels like the most dangerous thing I could ever do."

"That makes it sound like it's something you *need* to do," my friend said.

"I am married to an amazing Native woman," I said. "I know she loves me."

"Is your wife the first Indian woman who ever loved you?"

"Yes," I said, and thought about that first moment—whose details I will not share—when I realized that my wife *adored* me. I remember that her adoration made me tremble. I remember that I felt healed and challenged at the same time, I remember hoping that I would continue to deserve that adoration and that I would always adore her in return.

To be so romantically loved by a Native American woman was a *revelation*.

My late father loved my wife.

"Is she really as nice as she seems?" he asked me when Diane I were first dating.

"Yes, she is," I said.

My late mother loved my wife, too.

"She seems tough enough to deal with you," my mother said when Diane and I were first dating.

"Yes, she is," I said.

Monosonnet for the Matriarchy, Interrupted

When
A
Woman
Asks
You
To
Owl
Dance

(O, O, O, O, the owl dance, two steps forward, one step back, O, O, O, O, listen to the drummers attack that drum, O, O, O, O, if a woman asks you to owl dance, you have to accept her offer, O, O, O, O, but if you still have the nerve to decline, then you must pay her what she wants, O, O, O, O, give her some money, honey, fill her coffers, O, O, O, O, and then you have to stand in front of the entire powwow and tell everybody exactly why and how you refused her, O, O, O, O, and if you refuse to detail your refusal, you will be named and shamed out of the powwow, O, O, O, O, but, mister, why would you want to say no to your sister, O, O, O, O, but, brother, why would you want to say no to your mother, O, O, O,

O, all of these women are your sisters and mothers,
O, O, O, O, they're somebody's sisters and mothers,
so, mister, so, brother, dance with the women, mister, brother, dance with the women, mister, brother,
dance with the women, mister, brother, dance with
the women, mister, brother, they're everybody's sisters and mothers)

You
Should
Always
Honor
The
Chance.

I was joined in my sophomore year at Reardan by
my sisters, Kim and Arlene, twins who are a year
younger.

I was also shocked to see one of my childhood
bullies from the rez. She was one of those beautiful
Spokane Indian girls who had called me ugly, who
had called me Junior High Honky. And now she was
standing in the hallway of Reardan, my school, my
school, *my school*.

She saw me, smiled, and said, "Hello, Sher-
rrrrrman," stretching out my name in a mocking
fashion. I'd been known only as Junior on the rez,

and now she was already giving me shit for my new name, my new identity.

My sister saw it happen.

"What are you going to do about her?" she asked me.

"She better learn quick," I said. "This is not Wellpinit."

I was enormously popular in Reardan, with kids and adults, and I enjoyed the corresponding social power. But I also made a conscious effort to be egalitarian, to be friends with every social group. I was surrounded by kind people—and more than a few small-farm-town racists—and I was scared my bully would ruin all the good stuff.

"If she tries to fuck with me," I said to my sister, "I will crush her. If she leaves me alone, then I will leave her alone."

Because my bully was smart, funny, charismatic, and gorgeous, she quickly made friends with a few of her classmates. She was a year younger than me, so we didn't have any classes together. For a few weeks, it seemed like our social lives would be separate. I was on guard, vigilant, ready to defend myself against any social attack she might launch. If we'd been in a bigger school, we probably could have avoided each other, but our high school had one hallway and ten classrooms. So we were constantly in each other's sight lines. I found myself cast in a weird-ass John Hughes movie where two Indians were the leads.

I don't know what my bully was thinking during those few weeks. I imagine she was afraid. I imagine she felt lost. I imagine she felt powerless. She was the new kid, and that's always stressful. And, of course, she must have been puzzled by my popularity. How had I, the rez peon, become a white-high-school superstar? How could Junior Alexie, the omega dog, now be Sherman Alexie, the young man who was loved and respected? Hell, I started the drama club in that farm town and got thirty people to join.

I wonder if she ever considered befriending me. I wonder if I would have accepted and trusted her friendship.

Those questions are hypothetical, of course, because my bully could not help herself. She could not be happy in a world where she was not allowed to belittle me.

So, one morning, as I walked past her in the hallway, as she huddled with a group of her new friends, she turned my name into an insult: "Hey, Spermin'! Hey, Spermin'!"

She laughed. I stopped and stared at her. She smiled at me, as if she had won something. In Wellpinit, that behavior would have been acceptable. In Reardan, it was not.

My sister told me later that she'd seen all of that happen.

"She did that to you," my sister said. "And I knew it was over for her."

Over the next few hours, I whispered a few things to a few friends. Those whispered things were whispered to others. And those whispers continued to be whispered.

Within a few days, my sister ran up to me in the hallway and told me she had just seen my bully eating all by herself at a big table in the lunchroom.

"She looked so sad," my sister said.

A few days after that, my bully had transferred back to the school on the reservation.

It was a decisive victory.

I had saved myself.

Do I feel good about how I exiled my bully?

Yes, I feel great.

Do I also feel bad about how I exiled my bully?

More than three decades later, I still feel guilty. But I know it was necessary. I know it was self-defense. I know it was justifiable. But it also revealed to me how willing I was to socially torture another person.

You can call me vindictive, and I will not disagree.

I allowed my wife—who'd seen me naked and touched me thousands of times—to finally touch me in those places where I had hoarded so much of my pain and shame.

I called my sister and asked her what else she remembered about my battle with my bully.

"I want to know if you remember something I don't," I said.

"She was mad at me for years," my sister said. "And I had nothing to do with it. I was an innocent bystander."

"You've never been innocent."

My sister laughed. But she was laughing too hard for that small joke.

"What? What?" I asked.

"I bet if you stayed on the rez you would've married her."

"Fuck that!" I said, and laughed.

But it's not an inconceivable thought. My bully ended up leaving the rez school again and graduated from a different but mostly white high school. She graduated from college. She's always been ambitious, talented, and highly opinionated. She hasn't lived on the reservation for years but remains connected through family, friends, culture, and business. She also has plenty of enemies on the rez. My bully and I are the same kind of Spokane Indians.

I am laughing as I write this because I realize now, after all of these years, that my bully had followed me to Reardan. She had attempted to use my escape route. She had *emulated* me.

And I laugh even harder because I am quite sure she would absolutely deny that.

And now I am laughing at the thought that maybe she and I would have gone to the prom together. Or, heck, since it was a farm town, maybe she and I would have gone to the harvest ball.

Two Spokane Indians slow-dancing while surrounded by white kids. And hay bales festooned with blue ribbons. While Hank Williams, Jr., or Spandau Ballet played a love ballad.

That's the happy ending of the John Hughes movie about Indians, enit?

I allowed my wife—who'd seen me naked and touched me thousands of times—to finally touch me in those places where I had hoarded so much of my pain and shame.

But I have to keep asking: If I had stayed on the reservation, then whom do I think I would have married?

I bet I would have fallen in love with a white schoolteacher—one of those crusading liberals who come to the rez hoping to save Indians. Most of those teachers last for only a year or two. Saving Indians is a tough job with long hours and terrible pay.

But some of those white teachers stay for their entire lives.

During my travels to many reservations over the last twenty-five years, I have met a few white teachers who fell in love with and married Indian people.

I once met a TV news reporter, a white woman, who fell in love with an Indian man as she was interviewing him.

"On the rez, we were standing in a wild grass field overlooking the river valley," the woman said to me. "I was filing a report about environmental efforts on the reservation. And I just kept being distracted by the beauty of the landscape. And I looked at this Indian man. And he was so beautiful, too. And he and that landscape belonged together, you know? And I thought, 'Hey, I want some of that action!' And I have been getting that action for twenty years."

During high school and college, I fell deeply in love with two women. Both white. Marriage was discussed.

They both broke up with me.

And shortly after breaking up with me, they each met the white man they would marry. They are both still married.

I have always wished them well.

I remember them with affection and respect.

I suppose, in many ways, one never stops loving the people they loved during their youth.

Or hating the people they hated.

My bully reentered my life in 2005 or 2006. Maybe it was 2007. Or 2003. I was giving a reading at Auntie's Bookstore in Spokane. As always, I had reserved a section of seats for my mother, siblings, cousins, nieces, and nephews.

My siblings and mother took their seats early in the bookstore. But I was still in my hotel room getting ready. So my sister had to tell me what happened before I arrived.

"So we're sitting there," my sister said. "And *she* [the bully] and two other Spokane Indian women [who had never liked me either] come striding in and just took seats in the reserved section."

"Maybe they thought the reserved section was reserved for reservation Indians who had made a reservation," I said.

"Oh," my sister said. "That's a dumb joke. Anyways, they sat in our section and wouldn't even look at us. They looked all mad in the face."

I immediately noticed my bully when I walked into the bookstore. I don't even remember the two other Spokane Indian women who'd accompanied her. It was the only the second time I'd seen her since I'd exiled her from Reardan more than twenty years earlier.

I'd first seen her in the reservation trading post during the summer after I'd exiled her. I spotted her and tried to dodge behind a shelf. But she saw me and rushed at me, cursing. I don't remember exactly what she said. But she was furious at me. She knew that I had exiled her. She hated me for it.

I was sheepish, defiant, amused, and angry.

I don't remember what I said.

I wish I would have said, "I see that I hurt you. Do you have any idea how much you've hurt me over the years?"

But I imagine I instead offered her an empty apology, and I assume she rejected it.

So, now, more than a decade after that encounter, my bully was sitting in the front row at my reading. I wasn't even remotely the Indian boy she knew in Reardan or Wellpinit. I had become the kind of Indian man who can talk glorious shit to talk-show hosts and U.S. presidents on national television.

But, damn it, my bully still made me nervous. She was still smart and beautiful. She was still intimidating.

I heard "Junior High Honky" echoing inside my always-fragile head.

I performed my poems and stories. I improvised stories and jokes. I interacted with the audience.

And I watched my bully take notes the entire time. Battle plans, I assumed.

And I thought, "Holy shit! She is going to verbally challenge me in front of four hundred of my most ardent fans—in front of my hometown crowd. Is she really this brave and stupid? Doesn't she know how good I am onstage? Can't she see how I would win any war of insults against her?"

I have to admit that I was absolutely overjoyed at the thought of the impending confrontation.

And then I looked at my mother. At my sisters. At my nieces. At my female cousins. I looked at those Spokane Indians—those Native American women— and I thought about how much sorrow and pain they'd endured in their lives, how Native women everywhere are so targeted for violence by tribal and American society.

I love those Native women I call my family and friends.

But I don't love my bully. Not even a little bit.

However, I realized I had no need to win some imaginary fight with her. I had no desire to hurt her feelings. I didn't want to walk the circle of animosity anymore. I wasn't going to forgive her. I'm not a sap. She would have to actually apologize in order for me to think about forgiving her. But, stop, stop, stop, I wanted that shit to stop.

So when she raised her hand, I politely called on

her three separate times and answered questions about tribal responsibility, alcoholism, and negative stereotypes of Native Americans.

I declared a truce with her, at least within myself. Or maybe it's only a partial truce because a half-truce is really just a surrender, right?

In any case, I hope there is a future powwow when she, an elderly Spokane Indian woman, asks me, an elderly Spokane Indian man, for an owl dance.

"Yes, of course," I will say.

It won't be romantic. It won't be all that friendly. But it will be a clumsy acknowledgment of our life-long bond, however frayed.

On a Saturday morning in a hotel room in Bellingham—in an Oxford Suites that had three-dimensional art in the bathroom that spelled WASH in huge wooden capital letters—I said to my wife, "I am going to get naked and lie facedown on the bed. And I want you to look at my back. I want you to study my back. I want you to study my scars. I want you to tell me what they look like. I want you to touch the scars. I want you to trace their outlines with your fingertips. I want to feel you feeling my scars."

Diane did as she was asked. She touched the small scars. Ran her fingertips along the longer scars.

"What do they look like?" I asked.

"They're lighter than they used to be."

"Huh," I said. "Take some pictures with your phone and e-mail them to me. I will look at them later."

I thought it might take me weeks to look at the photos of my scarred back. Maybe months. Maybe I would never look at them.

So I was surprised to find myself downloading those photos onto my iPad only an hour later.

Diane was driving us home to Seattle. She almost always wants to drive, and I almost always want to sit in the passenger seat and daydream.

"Okay," I said. "I am looking at them now."

I laughed at how pale my back had become. I've lived in sunless Seattle for two decades. I'm an introverted writer who'd rather be inside reading or writing. And I haven't played outdoor shirts-and-skins pickup basketball in a long time.

Looking at my pale back, I realized that it had been at least fifteen years since I had been topless in direct sunlight.

So my skin had grown pale. Had grown from brown to slightly tan.

But my acne scars had also grown pale.

My skin and my scars were now almost the same color.

"You can't really see my scars all that much anymore," I said.

"Only if you look really close," Diane said. "Only if you're looking for them."

"I don't look burned anymore," I said.

"You're kind of mottled," Diane said. "Like a feather."

My wife and I traveled toward our home, toward our waiting sons. I closed my eyes and dreamed that I was entirely made of feathers. I dreamed I could hover like one feather, like a man made of feathers. And then I dreamed that each of my scars was a bird. And then I flew.

160.

Flight Hours

That bird, small and brown, wrecked
Against our kitchen window
And crashed dead to our deck.

"Avian suicide," I said
And walked out to retrieve
Its broken-feathered body—

And then I thought of my mother's coffin being
carried to the grave by her pallbearers. And realized
that I would be the bird's pallbearer. And that realization made me feel responsible for the bird, as if
its death needed to matter, as if it weren't just one
more member of an essentially endless species. So I

sat beside that dead bird and improvise-hummed an
honor song—

And startled when that bird lifted
Its head as if my song were a gift
That brought it back to life.

Of course, I did not resurrect
That bird. It had knocked
Itself out against our window

And was now regaining
Consciousness. But had it broken
Something? Maybe a wing?

Would it be able to fly?
Perhaps I'd have to watch it
Simply and slowly die—

And I knew that I shouldn't let the bird suffer. But I
didn't know if I could pick it up and snap its neck. And
as I imagined it struggling against my fingers, I knew
I wasn't cruel enough to smother it. So what to do?
How long would it take to die? Minutes or hours? A
day? And what would happen to the defenseless bird
if I left it alone on our deck? It would be easy prey for
all of the neighborhood predators—insects, rodents,
other birds, and all of the mass-murdering house cats.

I couldn't stand the thought of this poor bird being eaten alive while it was potentially paralyzed. So, yes, I was a weak-ass moralist unable to kill the bird and unsure if I had the patience to stand guard as it died. Then, as I pondered, the bird lifted a wing—

Ah, such a brave bird, reaching
Toward the sky, I suppose.
Or toward its God. I don't know

How birds die. But this bird
Shook that wing, shook
That wing, and then it raised

Its other wing and shook it, too.
Oh, I praised that bird
As it shook and shook and shook

Its wings, alternately
And simultaneously.
And then that little bird stood—

I wasn't home on the reservation when my mother died. My wife, sons, and I had visited her on Father's Day, almost two weeks before her death, and we'd said our good-byes. During our mother's final days and hours, my sisters and niece gently tried to get me to return. But I did not. I had thanked my mother for my life. I had told her that I loved her. Those weren't lies. And they seemed to give me enough closure to survive. I don't feel guilty about not being with my mother when she died. Or maybe I feel the proper amount of guilt. Or maybe I will feel more guilt as time passes. I don't know. But I certainly feel terrible that I hurt my sisters and niece. And yet, I'd also known that many other people would come to help my sisters and niece. When my mother died, there were at least ten cousins and friends in the room. My mother was surrounded by her most beloved ones. Everybody except me—

I applauded when that proud bird
Climbed to its feet and shook,
Shook, shook, shook, shook,

And shook its entire body.
Was it seizing? Or, wait, shit,
Were those its death throes?

No, no, I didn't think so
Because the bird walked slow
Circles around the deck,

Little oval miracles that became
Larger as the minutes passed.
And as it paced, the bird continued

To shake and shake and shake
Its head, wings, body, and feet,
But I wasn't sure why,

And then it walked to the edge
Of our deck, paused,
And then lifted into flight,

Around the corner
Of our house and then winged
Its way out of my life—

A few weeks after our mother's funeral, and a few days after my adventure with the bird, I sat with my therapist and told her about the little creature's pacing and shaking. "I don't know if I ever told you," my therapist said. "But I'm a birder. I love birds. And when they hit a window like that, or get hurt in any significant way, they have this ritual. They shake off the pain. They shake off the trauma. And they walk in circles to reconnect their brain and body and soul. When your bird was walking and shaking, it was remembering and relearning how to be a bird." Oh, wow. I couldn't say much after that intense revelation, but my therapist continued. "We humans often lose touch with our bodies," she said. "We forget that we can also shake away our pain and trauma." It seemed so simple. I openly doubted that it could be true—

But, that night, I stood on our deck
In the same place where that bird
Had fallen, arose, walked, shook,
And flew. And I performed

That ritual, too. I shook my arms,
Legs, head, and body. I paced
In small circles that grew larger
By the minute. I reached

Toward every other constellation.
I reached toward my sisters,
Niece, and brothers. I reached
Toward the memory of my mother.

And as I continued to shake, I felt
A sparrow-sized pain rise
From my body and—wait, wait, wait.
Listen. I don't know how or when

My grieving will end, but I'm always
Relearning how to be human again.

Acknowledgments

I sing an honor song for Nancy Stauffer, my agent and friend and compatriot since 1992. What is the official gift for a twenty-fifth literary anniversary?

I also sing for Reagan Arthur, my amazing editor. This is our first book together. But it's not the one I originally promised to her. That one is still on the way. It is *contractually* obligated to be on the way. But I might write and publish a different one. I don't know. Anything could happen. So, yeah, Reagan is incredibly patient.

More songs for every person on the Little, Brown team, in the adult and young adult departments. I am the author of this book, yes, but there are dozens of people who help present it to the world. Thanks to all of them.

Acknowledgments

Some of the words in this book were published, often in radically different forms, by Hanging Loose Press, *Superstition Review*, *Valapraiso Poetry Review*, and Limberlost Press.

Praise to Wendy Hathaway, co-pilot, navigator, engineer, lifeguard, EMT, and getaway driver of FallsApart Productions.

As always, I have relied on the love, emotional support, editorial advice, and constant inspiration of Kim Barnes, Shann Ferch, Kevin Taylor, and Jess Walter.

I give thanks for Jennings, Jeide, Williams, Lee, McBride, and Quirk—the Field House Gang.

I give a twenty-drum salute to the Neurology Clinic team at Harborview Medical Center in Seattle. You saved my life. You saved my brain. You saved my stories.

Special thanks to Grudge Judy, who helped me in the desert.

This book would not exist without the stories of the powerful indigenous women in my life. In particular, I want to honor Diane Tomhave, Kim Alexie, Arlene Alexie, Shelly Boyd, and LaRae Wiley.

And, forever and ever, I thank Alex Kuo, my teacher, who read one of my poems in 1987, and asked me, "What are you going to do with the rest of your life?" I said, "I don't know." And then he said, "I think you should write."

About the Author

Winner of the PEN/Faulkner Award for Fiction, the PEN/Malamud Award for Short Fiction, a PEN/Hemingway Citation for Best First Fiction, and the National Book Award for Young People's Literature, Sherman Alexie is a poet, short-story writer, novelist, and performer. A Spokane/Coeur d'Alene Indian, Alexie grew up in Wellpinit, Washington, on the Spokane Indian Reservation. He has been an urban Indian since 1994 and lives in Seattle with his family.

AUG - - 2017
3756087